*Race Over Party*

MILLINGTON W. BERGESON-LOCKWOOD

# *Race Over Party*

## Black Politics and Partisanship in Late Nineteenth-Century Boston

The University of North Carolina Press  *Chapel Hill*

*This book was published with the assistance of the Authors Fund of the University of North Carolina Press.*

The University of North Carolina Press has been a member of the
Green Press Initiative since 2003.

Library of Congress Cataloging-in-Publication Data
Names: Bergeson-Lockwood, Millington W., author.
Title: Race over party : black politics and partisanship in late
    nineteenth-century Boston / Millington W. Bergeson-Lockwood.
Description: Chapel Hill : University of North Carolina Press, [2018] |
    Includes bibliographical references and index.
Identifiers: LCCN 2017045426 | ISBN 9781469640402 (cloth : alk. paper) |
    ISBN 9781469640419 (pbk : alk. paper) | ISBN 9781469640426 (ebook)
Subjects: LCSH: African Americans—Massachusetts—Boston—History—19th century. |
    African Americans—Political activity—Massachusetts—Boston. | Partisanship. |
    Political parties—Massachusetts—Boston—History—19th century. | Reconstruction
    (U.S. history, 1865–1877)—Massachusetts—Boston.
Classification: LCC F73.9.N4 B47 2018 | DDC 323.1196/073074461—dc23
LC record available at https://lccn.loc.gov/2017045426

Jacket illustrations: front left, Boston Ward Nine ballot (used by permission of the Boston
Athenæum); front right, Boston Ward Nine voting precincts, 1878 (courtesy of the Boston City
Archives); back, photograph of Edwin G. Walker from P. Thomas Stanford, *Tragedy of the Negro
in America* (1897).

Portions of chapter four appeared previously in "No Longer Pliant Tools: Urban Politics
and Conflicts over African American Partisanship in 1880s Boston, Massachusetts," *Journal
of Urban History* 44: 2 (March 2018): 169–186.

*To my father, Millington, for his love of the past*

*and*

*to Zora and Millington Samuel, my hope for the future*

# Contents

# Illustrations

*Race Over Party*

# Introduction
## *The Folly of Political Solidarity*

On January 16, 1901, an interracial crowd of more than 1,500 men and women packed the Charles Street African Methodist Episcopal (AME) Church in Boston's West End to capacity. They were there to mourn the loss of Edwin Garrison Walker, one of the city's most notable black activists. A black Civil War veterans association escorted his body in procession to the church, and some of Boston's other prominent black leaders were among his pallbearers. "Walker was a fearless advocate for his race," one eulogy read, "he was proud of the fact that he was a colored man and as such sought the highest ideals in life."[1] Walker was the son of famous antislavery activist David Walker and had served as one of the first black men elected to the Massachusetts legislature. During his tumultuous career he was an outspoken critic of party politics, and the Republican Party in particular. Mourners remembered him as "among the first of the colored leaders of the country to perceive clearly the folly of political solidarity for the race."[2] A leading proponent of black independent politics, Walker advocated African American voters withholding support from the Republican Party, and even supporting Democrats until major party platforms reflected black interests and party members protected and expanded black rights. As one speaker eulogized, "He knew enough respecting the history of political parties in America and the real motives which have ever influenced their action on the negro question to understand how little can be obtained from them by slavish devotion to either one or the other at the polls."[3]

By the end of his life, Walker, like many other black activists, had grown increasingly bitter and disillusioned with not only the Republican Party, but with party politics generally. Black political independence had largely failed to transform American politics, and the conditions of African Americans nationally continued to deteriorate. With little to show for their decades of activism, and without the personal spoils of loyalty to a particular party, Walker and others looked to new organizations outside of party politics for the future of black political action.

The story of Walker and others who placed their faith in party politics and challenged the Republican Party is a tragedy. In the aftermath of the Civil

EDWIN G. WALKER, ESQ., ATTORNEY AT LAW.
HE WAS ELECTED TO THE MASSACHUSETTS LEGISLATURE IN 1863 AND
NOMINATED BY GENERAL BUTLER FOR THE POSITION OF JUDGE.

Edwin Garrison Walker, P. Thomas Stanford, *Tragedy of the Negro in America* (Cambridge, MA, 1897). (Manuscripts, Archives, and Rare Books Division, Schomburg Center for Research in Black Culture, New York Public Library, Astor, Lenox, and Tilden Foundations.)

War, they were believers in the power of partisan democracy to forge a greater future for African Americans. Some sought to transform the Republican establishment by staying loyal to the party of Lincoln. Others, like Walker, advocated independent politics as an alternative to what they recognized as the failure of the two major political parties, the Republican in particular, to improve and protect African American lives and rights in the aftermath of the Civil War. Even as independents criticized the current party structures, like loyal Republicans, they remained within the bounds of electoral partisan politics, hoping that one of the two parties would eventually emerge as the political vehicle for black progress. They worked tirelessly for decades, both inside and outside the official structures, to convince voters and party leadership of the importance of supporting black interests, from both a moral and politically pragmatic position, only to see white supremacy harden within American politics and the condition of black men and women worsen nationally. Their faith in partisan democracy had been tragically misplaced. The general failure of independent politics and black partisanship as a framework, however, is a tragedy with a silver lining, because it led black activists more firmly toward strategies of race-based organizing outside of the formal two-party political system.

Although black activists were divided between remaining loyal Republicans or advocating independent politics, the eventual failure of partisan politics as a vehicle for racial justice was less a problem of black unity and organization than a betrayal by a white-dominated government and political structure refusing to make black rights and lives a priority and to uphold the values of American freedom. Black partisan activists and independents misplaced their faith in a party structure dominated by racism, that, as became evident by the beginning of the twentieth century, was never going to support black interests, no matter how unified the black electorate ever became. Campaigns for independent politics were part of early civil rights struggles Shawn Leigh Alexander describes as "a bridge of ideas and activists," which inspired and provided a template for twentieth-century movements.[4] Abandoned by supposed allies and disillusioned with party politics as an avenue for black uplift, activists formed new organizations and cultivated strategies to continue the black freedom struggle themselves. While continuing to advocate political independence in voting, these groups emphasized mass mobilization and direct activism as tools in the black freedom struggle, rather than holding out hope that political parties would ultimately serve their interests.

In this battle over black partisanship, Boston became a central venue. Urban politics became the battleground, and they organized to use electoral politics to challenge the status quo at both local and national levels. What happened in Boston is part of a national narrative of black politics, but is very much rooted in black Bostonians' history of activism and the city's urban black political landscape.[5] It is a story of community-level organizing to respond to both local and national politics, and the turn toward independent politics was as much a strategy to address local concerns as it was a response to national political changes. Independent political sentiment in Boston had a particular longevity as debates over black partisanship captivated community politics for at least four decades, with activists such as Edwin Walker active for the majority of the period.

Boston is significant for the way its legacy of radical antislavery activism was combined in the postwar period with a commitment to electoral politics fostered by a unique political geography.[6] The concentration of black Bostonians in one ward allowed for African American electoral relevance beyond their population numbers, resulting in more black city- and state-level officials than in any other place in the North during this era. African Americans in Boston were highly active in the city's electoral machine and were willing to leverage their vote in pursuit of greater equality and civil rights protections. All the while, they were dedicated to the use of the ballot as a tool for black liberation. Struggles in Boston, even when they looked to national issues, were deeply personal, and attempts at independent politics could have severe consequences for those involved. Long-term victories were few and far between, and ultimately resulted in disappointment. This is a tragic tale about lost hopes and the limits of partisanship to achieve racial justice.

This history is part of the recent turn toward the study of Reconstruction and late nineteenth-century African American politics beyond the longstanding focus on southern black communities and mostly rural political movements.[7] Historians take seriously the northern urban men and women whose lives and experiences were as deeply shaped by this tumultuous period as their southern brethren. Northern city dwellers, who were no less affected by the rises and falls of post–Civil War freedom, were part of a national struggle for increased protection of rights and liberties, and black activists were hard hit, if not physically, then emotionally, by the crush of Jim Crow and white supremacist violence by the end of the century. Through a Boston-based study, this narrative expands our thinking by examining the ways in which urban electoral politics, and black partisanship especially, featured in the strategies of black activists and influenced the evolution of black politics in the final decades of the nineteenth century. The local study builds upon histories of black partisanship and independence that tell a more national story or focus on the biographies of key figures.[8] It challenges a narrative of northern urban political life dominated by histories of white ethnic activity, which have rarely focused on African American urban political and electoral organization.[9] Its central focus on urban politics identifies electoral activism as a significant element of black northern political life.[10] This book positions black urban electoral politics and partisanship as a central piece of the nineteenth-century black freedom struggle.

As black Bostonians engaged deeply in urban electoral politics, debates over partisanship became discussions over the place of African Americans in the U.S. body politic. Independents clashed with loyal black Republicans, and black voters of either position saw urban electoral politics as an invaluable tool to achieve full citizenship protections and exercise black political power. Independent politics emerged forcefully during what Gregory Downs calls an era of American "patronalism": "a revolution not just in what the American state could do but in what people believed it could do."[11] As expectations and demands on government increased, so too did black voters look to political parties as the conduit of resources. For both black Republicans and independents, having a political party respond to one's needs and interests was part of being a full and equal citizen. They also expected the same material concessions in the forms of jobs and political appointments as those being divvied out to other supporters.

They divided, however, over how best to achieve this vision. Republicans sought to prove their continued loyalty in the hopes of motivating the party from within. While not perfect, the Republican Party was the best choice in a sea of horrible alternatives. For black Republican loyalists, political independence in Massachusetts had to be stopped at all costs. They argued that black independents trod a perilous path, and that the best way to advance black rights was from within the Republican Party, despite its limitations. African American independents, however, were willing to take their chances and expected the parties to earn their votes. They rejected the idea that they owed any party loyalty or unanimity based on past deeds. What mattered was how the party acted as an advocate of black rights in the present, and whether it would protect those liberties from attack in the future. During this period, black Bostonians debated partisanship as a reflection of the place of African Americans in the nation. Were they to be respected members of the electorate whose interests would be represented in the platforms and actions of the major parties, or were they merely votes to be taken for granted by Republicans or suppressed by Democrats? Attempts to answer these questions shaped black politics in Boston during the final decades of the nineteenth century.

African American independents faced a difficult decision. In a city with one of the nation's strongest Republican machines, leaving the party was risky. In supporting Democrats, they turned away from a party associated with antislavery and black rights and toward a party associated with white supremacy. They also rejected the Republican-dominated Massachusetts political establishment in favor of a political insurgency and the possible loss of patronage that came with rebellion against the status quo. Further, and perhaps more importantly, declaring support for Democrats meant siding with the party growing in power across the states of the former Confederacy. To advocate for Democrats was to support the party of expanding southern white supremacy and Jim Crow. Thus, the risks of political independence were huge, and many who rejected Republicans paid for it with their political or professional careers. Yet, many refused to abandon their critiques and stood steadfast in their dedication to racial solidarity over partisanship.

By claiming independence, they sought a partisan middle ground. Nationally, as Bess Beatty describes, "despite its common usage . . . the term 'independence' never developed a definitive meaning."[12] Boston independents are part of the black political tradition of "flexible partisanship."[13] They made public declarations rejecting Republican loyalty without swearing formal allegiance to the Democrats. At times, they were "a Republican . . . who has dared to criticize the party," or "a Democrat within the true meaning of the word."[14] But most of the time they just declared themselves independent. Rather than backing *parties* in particular, they advocated backing any *candidate* who looked out for their interests, regardless of partisan affiliation. They hoped that by shifting their loyalties to other candidates, the Republican Party would renew its early calls for universal citizenship and federally protected equality. Alternatively, they hoped that support for Democrats would push that party to adopt more moderate positions on racial equality in their party platform. Black independents were willing to risk Democratic victories if that meant sending the message to both parties that African Americans no longer would be mere pawns in electoral politics. Strategically, they sought to show both parties that African Americans could not be counted on as reliable voters unless the parties made concessions in the form of political appointments and new government policies protecting their rights.

Black partisan choices were deeply connected to material gains and patronage. For black Bostonians, appointment to office simultaneously was a personal success and reflected on the race as a whole. These positions offered African Americans a gateway to official political offices that may have been inaccessible through electoral politics. A political appointment meant personal economic security, as a much-needed job in a very tight labor market. But rather than merely a "spoils system" of corruption and personal ambition, pursuit of patronage was a significant tool for black political power. Not only did African Americans in appointed positions of government authority have access to professional power and economic benefit, but the appearance of a black official had important symbolic value and was a public display of black uplift, inclusion, and equality.[15]

Black activists looked to political appointments as a reflection of how important the two major parties considered African American support to be. Seeking political appointments was about convincing other black voters to support a particular candidate or party in order to shift the balance of influence in the party system nationally. They, like white supporters, wanted to be rewarded for their campaign efforts, and, more importantly, they wanted party rhetoric of equality to be backed up by material concessions. The failure of either party to ultimately reward their black supporters in substantially meaningful ways further catalyzed black disillusionment with partisan politics, and rather than a symbol of black advancement, pursuit of patronage became a symbol of black complicity in a system of white domination.

This study understands the struggle over black partisanship in three phases. The first section details how black activists emerged from the Civil War eager to use electoral politics to their advantage. Initially they unified around the Republican Party and hoped to shape the future of that organization from within. They recognized the party's shortcomings, but were not yet ready to fully abandon the party. During this early period, however, cracks in this support emerged. Some black activists, such as Edwin Walker, openly criticized the Republican Party and were skeptical of the party's ultimate commitment to African American interests. During debates over Reconstruction and new constitutional amendments, they condemned reluctance by Republican congressional leaders to act swiftly on their behalf, especially on questions of suffrage. Yet, by and large, they remained loyal to Republicans and held out hope that the party could be kept loyal to black interests through persistent agitation.

During the demise of federal Reconstruction in the late 1870s, as described in the second section, an increasing number of black activists lost faith in the Republican Party, even as they kept to electoral and partisan politics as a strategy. In the 1880s, Boston became home to some of the staunchest advocates for black voters breaking from Republicans. Along with allies in other cities, they helped define the decade as an age of black political independence, when black partisanship was divided between those loyal to the

Republican Party and those willing to support other parties, Democrats included.[16]

In their departure from the Republican Party, black independents cast about for new allies. They supported local and national Democratic candidates. Most importantly, they campaigned for former Civil War general and congressman Benjamin Butler for Massachusetts's governor. Finding some success locally, they supported Democrat Grover Cleveland for president in 1884. They sought assistance from the growing Irish electorate in the city, and black independents were some of the strongest supporters of Boston's first Irish-born mayor and Democrat Hugh O'Brien. They backed Irish independence, and their support of Irish nationalism enhanced their commitments to racial unity.

Despite initial hope and optimism that these new relationships would usher in a new era of interracial freedom struggle, many of these alliances were ultimately problematic, fragile, and short-lived. Hopes for broader interracial and interpartisan coalitions faded by the end of the century. As their hope in Democrats diminished with the rising tide of white supremacy in the party, and they continued to be frustrated by the fecklessness of supposed Republican allies, they increasingly worked beyond the realm of partisan politics.

In the final section, black disillusionment and feelings of betrayal catalyze into extrapartisan organizing in response to the existential peril of racial violence. In the 1890s, antilynching became a driving concern, and inaction by the national parties became literally a matter of life or death. Black men and women formed organizations committed to black unity and eliminating anti-black violence. With electoral politics still an important part of their political vision, activists suffered crushing defeat when at the end of the nineteenth century their attempts at meaningful political leverage yielded few broad-based tangible results. In spite of black organizing, African Americans continued to be massacred by white mobs, and the major political parties stood silent in the face of atrocity.

By the beginning of the twentieth century, black independent politics was an inadequate strategy to challenge white supremacy and had largely failed as a discrete political movement. Although its leaders continued to advocate a political culture in which racial solidarity was paramount, and conveyed mistrust of affiliation with major political parties, they were ultimately disillusioned with partisan politics as a vehicle to bring about the transformative change they hoped for. As historian Bess Beatty emphasizes, African Americans "were active participants in the debate about their political future but . . . ultimately they were largely powerless."[17] Supporters of both parties failed at the national level to bring the majorities to their side and could not stem the rising tide of murder and violent discrimination. Their faith in black self-reliance, their political autonomy, and their experience in organizing, however, inspired future generations of activists who would carry these legacies into the foundation of the twentieth-century civil rights movement.

Abandoned by false and weak-willed allies in party politics, black activists of the next century renewed calls for organizations to represent and fight for the future of racial justice and equality. Never losing sight of the importance of partisan politics as a tool when necessary, and inspired by the independent politics of the nineteenth century, continuing generations depended less on white-majority political structures and institutions, as they looked to themselves as vehicles of transformative racial justice. Rather than seeking to transform existing structures and institutions, later activists built upon the work of black independents, like Edwin Walker, to forge new national organizations as strong as any political party.

# Part I
# All Outside Is the Sea

In 1872, Frederick Douglass addressed a national convention of African Americans in New Orleans and described black voters' relationship to the two major political parties. To Douglass, the choice was clear. "For colored men," the world-famous activist and orator explained, "the Republican Party is the deck." All other parties, the Democratic especially, "[are] the sea."[1] The reputation of the Republican Party, the party of Abraham Lincoln, the Great Emancipator, and the architects of Reconstruction, contrasted starkly with that of the Democratic Party, with its sympathy for slavery, secession, and a mild approach to former Confederates after the war. For Douglass, there was no alternative partisan path that would not conclude in Democratic victory and heightened oppression of black people. Any departure from the Republican fold, Douglass recalled later in his biography, would lead "away from our friends and directly to our enemies."[2] Leaving the Republican Party meant likely steering a perilous course in uncharted waters.

In the first decade after the Civil War, most African Americans tended to agree with Douglass. Black voters still viewed the Republican Party as the organization best positioned to expand and protect their rights. The party, still aligned with Lincoln, emancipation, and civil rights in the minds of African Americans, represented the obvious political home for black votes. Any trouble with the party, black supporters argued, could be resolved through internal pressure and reforms. Voting outside the party was not a viable option. Yet, cracks began to appear in the foundations of this unwavering support. Indeed, among the audience who heard Douglass speak in New Orleans in 1872 was a small delegation from Boston who embodied emerging questions over black partisan loyalty.[3] Lifelong loyal Republican George Ruffin listened alongside Edwin Garrison Walker, who was becoming increasingly skeptical of faith and allegiance to the Republican Party. Yet, even Walker held out hope that the Republican Party could be reformed. Black activists were not yet ready to rush headlong into the arms of Democrats or forge their political destiny entirely independent.

Events of the first postwar decade included great successes, but also disappointments that challenged this optimism. Almost immediately after the war, black Bostonians made gains that many thought evidenced a new era of black freedom. For the first time, city voters, including African Americans, elected black men to the Massachusetts state legislature, known as the general court. The same body passed new civil rights legislation protecting black access to public accommodation. Proud of local victories, black Bostonians watched the unfolding of Reconstruction closely and pushed for immediate expanded rights protections nationally, especially the right to vote. Many agreed with radical Republican allies that lasting change for African Americans could not occur and be maintained without aggressive black suffrage.

They grew quickly frustrated and disappointed with the pace of change, however. This was starkly evident during debates over the ratification of the Fourteenth Amendment, which, while preserving citizenship for African Americans, did nothing to protect black voting. Black activists, and Edwin Walker as a state legislator in particular, publicly denounced the amendment as a dangerous compromise and a sacrifice of black freedoms for the sake of political expediency. Despite this early anger and skepticism, the eventual passage of the Fourteenth and Fifteenth Amendments did much to mollify these concerns, and activists grew confident that black pressure on Republicans could bend the party to their interests.

African Americans entered the 1870s optimistic that the tools of electoral politics and support for political parties would yield the continued advancement of black freedom. They challenged the Republican Party to stay true to their founding principles and early fight on behalf of black people. The Republican Party, however, did not match black faith and support with action. Many white Republican former allies began to minimize the importance of black rights in their partisan action and argued that it was time for the nation to move on from such issues for the sake of white national unity. Even locally, former radical Republicans moved away from the black freedom struggle to issues of economic growth and industrial expansion. By the middle of the 1870s, most African Americans continued to heed Douglass's warning and stayed firmly aboard the Republican ship. There were, however, those who looked beyond the gunnels and were willing to risk a political life as independents in the uncharted seas of party politics.

## CHAPTER ONE

# An Atmosphere More Liberal, Although by No Means Unbiased

## Black Boston in the Late Nineteenth Century

In December 1901, the *New York Times* published a series of studies of north-ern urban black communities written by renowned sociologist W. E. B. Du Bois. The fourth in the series described African Americans in Boston. Du Bois celebrated the history of black Bostonians and gave a tempered, yet op-timistic account of racial advancement in the city. "In Boston," he wrote, "the atmosphere has been more liberal, although by no means unbiased.... On the whole, Boston negroes are more hopeful than those in New York and Philadelphia."[1] The limited successes and continued struggles, combined with the geography of the black community in the city, shaped the politics of black Bostonians and influenced their expectations of future progress.

From the early nineteenth through the beginning of the twentieth century, most black Bostonians made their homes along the narrow streets and steep incline of the north side of Boston's Beacon Hill and the West End.[2] Nearly half of the city's black residents lived in this area. Segregated to this area by a combi-nation of racist real estate practices and proximity to employment, they forged a tight-knit neighborhood that spawned strong community organizations and political networks. Boston's African American population increased nearly five-fold from 1865 to 1900. In 1865, the city's black population was 2,348 and made up 1.2 percent of the city population. By 1900, the population across the city had grown to 11,591 and made up over 2 percent of all city residents. A significant population in neighboring Cambridge and surrounding suburbs bolstered the black population of Boston proper.[3] Activists residing in nearby localities made regular trips to Boston for meetings and public rallies.

The small number of African Americans residing in Boston belies their significance. Although the population remained small relative to other north-ern cities, proportionally it was greater than or equal to that of New York, Chicago, Detroit, and Cleveland.[4] Further, the black community was unusually concentrated in the so-called Athens of America, and the city was one of the most racially divided in the United States.[5] This ward-level concentration made the black community a significant electoral interest in the city and provided the opportunity for political leverage.

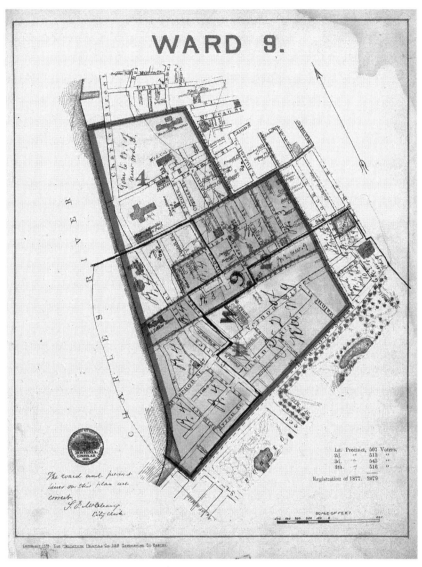

Voting precincts, Ward Nine, 1878. (Image courtesy of Boston City Archives,
Collection 4700.011, Ward and Precinct Maps.)

Within this urban landscape, most African Americans resided in Ward Six, later designated Ward Nine by the city government. Over 30 percent of the city's black population lived in this area.[6] Their concentration gave them electoral benefits despite their small population and proportion of the city's electorate. Within the ward, black residents lived in particular voting precincts north of Pickney Street and surrounding Cambridge Street near the newly constructed Massachusetts General Hospital. Over time, the population, especially new southern migrants, expanded into neighborhoods in the city's South End and nearby suburbs.

City officials redrew Boston's wards in 1875 and 1895. The 1895 redistricting divided the West End black community between Ward Eight and Ward Eleven. Most significantly, it merged a large portion of black residents into the much larger Ward Eleven, which lessened their impact on ward-level politics.[7] Further, government officials relocated the ward room, a major site of city politics, to a site farther away from the concentration of black residents.[8] By the end of the century, the population had migrated to southern wards, which, coupled with redistricting, resulted in a dilution of urban black electoral strength.

## Traditions of Politics and Protest

As Du Bois noted in his Boston profile, although the racial climate in Boston was more progressive than elsewhere, black residents still struggled, especially economically. While far from the poorest black urban community, black Bostonians suffered per capita wealth below that of northern cities such as Philadelphia and Cleveland.[9] As historian Elizabeth Pleck notes, "Black poverty in late nineteenth-century Boston was less a question of starvation than of nagging and almost inexplicable inequalities."[10] While the political leadership of Boston tended to be of a more educated and professional class, most African Americans remained confined to lower-skilled laboring jobs. Nearly 80 percent of black Bostonian workers during the end of the nineteenth century held low-wage occupations.[11] Most black men were employed as laborers, porters, or household servants, while most women worked as laundresses and domestics.[12] Further, levels of black home ownership in Boston were very low; never more than 6 percent in the late nineteenth century. These levels were roughly equal to those in other Eastern Seaboard cities but lower than in southern and midwestern cities.[13] Those who could purchase homes often did so at great expense.[14]

Despite diminished economic status, rates of literacy and education remained relatively positive. The literacy rates for black Bostonians and the percentages of African American children attending school tended to be higher than in other cities.[15] Even postwar southern migrants tended to have higher rates of literacy. Between 1866 and 1868, for example, more than 1,000 formerly enslaved men and women migrated from southern states to Boston and Cambridge with the assistance of the Freedmen's Bureau.[16] These migrants tended to come from southern cities and were better educated than their rural brethren. Many of these men and women traveled to Boston on steamships that sailed weekly from Norfolk, Richmond, and Baltimore.[17]

Despite having certain advantages, black life in Boston was not without its difficulties, and Bostonians' northern locale did not remove them from the national climate of racial discrimination or white supremacy. As mentioned, racism in employment kept black Bostonians in lower economic employment and in lower quality, primarily rented, housing. Additionally, they faced racial discrimination in places of public accommodation, and especially amusements.[18] As one victim noted, "So you see . . . you need not go south to experience indignities . . . yea, almost under the shadow of 'the Athens of America' you are ejected on account of your color."[19]

Black Bostonians fought vigorously against racism in their city and across the country. Activists in the late nineteenth century tapped into a long legacy of political organizing and resistance to racial oppression. Antebellum Boston was home to one of the nation's most politically active African American communities, and both northerners and southerners viewed the city as one of the epicenters of antislavery activism. Men such as Robert Morris and Lewis Hayden worked with women such as Mariah Stewart to end the institution of slavery, protect fugitives, and work for full citizenship on local and national levels.[20] From within its boundaries emerged national antislavery publications such as William Lloyd Garrison's *Liberator*. Black Bostonians also petitioned state and local government for equality in places such as public schools and accommodations.[21]

Black Boston's traditions of politics in the postwar decades were connected to the antebellum period by more than just ideology. Many of the men and women who fought against slavery and for black Bostonians' civil rights continued to be active after the Civil War. For example, Lewis Hayden, a vehement opponent of slavery and the Fugitive Slave Law, became the grand master of the Prince Hall Masons and was elected to the Massachusetts legislature in 1873. Boston's traditions of political involvement also transcended generations. In addition to Edwin Garrison Walker, the son of outspoken antislavery activist David Walker, twentieth-century editor of the *Boston Guardian* William Monroe Trotter's father, James, served in the Massachusetts Fifty-

Fifth Regiment before returning to Boston to become an outspoken advocate of independent politics.[22]

Black activists drew heavily on an active press to publicize their activities and attract allies to their cause. The city was home to several large presses, most of which had strong partisan affiliations. During the hotly contested political races of the late 1870s and early 1880s, the newspapers contained significant coverage of black political activity and opinions. Coverage of black politics increased in the months prior to an election and tended to be divided along partisan lines, although there was often significant overlap. That the opinions of African Americans often appeared in the pages of the Boston press is further evidence of the important part played by black Bostonians in the political debates.

African Americans in Boston also owned and operated short-lived newspapers of their own. In the 1880s, for example, African Americans founded the *Boston Advocate* and the *Hub*. These papers took distinct sides in debates over partisan support and provided a widely distributed platform for this discussion. Although they were significant organs of black Bostonian opinion, both newspapers lasted less than a decade before closing due to lack of funding. Despite their brief existence, these papers provided a significant forum for black political debate and are a rich source for understanding the political discourse of the period.

Black Bostonians were also constant contributors to one of the largest African American newspapers of the era, the *New York Globe*. Founded by editor Timothy Thomas Fortune, often a guest at Boston political meetings, the *New York Globe*, later the *New York Freeman* and the *New York Age*, provided a forum for Bostonians to present their opinions and provide news of their activities to African American readers across the nation. Nearly every week from its founding in 1883, Fortune's newspaper offered coverage of black Boston's social and political gatherings, transcripts of significant speeches, and letters to the editor and editorials written by members of Boston's African American community. The *Globe* also provided space for Bostonian correspondents to hone their journalistic craft before founding their own papers. J. D. Powell Jr., for instance, served as the original Boston correspondent to the *Globe* before leaving to found the *Boston Advocate*. Further, Fortune, as a supporter of African American independent politics, often featured discussions of Massachusetts elections and issued endorsements for candidates.[23] In this way, Boston and its black residents became featured topics and contributors in the national public sphere of black politics, transcending their seeming isolation in New England.

Besides the press, African Americans in Boston used public meetings of political organizations to galvanize support for candidates and to debate crucial issues. These meetings were sometimes small conferences by invitation only, but often they were large-scale affairs coupled with a parade or dinner. Meetings took place in spaces such as Faneuil Hall or in the sanctuaries of the city's African American churches. The accounts of the meetings present a diverse crowd of men, and sometimes women, engaged in discussions of the political identity of African Americans. Organizations such as the Bay State League, Colored Butler Clubs, and the Sumner National Independent League were overtly political and not only contributed to the political literacy of Boston's black community, but also were engaged in the development of an internal sphere of politics that was in conversation and occasional conflict with the external arena of electoral politics.[24] Further, black Bostonians maintained a strong associational life in fraternal organizations and clubs that provided areas for increased political discourse.[25] By organizing rallies, parades, speeches, and so on, black Bostonians created public forums for debates over political identity and definitions of American citizenship, especially as it manifested in voting and partisan politics.

## Black Bostonians and the Ballot

Boston's tradition of black activism, along with organizing experience, was a great asset in postwar electoral politics. Although black Bostonians faced regular racial discrimination, Boston, unlike many other cities both North and South, had few limits on African American suffrage.[26] African Americans in Boston, as in all of Massachusetts, had been guaranteed the right to vote by state law since the early decades of the nineteenth century; Massachusetts had no explicit laws disenfranchising citizens based on race. However, Massachusetts restricted voting to men over the age of twenty-one, required all voters to pay a poll tax, and, in response to increased foreign immigration, required all voters to be able to read the Constitution and sign their names. These regulations, however, made little impact on access to the polls.[27] Literate African American men could vote in all elections, and by the 1880s black women could cast ballots for local school board elections. Men and women in Boston had a tradition of active participation in electoral politics, making them fierce opponents to limitations on black voting in other parts of the country.[28]

Boston's black voters came from a variety of socioeconomic backgrounds. Although the political leadership of black Boston tended to be drawn from the more educated and economically successful, this was not universal, and did not necessarily exclude the lower classes from participation. In 1864, lawyer and activist George L. Ruffin collected the names of voters, their addresses, and whether they paid their poll tax. Among the names was a cross section of Boston's black community from both skilled and unskilled occupations. For example, Ruffin's record lists carpenter John Austin, porter Wesley Bishop, and laborer William Elisha. While Boston's black political leadership tended to be relatively wealthy or work as attorneys, journalists, or statesmen, the majority of the city's black voters were laborers.[29]

This electoral participation resulted in the election of African American representatives to the Massachusetts State House. From 1867 to 1902, Bostonians elected fourteen black state representatives with large support from the African American community. The men elected were leaders in the community, serving in social and fraternal organizations and often as spokesmen before and after their official public service. Many of the men eventually elected to state-level positions first gained experience serving as representatives to Boston's common council.[30]

Through elected officials, black Bostonians hoped to influence municipal and state politics from within the halls of government, rather than relying solely on outside agitation. Additionally, there was regular cooperation between internal and external elements. Working within the government provided experience that would inform political activities outside formal structures. This public service helped African Americans lay claim to the local and national citizenship that would shape their activism. Despite earning praise for making significant breakthroughs in black political representation, African American representatives often found themselves under scrutiny by members of the black community who felt that black legislators did not take a large enough role in uplifting the race, or were pandering to the state and national leadership of the Republican Party. Electoral success in Boston inspired confidence as they attacked political discrimination nationally and in the South especially.

Some black Bostonians had direct experience with southern-style racism, and this background shaped their activism. Following the end of the Civil War, returning veterans and former slaves from the South arrived in Boston and made their homes along its streets. Although the bulk of the African American community continued to live in city wards in Boston's West End, these new arrivals were some of the first African Americans to settle in the South End, and they helped begin the African American migration to that area. Some of these southern migrants influenced Bostonian institutions and became leaders in the community. For example, Julius C. Chapelle, born in South

Carolina, migrated to Boston in 1870. Chapelle was eventually elected to the Republican State Central Committee, the Boston City Council, and in 1883 the Masssachusetts General Court, where he supported bills improving the economic and political conditions of black Bostonians.[31]

Black Bostonian politics was additionally shaped by the influx of Irish immigrants during the middle and late nineteenth century. In the 1840s and 1850s there was a massive influx of new Irish residents, but despite their numbers, the nativist and anti-Catholic climate of the city stunted their political aspirations. However, by the 1870s the Irish began to be a politically significant force in Bostonian politics, and by the beginning of the twentieth century Bostonians elected several mayors of Irish descent.[32] During this period there was also some cooperation between Irish immigrants and the African American community. For example, Edwin Garrison Walker often represented Irish clients and admired Irish resistance to British rule.[33] Further, John Boyle O'Reilly, a former Irish revolutionary who became editor of the *Boston Pilot* following the Civil War, advocated African American civil rights and encouraged African Americans to use Irish nationalist movements as an organizational inspiration.

African American women also played important roles in organizing and engaged in debates over black politics and electoral partisanship. As historians such as Stephanie Shaw have demonstrated, women's collective activism of the 1890s in Boston had roots in the decades preceding and immediately following the Civil War. As Shaw explains, rather than the beginning of an era of black women's activism, the organization of women in the 1890s "represents another step in an internal historical process of encouraging and supporting self-determination, self-improvement, and community development."[34] Prior to the war, Boston was home to some of the most active black female public speakers and activists. During the Civil War, Boston's women organized to recruit soldiers for the black regiments as well as to raise funds for the Union forces. In the immediate aftermath of the war, women again came together to aid recently emancipated men and women, whether by raising funds for schools or by traveling south to work as teachers.

Many of the most prominent and politically active women in the city were engaged in various societies. These organizations not only provided a forum for members to engage in vigorous discussions about current events, but also served as a political training ground where women perfected the art of public speech and debate. Further, some of these organizations provided instructions in parliamentary procedure, thereby creating a cadre of African American women highly literate in the intricacies of formal politics. These skills would be very important as Boston's black women founded formal political organizations that attempted to guide the national destiny of the race.

African American women in Boston were in a unique position to access the public sphere of electoral politics. In 1879, after years of failed attempts, the Massachusetts General Court approved a law allowing women voters to cast ballots for local school committees; African American representatives to the general court had submitted petitions advocating woman suffrage and voted for its legalization. Following this significant victory, both black and white women would continue to campaign for full electoral equality. Woman's suffrage faced significant obstacles in Massachusetts. In addition to confronting an active antisuffrage opposition, many in the Republican majority of the state legislature opposed woman's suffrage for fear that these new voters would bolster the growing support of the Democratic Party in Massachusetts. In this way, women were caught in the middle of a male-dominated power struggle over partisan dominance.[35]

Through social clubs such as the Woman's Era Club and national organizations such as the National Association of Women's Clubs, these women influenced the larger discussion, and through publications such as *Woman's Era*, they were a commanding force in the discourse of politics nationally. Further, black women such as Josephine St. Pierre Ruffin were active in female suffrage organizations. They took the stage alongside men and were outspoken advocates of a national racial consciousness and uplift ideology.

With their strong institutions and traditions of activism, African Americans in post–Civil War Boston became a significant force in urban politics. They effectively mobilized to increase black political strength in the city. They utilized black-led political organizations to campaign for local political officials. They expressed their political viewpoints in the pages of Boston's general press and established black-owned and -edited partisan newspapers to wage battles over black support for local urban and national candidates. Success on the local level in Boston encouraged African Americans in the struggle for black uplift nationally. Inspired by antebellum legacies of antislavery and civil rights activism, and bolstered by the electoral strength of their demographic concentration, black Bostonians entered the postwar period mobilized to fight for their liberties both in the city and across the nation. Committed to the use of the ballot to effect change, they found a political home in the Republican Party and hoped to keep black interests at the forefront of party policy. As events of Reconstruction began to unfold, activists soon realized this would be no easy task.

## CHAPTER TWO

# No Peace until the Suffrage Question Is Settled

*Black Politics in the Age of Reconstruction*

On December 1, 1865, prominent African Americans from throughout New England joined Frederick Douglass in the Twelfth Baptist Church on Phillips Street in Boston's West End "for the purpose of taking action on matters concerning the colored man and his status in the United States."[1] The attendees made clear that they saw their political destiny as connected to the state of African Americans across the nation. George T. Downing from Rhode Island declared, "The colored people of the North could not be secure in the partial rights which they now possess, so long as the colored people of the South were denied justice."[2] One of the major topics discussed was the future of African American participation in American politics as voters.

For the members of the convention, African American suffrage had to become the primary focus of Reconstruction, and without it, all other gains would be meaningless. Bostonian Charles Remond, president of the convention, stated that he did not care about military gains, or even the surrender of the Confederacy. Rather, he announced, "the nation would have no peace until the suffrage question was settled." In the convention's official statement, the attendees affirmed the primacy of legal equality and voting rights as they sent a delegation to Washington to pressure the president and Congress to pass legislation. "Until the colored man is made equal before the law," they warned, "an earnest, unceasing agitation will be pressed, which will necessarily obstruct the wheels of progress in every avenue of material prosperity in the land, which will be unclogged only when justice is done in the matter."[3] For the delegates to the New England convention, suffrage was central to their political agenda, and in the coming decades they would make good on their threats of agitation until their goals were achieved.

African Americans in Boston were quick to emerge as prominent figures in city and state politics in the early years of Reconstruction. Soon after the conclusion of the war, black voters in Boston and Charlestown elected the first black members of the Massachusetts legislature. The officials, Edwin Garrison Walker and Charles L. Mitchell, were the first African Americans elected to any state legislature in the postwar nation. During the campaigns, black Bostonians embraced the ballot as a powerful tool for uplift, and the right to suffrage became a central rallying point. African Americans organized by canvassing for votes, managing precincts, and founding political organizations dedicated to the election of a party or candidate. These campaigns reflect varied interpretations of Reconstruction's aims, and they affected African American notions of party loyalty.

Once in office, Walker and Mitchell wasted little time before presenting the interests of their black constituency to the state. In particular, Walker expressed the view of many black Bay Staters as he opposed ratification of the Fourteenth Amendment to the U.S. Constitution in 1867. Through this opposition, black citizens questioned the motives of the national government and party structures. Even after the passage of the Fifteenth Amendment, black Bostonians remained hesitant to place complete trust in federal authority and national party leadership.

In their challenges, African Americans' definitions of citizenship were inextricably tied to the right to vote and partisanship. Through the ballot, they pressed for an accumulation of black political power. Pronouncements of equality and freedom rang hollow without the power to shape their political destiny. Rights of citizenship could be protected only by black voters exerting meaningful influence over civic life. Black Bostonians' visions of full citizenship included membership in a responsive political party, and calls for full voting rights also merged with growing calls for partisan accountability. Even as black supporters criticized party priorities and demanded immediate action, most remained loyal Republicans. Not yet ready to depart the party, they hoped that by appealing to the Republican antislavery past and commitment to black freedom during the war, coupled with the leverage of black voting power, they could continue to hold the party accountable and force its commitment to the black freedom struggle.

Although nascent, the seeds of political independence and disillusionment with party politics were planted during these early years of Reconstruction. Black activists saw early on the willingness of white Republicans to abandon black interests for the sake of political expediency. Over the next decade, African Americans would go to great lengths to keep the radical flame alive within the party. They organized at the city level to advance a national agenda, and federal protection of black voting rights across the nation was paramount. They fought for political recognition and held the Republican Party accountable for deserting its ideological origins. When the Republican Party fractured and began to de-emphasize the importance of black equality in its platform, some black supporters sought an independent political destiny beyond strict party loyalty.

## Black Electoral Success

Black Bostonians mobilized in the immediate postwar years to confront aspects of state government that they viewed as public displays of black marginality or official recognition of inferiority. In doing so, they united Boston struggles with the national struggles for black equality. In 1867, black Bostonians petitioned the city government for the removal of all racial identifiers in the official tax and voting registers.[4] They viewed these labels as a sign of a second-class citizenship. In the previous decade, the publishers of the city directories had stopped including racial identifiers, and by removing one of the last bureaucratic labels from the government records, African American petitioners sought physical proof of equality in the eyes of the state.

The attack on racial designation in the voting rolls was part of the expansion of black electoral strength during this period. Almost immediately following the war, black Bostonians took advantage of their voting power and began electing representatives to the Massachusetts General Court.[5] During these campaigns, questions of partisan affiliation, cross-party alliances, and cooperation with Irish Bostonians emerged and would grow stronger in the coming decades.

The majority African American Ward Six attempted to elect a black representative for many years, but tended to divide the vote among several candidates. After attempting to nominate John J. Smith in 1865, black Bostonians successfully nominated black candidates in 1866 following the decennial reapportionment that gave Ward Six an additional legislative seat.[6] In November 1866, residents of Boston's Ward Six and nearby Charlestown's Ward Three elected the first African American representatives to any state legislature in the nation.

Initially, however, it appeared to observers that in both cases, the black candidates would be defeated. In Ward Six, due to calculation error and confusion caused by a raucous wardroom crowd, Charles L. Mitchell was first nominated, but then found to not be among the top three vote getters, falling just ten votes behind the third-place finisher, white lawyer and incumbent legislator Harvey Jewell.[7] Charles Mitchell was a printer and worked for several years in the office of the antislavery newspaper the *Liberator*. During the war, Mitchell also served in the Fifty-Fifth Massachusetts Regiment, where he was one of the few black soldiers to be awarded the rank of lieutenant.[8] In the primary, Lewis Hayden received fifty-nine votes, which split portions of the black vote.[9] The exclusion of Mitchell raised fears among Republican leaders of losing black voters in the ward, and the winner of the primary, insurance executive Benjamin Stevens, declined his nomination to make room for

Mitchell on the ticket.[10] According to the *Boston Daily Advertiser*, the change was well received and "will satisfy the views of all concerned."[11]

In the election that followed days later, Mitchell won a seat in the statehouse, and black Bostonians from Ward Six celebrated. A large gathering of black supporters, several with loud drums, paraded through the ward until after midnight, "singing and hurrahing as they marched."[12] At a gathering at Faneuil Hall celebrating the result, black Rev. Leonard Grimes explicitly thanked the Republican Party. "God bless the Republican Party," Grimes began, "and may it go on in its good work till every black man who is loyal and true may go to the ballot box as well as the cartridge box to do his duty."[13] As black Bostonians celebrated the election of the first black men to the legislature, they also declared their partisan loyalty.

Across the Charles River, in Charlestown the election of Edwin Garrison Walker was also contentious, but lacked demands of party fealty. Edwin Walker was born in 1831 in Boston. His father, David Walker, was the author of the controversial pamphlet *Appeal to the Colored Citizens of the World*. Soon after David's sudden death, Eliza Walker gave birth to Edwin.[14] Walker moved with his mother to Charlestown, where he enrolled in the public schools. Following school, he worked as a leather worker, and in 1857 he opened his own business. Walker was active in the antislavery movement and may have taken part in the rescue of fugitive slaves. He spoke out against emigration and the African Civilization Society at a meeting of black men of New England in 1859. In the 1850s, Walker studied the law and was admitted to the Suffolk County bar in 1861. In the years after the Civil War, he worked closely with other antislavery activists, especially Robert Morris and George T. Downing.[15]

Republicans in Charlestown's Ward Three nominated Walker as their candidate.[16] Although this ward housed Charlestown's largest black population, it was small enough that Walker's victory depended on the ward's white majority. His supporters were confident, however, of his election.[17] A leading Republican wrote to the *Charlestown Advertiser* endorsing Walker, arguing, "Republicans should show their consistency in this matter, and not advocate impartial suffrage in the South, while denying support to a citizen of Massachusetts on account of his color."[18] According to the paper, this appeal was "written in the view that it is hinted certain Republicans propose to 'bolt.'"[19]

Fears of Republicans not supporting Walker continued to Election Day, and it would ultimately take Democratic support to secure him the victory. According to press reports, the Republicans did not make his nomination in good faith, and on the day of the vote the odds of election were stacked against Walker. Despite early pessimism, by the time the polls closed at four o'clock in the afternoon, fifty registered Democrats, mostly Irish, had crossed party lines and voted for Walker, helping him win by a vote of 342 to 324.[20] According to a *New York Times* report, it was Walker's support of Irish radicals' incursion into British Canada, his "warm interest in the Fenian cause," which helped him get Democratic votes.[21] A black delegation from Boston joined Walker in celebration across the river, where he thanked his white supporters for "the honor they had done him in overcoming their prejudices and voting for a man irrespect of color."[22]

By supporting the Irish nationalist Fenians, Walker attracted the support of Democratic Irish residents. "It is stated," the *Times* recorded, "that the [Democratic] party did as much toward his election as the Republicans, though he has always been identified with and [as an] exponent of the principles of that party."[23] Walker would not have won the general court seat without Irish support, and his sympathy for the cause of Irish independence would continue to inform his politics in the coming decades. The lack of support by Republicans influenced Walker's skepticism of Republican Party loyalty to its African American supporters throughout his life, beginning during his term as legislator.

Other black candidates also benefitted from Irish Democratic support. In Boston's Ward Three, Richard S. Brown accepted the Democratic nomination for city council after failing to gain a place on the Republican ticket.[24] On the day of the municipal election in December 1866, according to a press report, "the Irishmen and the colored men clasped hands in [Ward Three] and pulled together."[25] When the votes were counted, however, Brown was tied with Republican candidate Edward R. Merritt, causing a special election. While Republicans in the ward praised the Democratic nomination of a black candidate, they used the nomination of Brown to point out the racism among the Democrats. "A little practice of that sort," the Republican *Boston Daily Advertiser* argued, "may enable them to adopt more Christian and civilized views as to the general relations of that race." Republicans, however, "who need no training of this sort, can afford to vote for a regularly nominated white man."[26] On the day of the special election, excited voters from both parties streamed into the wardroom, and throughout the day the vote totals remained close. As the polls closed, the Republican Merritt won. Despite the opposition's victory, Ward Three Democrats were pleased with such a large turnout for an African American candidate.[27]

African Americans, too, used the opportunity to highlight their partisan independence. When, in 1867, Brown refused renomination, Ward Three black voters declared "the right to reject at the polls any candidate of any party who refuses to any class the privileges and dignities of American citizens." "They had not," the press reported, "sold themselves to the Democrats or any other party, but had acted against political demagogues."[28] In both Brown's failure and Walker's success, African Americans depended on and asserted partisan flexibility. The willingness to cross party lines had roots in this immediate postbellum era and would intensify over the coming decades.

Following the 1866 campaigns, the Boston press praised the nomination of black candidates as affirming Massachusetts's historical commitment to liberty. "It is fitting," authors of the *Right Way* declared, that "this mode of exemplifying the great doctrine of political equality should commence where the Revolutionary War commenced."[29] The *Commonwealth* echoed the sentiment: "These elections show that Massachusetts is consistent in theory and practice, and had taken a step in progress which must make every believer in equal and exact justice rejoice."[30]

As they celebrated, the press also cautioned white opponents of Walker's and Mitchell's election not to overreact. The election of black men in Massachusetts, they advised, was limited to majority black wards and did not reflect an overthrow of state politics. "For Massachusetts to put a black citizen in the place of Governor Bullock or of Senator Sumner," editors for the *Boston Daily Advertiser* argued, "would be indeed a subject for the derision of the rebel press, and the apologies of our injudicious friends; but for the ward in Boston which contains a large population of this color to give a veteran soldier of a colored regiment a seat . . . is most appropriate and commendable."[31] Reporters for the *Right Way* also argued that black representation was limited. "Massachusetts has now," they wrote, "the same proportion of colored men in her Legislature, that she had, by the last census, of colored inhabitants in her population. This is just, and no more than just."[32] While the press regarded the election of Walker and Mitchell as a triumph, they made it clear that white legislators were still in control.

Despite the controversy and limits to their power, the arrival of the two black legislators in the general court gave African American Massachusetts residents the first representatives of their race in government. Through them, they could communicate concerns to the chambers of government directly and become vocal and influential voices on the policies and programs of Reconstruction. For the first time, black legislators would guide decisions affecting African American men and women both in the state and nationally. They would not have to wait long, for soon after the election, Walker and Mitchell contended with one of the most significant pieces of Reconstruction legislation, the Fourteenth Amendment to the U.S. Constitution.

## Criticism of the Fourteenth Amendment

On June 13, 1866, the U.S. Congress passed the Fourteenth Amendment and sent it to the states for ratification. During the drafting of the amendment in Congress, Radical Republicans, moderate Republicans, and Democrats compromised on directly conferring on African Americans the right to vote. Instead, they left the governance of voting up to the individual states, with a penalty of loss of representation for those states that denied black suffrage.[33] Although Republicans in the Senate, bound by a caucus decision, voted unanimously for its passage, they did not universally support the amendment. Radical Republicans such as Charles Sumner criticized it for its lack of guarantee of black suffrage. Moderate Republicans, however, argued that an endorsement of equal black suffrage was a political liability and advocated forestalling the issue until a later date.[34] The compromises drew the ire of many Massachusetts's Radical Republicans, and those in the general court adamantly called for a delay or the defeat of ratification. Debates over ratification sent signals among the black community that their Republican allies were willing to compromise black rights away for the sake of political expediency.

African Americans joined with white opponents in a critique of the amendment's second section because it left open the possibility of disfranchisement. Through their petitions and representation in the general court, African Americans expressed their criticism and participated directly in the ratification process. They appeared before the Joint Committee on Federal Relations to express their concerns.[35] They asked that Massachusetts reject the amendment in favor of a substitute that better protected African American suffrage and civil rights.[36] Charles Mitchell, for example, presented a remonstrance decrying the amendment, which was signed by former antislavery activists and members of the African American community, including Twelfth Baptist Church minister Rev. Leonard Grimes, prominent attorney Robert Morris, and nationally known leaders such as Charles Remond and Lewis Hayden.[37] "Our reason for this petition," the preprinted form read, "is the danger to the liberties of the people from conceding to any State . . . the right or possibility of denying to any class of its loyal citizens the natural right of representation and the elective franchise."[38] The same language was mirrored in four other petitions brought before the general court.

In addition to submitting petitions, Boston's African American community was uniquely situated to contest ratification. As members of the general court, Walker and Mitchell provided direct African American opposition and worked to shape the legislature's opinion of the amendment. Walker was especially well positioned to provide his input. As a member of the House Committee on Federal Relations, he was among those responsible for issuing a report recommending the preferred course of action. On the committee, Walker joined influential Radical Republicans such as Francis Bird, who also opposed ratification.[39] Through participation in the authorship of the majority report opposing ratification, Walker provided an influential voice to the proceedings and was one of the few African Americans nationally to participate directly in the amendment's ratification. In this case, black political participation transcended the petition process and was given a voice with which the rest of the legislature had to contend.

In their report, the committee requested that the legislature recommend debate on the bill to the next general court session—in effect, rejecting the amendment. Massachusetts was the last state in the Northeast and one of the last states in the former Union to vote on ratification, and the Committee on Federal Relations cautioned the general court to be patient.[40] Ratification by other states did little to sway the committee's opinion. They argued that Massachusetts "can afford to stand alone on her convictions, but cannot afford to 'follow the multitude to do evil.' "[41]

Taking the amendment section by section, the committee majority argued that the legislation extended too much protection to the states of the former Confederacy to determine voting qualifications. Congress had and should exercise the authority to set and regulate voting in those states. "Conquered rebels have forfeited every right," the committee declared; "almost infinitely less has he the right to political power." In particular, the committee took issue with the second section, deemed "one of the most objectionable features of the amendment," which called for proportional representation of the total population and imposed penalties upon states that abridged voting rights.[42] The second section stipulated that if any state denied the right to vote to any male citizen over the age of twenty-one, its population on which representation was based would be reduced in proportion to the number of disenfranchised voters.[43] "This section," the committee concluded, "confessedly permits the disenfranchisement of colored citizens, and obviously attaches no penalty adequate to the punishment or prevention of this crime."[44]

By focusing a majority of their report on section two, legislators expressed the primacy that they placed on suffrage as a right of citizenship. For Edwin Walker and other committee members, securing African American voting rights was a fundamental precondition to integrating black men as full participants in the body politic. The black vote would almost certainly guarantee the establishment of Republican control over southern legislatures and thus the continuance of the U.S. Congress's progress in preserving black gains and assuring further progress. For those who cautioned against the ratification of the Fourteenth Amendment without an initial guarantee of African American suffrage, all other Reconstruction legislation was in jeopardy.

The majority argued that black citizens had served honorably in the Civil War and therefore deserved constitutional protections that were absolute: "From the first shot upon Sumter, the negro held the fate of the Union in his hands." Black military service greatly contributed to the Union victory, and thus veterans and their descendants deserved better than the Fourteenth Amendment offered. "What treatment is due to such allies?" the committee asked. "Disenfranchisement by the government they saved! Was this the entertainment to which Massachusetts invited the gallant recruits of her first black regiments?"[45]

The inclusion of the penalty in section two reducing representation did little to convince the Federal Relations Committee that southern whites would willingly enfranchise African Americans. "The madness of slavery and the providence of God has given to our government the golden opportunity to eliminate this oligarchical feature," the report continued; "this second section relinquishes this great power, rehabilitates the Southern oligarchy, and gives new life to this fruitful source of our woes."[46] The majority argued that former Confederate politicians could not be trusted to protect the voting rights of African Americans, and that regardless of penalty, Congress was placing southern governance in the hands of former slaveholders and leaders of the rebellion.

The restoration of former Confederate leadership would inevitably lead to voter disenfranchisement. Under the second section, white southerners would be "free to exclude from voting every colored citizen." The majority argued that white southerners would not enfranchise African Americans regardless of the penalty. The committee pointed to the so-called three-fifths compromise in the original U.S. Constitution as evidence. "For seventy-five years [the former Confederacy] acquiesced in the loss of representation for two-fifths of their slaves, rather than emancipate them," the committee explained. "Have we any right to assume that this same oligarchy will enfranchise their blacks?"[47]

The majority report also advocated African American participation in Reconstruction and the crafting of new constitutional amendments for civil and political rights. The report recognized that white politicians dominated nearly all state ratification proceedings. In Massachusetts, however, as a committee member, Walker was one of the few black men in the country who had the opportunity to formally weigh in on ratification. "It is easy," the report argued, "for white men, who practically wield the whole political power of the country, to regard with comparative indifference the rights of the long proscribed classes."[48] However, with Walker on the committee, the Massachusetts legislators argued that they could "view this subject from the stand point of the disenfranchised race, and adopting the fundamental principle that 'all governments derive their just powers from the consent of the governed,' we owe it to ourselves to demand, that the rights of underrepresented classes shall not be betrayed."[49] The report concluded that African Americans, including Walker, opposed the amendment, and that no legislature should make a decision regarding its ratification without their agreement. "It would be antirepublican and dangerous" to ratify the amendment, "not only without their consent, but against their universal protest."[50]

Walker and the other authors of the report advised the general court to delay ratifying the amendment until Congress had prepared another amendment that would explicitly protect suffrage. They feared that if the Fourteenth Amendment were ratified prematurely, representatives from former Confederate states would block future progress. It was only by securing the vote for African Americans that the Republican Reconstruction agenda could be protected. Disenfranchisement, they argued, would relegate the goals of Reconstruction "to a far off and uncertain future." "If Reconstruction be initiated and organized on the basis of this amendment," the report concluded, "it will inevitably be under rebel control, and as inevitably, the blacks will be excluded from all agency in the work."[51] After the committee issued its report, debate came to the House floor, where Walker continued his fierce opposition.

In a fiery speech on the House floor in March 1867, Walker denounced the amendment as giving control over the future for black men and women back to former slave owners. While supporting the majority of the amendment, Walker explicitly attacked the second section that "placed in the hands of the people of the rebel states the entire black population."[52] The amendment was an act of compromise with the southern states that did little to protect the rights of African American voters. "The amendment," Walker charged, "carefully guards everything else but the interests of millions of blacks in this country."[53] He concluded that support for the amendment was tantamount to yielding to the former confederacy and betrayed the reformist character of Massachusetts. "Massachusetts has always led the van in reform," Walker concluded; "the passage of the amendment, with the second section in it, would not be doing justice to the true, manly sentiment of Massachusetts."[54] The amendment was further evidence of the federal government, and the Republican Party, choosing political expediency over securing black rights.

Walker drew on the history of emancipation during the Civil War to show how tentative the federal government had been in freeing enslaved men and women. He recognized that members of Congress had hesitated to pass legislation that benefited African Americans for the sake of preserving the Union. By extension, the Fourteenth Amendment was another case of the federal government's bowing to the interests of the former slave states for the sake of political expediency and rebuilding the Union. "While the slaveholders were fighting us, seeking to destroy the last vestige of liberty on this continent," Walker declared, "the people were declaring that if the government and slavery could be saved they would be saved, if one should die it should be slavery. . . . That was another bow to slavery . . . the last bow to slavery comes in the shape of this second section."[55] Suspicion and criticism of this kind of the Republican Party and the federal government would help build the foundation for more staunchly independent political positions at the end of the 1870s, which expanded by the end of the century.

Despite Walker's opposition, the legislature eventually ratified the amendment. Ultimately, an overwhelming majority of the Massachusetts House of Representatives supported ratification, but both Edwin Walker and Charles Mitchell voted against the amendment's adoption instead supporting a request to Congress for a new constitutional amendment "prohibiting disenfranchisement of any citizen on account of color."[56] Despite ratification, in their opposition, and especially through Walker's committee representation and public oratory, African Americans demonstrated that they refused to be silent party loyalists, that they were going to be active participants in the questions of Reconstruction and were willing to confront Republican leaders if necessary.

Additionally, opposition to the Fourteenth Amendment demonstrated the importance of suffrage as a fundamental component of black visions of Reconstruction, and the reaction of men such as Edwin Walker showed the uncompromising position black activists took against potential disfranchisement. The right to vote was central to their worldview and definitions of citizenship, and it was only through the use of the ballot, along with federal protection, that African Americans could stand up to the persistent southern commitment to white supremacy. For Walker and the other opponents, it would be better to have no amendment at all than to have one that did little to protect black suffrage.

In the years following the ratification of the Fourteenth Amendment, African Americans continued to mobilize politically and campaigned for black candidates to succeed Mitchell and Walker. In these elections, despite their misgivings, black Bostonians declared their increased support for the Republican Party, and there seemed to be a general consensus that African Americans were best served by casting their lot with the party of Lincoln. In 1867, for example, Lewis Hayden presided over a meeting of black residents during the successful campaign of black Republican John J. Smith to succeed Charles L. Mitchell as a representative from Ward Six. Hayden as well as other members of black Boston's political elite declared unwavering support for the Republican Party. The attendees passed resolutions "recognizing the Republican Party as the party that secured the freedom of the slave, and his investment with all the rights of the citizen; and declaring that in their political course the colored men of Boston will support no organization whatever which seeks to undermine and destroy the efficiency of the Republican Party who are committed to the Reconstruction measures."[57]

While black Republican strength helped John J. Smith win in Boston, Edwin Walker lost reelection in Charlestown "because of the number of liberal candidates in the field."[58] Later commentators attributed his loss to his outspokenness and public condemnation of the Fourteenth Amendment.[59] That speech, they argued, "practically severed his connection with the Republican Party."[60] Loyal black Bostonians from Ward Six continued to support Republicans and elect black candidates to the state legislature, but Walker's sentiment of political independence continued to grow and was present even in near-universal celebration of the Fifteenth Amendment several years later.

## The Fifteenth Amendment and Debates over Partisan Loyalty

The ratification of the Fifteenth Amendment in 1870 affirmed black Republican support and assuaged some of the critics of the Fourteenth Amendment. Unlike the previous amendment, which discouraged and penalized but did not prohibit voter disenfranchisement, the Fifteenth Amendment explicitly stated that the right to vote "shall not be denied or abridged by the United States or by any State on account of race, color, or previous condition of servitude."[61] The amendment, however, did not universally guarantee the right to vote. It only prohibited federal and state disenfranchisement based on race and did not establish a right to hold office or prevent states from enacting other voting qualifications. Northern Republicans especially were hesitant to enact sweeping legislation, fearing the political power of foreign, poor, or illiterate white Democratic voters.[62] Allowing continued restrictions created the opportunity for states to enact much of the legislation limiting black enfranchisement in later decades.

Immediately after passage of the amendment, however, African American communities celebrated, with little attention to the possibility of future exclusion. When Massachusetts governor William Claflin presented the amendment to the general court in early March 1869, the earlier controversy that had surrounded ratification of the Fourteenth Amendment was gone. The legislature ratified the amendment quickly, with 192 supporting and only 15 opposing. John J. Smith, who succeeded Mitchell and Walker in 1868 as the only African American representative in the general court, voted in favor.[63]

In the following year the amendment was officially ratified nationally, and jubilant African American communities throughout the country celebrated. In Boston, there was a massive parade through the city that culminated in a grand ceremony and speeches at Faneuil Hall. John J. Smith and Charles L. Remond, the president of the celebration, led the march through the West End. The parade included members of the Fifty-fourth and Fifty-fifth Massachusetts regiments and black fraternal lodges from Massachusetts and Rhode Island. At the conclusion, the throng packed Faneuil Hall. "The floor," the *Boston Daily Advertiser* reported, "was occupied by the various societies, the galleries by ladies, and the space beneath galleries by everybody who could get standing room."[64] The crowd heard speeches by prominent black and white former antislavery activists and political leaders including William Lloyd Garrison, Wendell Phillips, George L. Ruffin, Robert Morris, and Edwin Garrison Walker. Charles Remond declared that it was "the colored people's Fourth of July."[65] The speakers, though all gathered for the same event, shared diverse perspectives on the passage of the amendment and future strategies for black uplift. These discussions exposed early instances of growing tensions, particularly around black support for political parties.

George Ruffin presented a series of resolutions commemorating the event foreshadowing his future as a powerful voice for Republican support in the city. Ruffin was born of free parents in Richmond, Virginia, in 1834. After moving to Boston as a child, he attended public school and worked as a barber. He eventually began legal studies and graduated from Harvard University Law School in 1869. Voters in Ward Six elected him to the Massachusetts legislature in 1870. He also served on Boston's Common Council in 1875 and 1876. He remained an active participant in Republican politics, serving on both the ward and city committees. Controversially, he would be appointed to a Massachusetts judgeship over Edwin Walker in the 1880s. He was later made a consul for the Dominican Republic. Ruffin was married to Josephine St. Pierre Ruffin, a national leader of African American club women, founder of the Women's Era Club, and, with her and Ruffin's daughter Florida, editor of the *Women's Era* newspaper.[66]

In his celebration of the Fifteenth Amendment Ruffin not only lauded its importance but used the opportunity to dedicate the loyalty African Americans had to the Republican Party. Ruffin declared, "We recognize the Republican Party, which has enacted the just wholesome laws of the past ten years and securely fixed in the Constitution of our country the beneficent provisions. . . . We here offer the members of that party our heartfelt thanks."[67] Other speakers were more muted in their celebration and pointed out the continued hardships facing African Americans.

As Edwin Walker spoke, he addressed continued racial prejudice and the political obstacles facing the race. Walker avoided telling the audience to be "loyal to this party or that party, for such advice is unnecessary."[68] He argued that while policies of Reconstruction attempted to enforce black voting equality in southern states, they neglected continued restrictions and prejudice in the North. He lamented that "with the death of slavery came another species of caste."[69] Incidents of racial discrimination in the state muted hopeful celebrations of coming racial equality. "There was not a town in Massachusetts," Walker announced, "where a black man could be elected by popular vote . . . because of caste." He expected "to see black men in the city council of Richmond before they would be in Boston."[70]

Walker seized the occasion to question why, as southern states were sending black men to Congress, the North did not do the same. By criticizing the state of electoral politics in Massachusetts, Walker exposed the hypocrisy of a Republican platform that sought to mandate black voting and office holding in the South, even while maintaining restrictions on them in the North. Walker cautioned that although the passage of the Thirteenth, Fourteenth, and Fifteenth Amendments was significant, discrimination persisted. Even in Massachusetts, most African Americans had little chance at a career in electoral politics.[71]

Another speaker, attorney and former antislavery activist Robert Morris, was a mentor to Walker and similarly skeptical about racial progress following passage of the Fifteenth Amendment. He urged African Americans to rely less on white party leaders and take control of their own political destinies. Morris had seen firsthand the duplicity of supposed white allies. He remembered that early in the Civil War, when he had approached leaders in the State House regarding raising an African American regiment, he was rebuffed. Once the regiment was formed, Morris lamented, African Americans were not given leadership over the regiment, in contrast to Irish regiments where "Yankee officers were never put over them."[72] White political leadership was happy to use African Americans as soldiers and as voters, but was resistant to yielding control to black leadership.

Now was the time, Morris declared, for African Americans to take control of their own national fate, by force if necessary. In the face of recent incidents of racial violence in the South, Morris proposed "to send two black regiments down there with a black brigadier in command. Then there would be no trouble, and they would soon have Georgia as peaceable as Massachusetts."[73] In addition to the military, Morris concluded that black voters should also take control of the Republican Party: "The Republican Party had ridden into power on the Negro's back, but now the blacks had mounted, and, having seized one party by the ears and the other by the tail, would ride the jack themselves."[74] African Americans, Morris argued, had the electoral power to drive party policy, but must be willing to exercise it.

It was not only African Americans who advocated political independence. White former abolitionist and famous orator Wendell Phillips supported Morris's comments by calling for African Americans to use the vote to defend themselves from those, even Republicans, who would undermine the progress of Reconstruction. Phillips called on black voters to look beyond a candidate's party affiliation and judge him on his dedication to the advancement of black citizens. He advocated a root principle: "the nation knows no distinction of race." He condemned any black support of candidates who upheld racial distinctions. "If I ever see a black man," Phillips proclaimed, "go to the ballot box to record a vote to lift into office a man that knows any distinction of race in the political arena, that man I shall regard as recreant to his own race . . . as poisoning the fountain out of which his own children are to be fed."[75] Like Morris, Phillips encouraged African Americans to exert electoral influence on Republicans and hold accountable those who marginalized black supporters.

Phillips called on black voters to be the primary defenders of their civil rights and to punish without mercy any elected official who would perpetuate racial division. Phillips declared, "Never forgive at the ballot box."[76] He continued, "If you know a man who in yonder legislature . . . has given a vote that is unjust to a black man, because he was black, no matter if the very next year he does as much for your race as Charles Sumner and Benjamin Butler . . . never forgive him."[77] He urged black Bostonians to monitor and keep track of the voting record of their representatives on issues of civil rights and be prepared to confront those persons when they campaigned.

Finally, Phillips, also a strong advocate of women's suffrage, charged African American women to play a role in the battle against racial prejudice in politics. "Mothers," he commanded, "never forget the name of the man in political life who has either ignorantly or maliciously given a vote against your race." Phillips instructed black women not only to influence the votes of their husbands and sons but also to look toward the time when they too would vote. He focused on women in the audience as potential models of independent voters. "When the laws give you the right to vote," he maintained, "go out also with a firm determination, no matter what his party or name may be, if he has voted against you strike his name from American politics and bury it as completely as if he was forty feet under the Rocky Mountains."[78] Phillips urged black voters, male and female, to stand firm on ideologies of racial uplift and equality, regardless of a candidate's party.

Walker, Morris, and Phillips urged African Americans, both voters and nonvoters, to be skeptical of all politicians regardless of partisan affiliation. They advocated the support of candidates based on their support for black political and civil rights, not their affiliation with the Republican Party. These arguments cut against the Republican Party's objectives for the Fifteenth Amendment: to recruit and maintain the loyalty of black voters in both the South and the North. On this day, a day celebrating constitutionally guaranteed black male suffrage, leaders called African Americans to use their vote strategically, even if it meant defeat of Republican candidates. Here was the emerging divide between loyal Republicans such as George Ruffin and independents such as Morris and Walker. These schisms continued to coalesce during the fervor that accompanied the presidential election of 1872 and would grow over the coming decades. Those who declared in 1865 that there would be no peace until African Americans were fully enfranchised would find that as that battle continued, new fronts were emerging in the realm of partisanship.

## CHAPTER THREE

# Vote, That the Work Might Be Finished

*Black Electoral Politics and the Presidential Election of 1872*

While African Americans celebrated the adoption of the Fifteenth Amendment, they viewed it as just another step on a longer journey toward full and meaningful citizenship. Progress was slow, but black activists had faith that through diligent organizing and hard work through the Republican Party, they could prevent backsliding and assure further advancement. As the first presidential election after the passage of the Fifteenth Amendment approached, most black activists remained loyal Republicans and dedicated their service to electoral victory. "Vote," George Ruffin told a Boston convention crowd in 1872, "that the work, begun under the immortal Lincoln, may be finished under Gen. Grant."[1] Even while increasingly skeptical of white Republican loyalties, black voters remained overwhelmingly committed to the Republican Party as the primary vehicle for racial progress. Some of their white former allies, however, began to distance themselves from the cause of black equality in favor of other issues. In what historians have described as a shift from "ideological" to "pragmatic" politics, former Radical Republicans were less willing to take the political risk of casting their lot with black activists. This left African Americans as the national standard bearers for lasting freedom and enforcement policies.

At the beginning of the 1870s, as the Republican Party continued to splinter, black activists remained committed to civil rights. Disillusioned with the Republican establishment, they supported insurgent former Civil War general and Massachusetts congressman Benjamin Butler for gubernatorial nomination. Running as a Republican, however, Butler failed to receive the nomination from the statewide conventions. Many white Republican Party leaders opposed the general for his antebellum loyalty to the Democratic Party and his increased denunciation of big business and hard money.[2] Butler's defeat further galvanized black skepticism of the Republican Party, which spilled over into national elections.

In 1872, what had been a minor skirmish at the state level became a national battle during the presidential election. Many Republicans increased their distance from their radical past when they supported New York newspaper editor Horace Greely over the incumbent president Ulysses S. Grant.

These so-called Liberal Republicans joined with the Democratic minority to form the Liberal Republican and Democratic Party. As members of this "New Departure" distanced themselves from the racist traditions of the Democratic Party, Liberal Republicans maintained some calls for black civil rights. Indeed, former Radical Republicans such as Francis Bird joined the coalition.[3] Historians Eric Foner and Heather Cox Richardson explain that the transition of former Radical Republicans came more from hostility to perceived corruption in the Grant administration and a desire to preserve the free-market economy than from antipathy toward African Americans. Whatever the motives, they had limited support for black interests. For Liberals, over-reaching federal protection of black freedom undermined fundamental ideas of free labor and equal opportunity. "Freedom [to liberal reformers]," Foner explains, "meant not economic autonomy or the right to call upon the aid of the activist state, but the ability to compete in the market place and enjoy protection against an overbearing government."[4]

Liberal Republicans were explicit in their opposition to extended federal interference in and control of the state-level elections. They acknowledged the Fourteenth and Fifteenth Amendments as the law of the land and trusted state governments to enforce the provisions.[5] They rejected calls for federal protection of the polls and more direct voters' rights protection; these they thought violated the rights of states to govern their own elections and decide their own voting qualifications. While the states could not explicitly discriminate based on race, color, or previous condition of servitude, under Liberal doctrine, other qualifications, such as property ownership or literacy, were permissible and constitutional.[6]

Massachusetts's Liberal Republican and Democratic Party influenced presidential politics. In 1872, it played a key role in securing the nomination of New York newspaper editor and former radical abolitionist Horace Greeley as a candidate and winning the endorsements of prominent Radical Republicans.[7] Greeley's nomination signaled the demise of Republican ideological unity and generated debate among black Bostonians. A majority of African Americans continued to support President Grant for reelection, but some African Americans, including activists Robert Morris and George Downing, supported Greeley.

The Greeley campaign hoped it could call on the public endorsement of former Republicans to secure the loyalty of black voters.[8] Both Republican leader Francis Bird and longtime senator and supporter of black civil rights Charles Sumner endorsed Greeley.[9] Black activists such as Downing hoped that African American support for the liberals would press Republicans and the

Grant administration to reaffirm their commitments to protecting black rights, rather than merely paying lip service to ideas of equality.[10] Still, there were barriers to broad African American support for the Liberal Republicans as they recalled past Democratic support of slavery and opposition to Reconstruction amendments. As other issues took precedence for white politicians, for African Americans, issues of racial justice remained paramount. Black activists rejected traditional Republican leadership and sought candidates, regardless of party, who were willing to stand with them in the fight for justice.

## Black Boston and the "Beast"

In 1871, the Massachusetts Republican Party was in disarray, weakening the power of the state establishment and creating room for Benjamin Butler to mount a statewide campaign for the Republican nomination for governor. Since the Civil War, Butler had endeared himself to black Bostonians. Although a Democrat and an opponent of the Civil War in the 1850s, Butler transformed during his time as a Union general into an outspoken advocate of African American rights. During the war he was one of the first officials to protect those fleeing from bondage to Union lines as "contraband," and his enforcement of black rights and brutal treatment of Confederates while in command of Union-occupied New Orleans earned him the respect of African Americans, even as southerners condemned him as "Beast Butler." After the war, Butler represented Massachusetts in the U.S. House of Representatives, where he was a major author and advocate of civil rights legislation and continued federal protection of African Americans' rights. He grew in popularity among African Americans, due in particular to his work on behalf of enslaved people during the Civil War and his fervent advocacy of civil rights as postwar congressman in the House of Representatives. Butler's original authorship and advocacy of the third enforcement act, also known as the Ku Klux Klan Act, played a large part in galvanizing his black supporters. This legislation declared that conspiracies to limit voting rights, office holding, jury service, and equal legal protection could be prosecuted in a federal court if local authorities failed to act. The act also empowered the president to deploy the military and suspend the writ of habeas corpus in extreme cases.[11]

While Butler cultivated a new reputation as a radical reformer, former Boston radicals became the champions of the free market and protections of Boston's business interests. In addition to distancing themselves from civil rights struggles, their embrace of probusiness policies also placed them at odds with Boston's working class. Benjamin Butler forged a coalition of white workers and disillusioned African Americans as he mounted a campaign committed to workers' rights and continued protection of black rights in the South. In this race, for the first time, black Bostonians supported an insurgent against the Republican Party establishment. Although they still remained loyal to the party generally, their support of Butler indicated their willingness to place ideology over pragmatism.

In April 1871, leaders of black Boston invited Butler to speak before an audience at the North Russell Street Church to "address upon us the political issues of the day." They praised the support of the Ku Klux Klan Act and Reconstruction policy by Massachusetts's congressional delegation and Butler in particular. "We desire to show our respect and gratitude," Lewis Hayden and other black leaders wrote in a letter of invitation, "for the fidelity with which you have supported in Congress the rights of Southern loyalists. . . . Our thanks to you are the complement of the abuse heaped upon you by all who hate the Union and by all who hate freedom."[12] Quoting from Senator Charles Sumner's endorsement of the legislation, the signatories endorsed "the imperialism of equal rights," the power of the centralized federal state to protect black freedoms.[13] The use of active state power was central to their vision of freedom and a major catalyst for their endorsement of Butler and the Grant administration.

On the evening of May 8, Charles Remond introduced Butler to the mostly black audience. Butler opened by explaining the shift in congressional priorities away from Reconstruction and highlighted the rise of southern racial violence. "Scarcely at any period before," Butler declared, "were your interests more in jeopardy or had you more at stake."[14] He highlighted his role as author and chief advocate of the Ku Klux Klan Act and argued that the Fifteenth Amendment was of little use without federal protection of African Americans' rights. "The ballot," Butler argued, "is no protection against the bullet when he who holds the ballot is unarmed, homeless and landless." Only with federal protection from armed intimidation and violence could African Americans fully exercise their right to vote freely and "use the ballot to protect [themselves]."[15]

Although by the end of the decade Butler would reject Republican affiliations, in 1871 he made strong partisan claims pressing for increased black turnout and against Democratic support. He cautioned against believing Democrats' rhetoric that they would leave the amendments in place if elected. "If the Democratic Party shall come into power," he warned, "all benefits of those Constitutional guarantees will be taken away from the colored man."[16] While Butler disagreed with members of the Republican Party, he was adamant against leaving the party.

As he concluded his speech, Butler decried claims of African American inferiority and ignorance. He celebrated the success of his black colleagues in the House of Representatives and rejected the argument of white southerners that it was African American freedom that was causing unrest across that region. It was whites, Butler declared, who were the true perpetrators of violence and responsible for undermining the successes of Reconstruction. "Which knows most of the necessities of the South," Butler asked, "the negro or the white man?"

> The Negro builds churches and school-houses; the white man burns them. The negro works industriously to provide something from the soil; the white man refuses to labor, and endeavors to create anarchy because he can no longer live in idleness upon the labor of others. The negro, after the day of toil, is well-taught enough to go to his peaceful home and quiet rest. He knows enough to respect every man's right to person and property; and the white man rides at night masked, disguised and armed, to the terror of the people, and for the purpose of murdering the officers of the law, or of burning the cabins of the peaceful. Finally, the colored men everywhere knew enough . . . all to vote the Republican ticket, and that steadily; and that is sufficient political knowledge, in my judgment, for anybody.[17]

Butler concluded that white southerners were responsible for the slow pace of black progress, which they used as justification for the abandonment of Reconstruction policy all together.

As he ended his speech, Butler recognized the bravery of black soldiers during the Civil War and used this as evidence of the willingness of African Americans to resort to armed conflict to protect themselves if necessary. He warned that those responsible for racial violence "better not trespass too far"; that while southern black residents desired peace, they would fight back, especially if the federal government failed to protect them. "His hunters will quail and flee before the determination of his defense and the courage of his battle . . . and stand aghast with horror at the cruelty . . . when it bursts the bounds of patience under accumulated suffering and wrong."[18] In closing, he declared it the duty of all statesmen to study closely the positive facts of black emancipation and "say whether such a race is not fit for the responsibilities and rights of self-government."[19]

Butler's speech increased his profile among the Boston black community, and they declared their support. In letters, they praised Butler and offered their service in aid of his candidacy. William Cooper Nell, the noted black historian and abolitionist, reflected support based on Butler's Civil War service. "The name of General Butler," Nell declared, "always rises to my lips when I am reviewing the deeds of Northern Patriots who were most aggressive and potential in putting down the slaveholder's rebellion."[20] Black residents of Ward Six attested to black voting strength and pledged to work on Butler's behalf. One black supporter noted, "the colored people hold the balance of power in the Sixth Ward."[21] Others pledged to use what resources they had to secure the Republican nomination for Butler. "I will do all in my power to make the election a success," another supporter announced. Such pronouncements continued as black and white Republicans moved toward the nomination.

Discord within the Republican Party was evident, and African Americans were at the center of the tumult during ward caucus meetings to select delegates to the Republican nominating convention. During what the anti-Butler *Boston Daily Advertiser* called a "disgraceful scene," African Americans joined with Butler supporters in advocating delegates loyal to the general over those of the Republican establishment.[22] Butler's opponents decried the day's events as the height of political corruption and alleged that "there was never a more complete example of the worst form of caucus packing."[23]

While there were clashes between Butler opponents and supporters in all the wards, commentators made note of the considerable black presence in the adjacent Wards Three and Six caucus meetings. In the Third Ward, reporters for the *Boston Daily Advertiser* remarked that "the caucus was packed for Butler." They criticized Irish voters as they highlighted the role of black poll workers in the day. "It was amusing," they reported, "to see Irish novitiates in republicanism bundled in and put through by officious colored men, whose faces beamed with exultant smiles as they were made conscious that one more vote had been cast for their favorite."[24]

In nearby Ward Six, the caucus meeting was particularly contested, and reports of the day singled it out as the most controversial. Here, too, black participation was particularly noticeable. Newspapers alleged that Butler supporters "collared" black voters and forced them be counted with them.[25] George Ruffin, now the Ward Six representative in the state legislature, pressed the organizers to amend their current checklist of voters with one he had brought "of persons who should not be deprived of their rights."[26] When the meeting ultimately fractured and the anti-Butler faction attempted to take the official checklist to a separate meeting at the Charles Street Church, a group of black voters attempted to intervene. As the scene turned more violent, the police arrived and, as the Democratic *Boston Post* described, "used their clubs liberally."[27] The riotous crowd overturned tables and some "made rather un-dignified exits from the windows into the area."[28] When the dust settled, two separate meetings resumed, and each selected a different slate of delegates to the convention. African Americans were represented among both delegations. The anti-Butler caucus passed a resolution declaring itself "the only legal and just" voice of Ward Six Republicans.[29] Other black Bostonians remained loyal to Butler. In an interview with the *Boston Post* days after the meeting, George Ruffin affirmed that Butler still had much support from the black community. Declaring that "the Butler men carried the day," Ruffin opposed seating the anti-Butler delegation at the convention.[30] He maintained the loyalty of a ma-jority of the black voters for the general and affirmed Butler's military and congressional service as a leading cause.

Butler's Ward Six delegates were cautiously optimistic that despite the events at the caucus meeting, they would be seated fairly at the convention in Worcester. These hopes were quickly dashed as the convention rejected But-ler's nomination.[31] Dejected, black delegates returned to Boston more con-vinced that their interests did not lie with party leadership. Butler returned to Washington as a congressman and did not seek a statewide office again until 1873, but his mark on Boston's black community persisted, and his 1871 cam-paign laid the groundwork for African American support for him during his emergence as the face of the Massachusetts Democratic Party in the late 1870s. Other black Republicans left the party briefly. George Ruffin, for ex-ample, joined the newly formed Labor Reform Party as nominee for attorney general.[32]

## Partisan Debates and the Growth of Independent Politics

The year 1872 marked a significant point in African American politics and par-tisanship. This was a moment of heated debate over African American parti-san affiliation that reflected the importance African Americans placed on the election. As 1872 was the first presidential election after the passage of the Fif-teenth Amendment, many felt that the future of Reconstruction and the fate of African Americans would be determined by the contest between the former general and the newspaper editor. The election marked the first large-scale Af-rican American mobilization in any presidential contest. Black Bostonians or-ganized campaign committees, deliberated in meetings, and gathered in public rallies. In these meetings, black voters again questioned fidelity to the Republican Party. They viewed themselves as a significant electoral force in the city, and detailed reports of black organizing circulated in the city's press.

As the election approached, black leaders came together to discuss their endorsement of candidates and how best to approach the campaign. Although they were generally united around ideologies of racial equality and civil rights advocacy, they expressed divergent views about black partisan allegiance. While there had been disagreements over party affiliation in previous years, the election of 1872 meant the debates potentially had electoral consequences. For supporters of Grant, a Republican election meant continued racial progress, while Greeley's victory would mean the end of Reconstruction and the potential decline of black fortunes. Meanwhile, for supporters of Greeley, Grant's administration did not do enough to protect African American rights and property, while it agitated antiblack sentiment.[33]

Partisan affiliation was a significant subject of heated discussion, and early divisions were on display during a March 1872 meeting of African American men from throughout the state at the Twelfth Baptist Church. Loyal Grant supporters proposed resolutions celebrating current racial progress, urging continued civil rights agitation, and praising the Republican Party: "We look upon the assemblage of any body of colored men at this time with solicitude and cheerfully commit to their hands our interests and the proper direction of our influence for the future."[34] The resolutions did not merely thank the Republican Party for its service, but pledged African American loyalty to its candidates. Speaking of the upcoming national Republican convention in Philadelphia, the resolution committee agreed to endorse the chosen Republican candidate. The members affirmed "our duty as colored voters to reindorse [sic] the platform which has served as a basis for the settlement of the difficulties of Reconstruction . . . and as it has thus far led us toward the fruition of our hopes we again express our loyalty to the Republican Party."[35]

Members, however, expected continued progress on civil rights as a prerequisite for further loyalty. They urged the passage of aggressive civil rights legislation and declared that "while our faith in the Republican Party is as firm as ever, and our confidence remains unshaken, nothing but a complete recognition of our rights and the breaking down of all barriers of color distinction will show us whether that confidence has been misplaced."[36] Although most of the resolves were passed unanimously, some of the members took issue with declarations of loyalty to the Republican Party.

Robert Morris, in particular, opposed the offer of African American votes to whoever was chosen at the Republican convention in Philadelphia. Morris demanded that the convention endorse political independence and allow black voters to choose their own allegiances. He "was not yet ready to say that he was going to vote for the present incumbent . . . neither was he ready to take a jump into the dark."[37] Echoing his earlier statements, Morris urged black voters to choose candidates who would support black equality without compromise or hesitation. "I want the man who is to be the presiding officer over this great nation, willing to say that every black man shall have the right to go from one end of this mighty country to the other, without let or hindrance, and to say that unequivocally."[38] While Morris was unsure of what allegiance to Greeley would resolve, he was increasingly certain that the Grant administration was not the ally other African Americans supposed it to be. Morris was supported by another speaker who "was pledged to no party . . . and was in favor of accepting anyone who would do the most for them."[39]

George Ruffin, by contrast, had helped write the meeting's resolutions and immediately responded to Morris, defending loyalty to the Republican Party. Although he stated that the resolution "did not commit them to anything but principle," Ruffin declared, "he was in favor of the committee expressing itself as being good Republicans as anybody, and was willing to abide by the action of the gentlemen who were to meet at Philadelphia." Convention president Charles Remond supported Ruffin and declared, "those who start away for a new party take their chances on an uncertainty."[40] Following a sometimes biting debate, the endorsement of Republicans was voted down by a vote of twenty-five to eighteen.[41] Despite the favorable support for Grant, the majority of meeting attendees were not willing to commit universal loyalty to the Republican Party.

Despite the disagreements, at the conclusion of the day's meetings, the convention formed a state central committee, made up of seventeen members, to organize African Americans across Massachusetts. While most of the committee members were from Boston, there were representatives from black communities throughout Massachusetts.[42] In forming the state central committee, the members of the convention emulated the major political parties who used state central committees to unify political strategy across the state. The organizers hoped that through the central committee they could effectively communicate with black communities across Massachusetts in order to organize black voters as an effective political bloc.

While they generally supported the state Republican Party, the committee stood outside of the official Republican organization and was uniquely concerned with the interests of the black electorate. The primacy of racial interest sometimes brought members of the committee into conflict with the

Republican Party and each other. Among the committee members were men such as Morris and Ruffin who had very different ideas about African American participation in politics. Although these disagreements persisted, it did not stop them from serving as representatives to the same body. While political disagreements were muted for the time being for the sake of racial unity, as the election approached, divisions over partisan affiliation would become starker.

In the months following the formation of the central committee, the debate over black allegiance to the Republican Party increased, and African Americans chose candidates who tested black political unity. As the election approached, public statements took on a more partisan valence. In July 1872, black Bostonian supporters of General Grant met at the Phillips Church to declare publicly their support for the Republican Party. Newspapers publicized the event as a Republican rally, and the participants were explicit in their support for the Republicans and their denunciations of the Democratic Party, which endorsed the liberal ticket. Lewis Hayden recognized the significance of the moment and declared that "the pending election was the most important to the colored men of any that had occurred since the election of Lincoln."[43] Speaking about increasing divides within the Republican Party, Hayden explained that while in previous elections "all their friends were all united and working for the common cause," now some had joined their opponents, and "for this reason he adjured the colored men of the nation to stand firmly together."[44] As white Republicans and some black voters defected from the Republican Party, many such as Hayden perceived the black electorate as a strong barrier between political power and the Democratic Party.

Continuing to emphasize the seriousness of the coming election, George Ruffin declared that the current campaign was "a continuance of the old antislavery struggle." For Republicans such as Ruffin, the election of Greeley meant the demise of postwar black progress and a rollback of federal Reconstruction policy. Less than a decade had passed since emancipation, and black Republicans feared that a Democratic administration meant the return to power of slavery's advocates. "The fruits of victory already gained," Ruffin warned, "were sought to be wrung from the colored men by treachery."[45] Ruffin continued to emphasize the contributions that Grant had made to African American civil rights and decried Greeley despite his antislavery background.

The Democratic New Departure by which northern Democrats sought to distance themselves from white supremacy drew pointed criticism from Ruffin as a "death bed repentance." For Ruffin, the Democratic Party in any iteration was the party of slaveholders, and he urged black voters to judge the parties on their past records and current advocacy of Reconstruction. He praised Grant's record, and without Democratic support of concrete policies protecting African American rights, his opposition was resolute. "Let the Democrats, if they have changed their views," Ruffin declared, "bring forth fruit meet for repentance.... Let them show action to correspond in the States where they are in power."[46] He rejected the moderation of northern Democrats, and instead tied their destiny to the plight of black citizens in the southern states. As long as black oppression continued in states controlled by the Democrats in the South, Ruffin argued, African Americans should oppose all Democratic candidates, regardless of their past support of African American interests.

Another speaker, former black abolitionist and author William Wells Brown, cautioned black voters against being swayed into supporting Democrats by Greeley's past antislavery activism and Charles Sumner's surprising support of the Liberal Republicans. Brown called for "unity of action" and urged black Bostonians to travel to the South to advise southern black voters against voting for Greeley.[47] Brown looked to black Bostonians as potential national political leaders and called on them to organize beyond the borders of Boston or the Bay State. Exemplifying the relationship between black Bostonians and southern black communities, John Oliver from Richmond, Virginia, rose to speak and pledged the support of black Virginians for Grant as he affirmed fears that the Democratic Party in that state advocated school segregation and qualified suffrage.[48] The attendance of Oliver brought Bostonian attendees into conversation with residents of states most vulnerable to shifts in Reconstruction policy.

At the conclusion of the meeting, the members resolved to support the Republican incumbent and attacked the Democratic Party as enemies of black civil rights. "We, the colored citizens of Boston," the resolutions began, "declare our hostility to our common foe, the Democratic Party of the United States.... Its infamous record in causing a bloody war, with all its consequences, is not by us forgotten." The resolutions affirmed the Republican Party as the chief defenders of black liberties and equality. Therefore, the black Bostonians in attendance announced, "we shall as a people cast our vote ... for the nominees of the Republican Party."[49] Although the convention agreed "as a people" to cast votes for Grant and Wilson, there were others in Boston who stood steadfast against universal allegiance to the president and instead sided with the Liberal Republicans.

Foreshadowing tensions that would increase in the coming years, Robert Morris and others supported Greeley, which drew the ire of many of Boston's black Republicans. At an August meeting of Boston's black Republicans, Charles Remond issued a severe condemnation of Greeley's black supporters and pronounced them "traitors to the cause of the black men."[50] When one of the Greeley supporters rose to rebut Remond's attacks, the meeting's organizers refused to grant him permission to speak and urged him to schedule his own meeting at another time.[51]

Morris blamed Grant for continued black oppression. At a meeting of black and white Greeley supporters held in Ward Eleven in September, he explained his support and acknowledged criticism of his position by black Republicans. Boston's black community, he explained, "had made it pretty warm for him lately," but he refused to back down from his independent position. "He had never been accustomed to having a whip cracked over his shoulders," the *Boston Globe* reported him saying, "but had been accustomed to do his own thinking and talking."[52] Morris's declarations for Greeley were more a result of his dissatisfaction with the improvement of African American conditions under Grant than a specific endorsement of any Liberal Republican policy.

Unlike black Republican supporters, who praised Grant's resistance to the Ku Klux Klan, Morris blamed the president for not acting more aggressively and quickly. He argued that if empowered by the federal government, he and other African Americans could do a superior job of suppressing Klan violence.[53] "Give him a good black sheriff and a regiment of black men," Morris said, "and he would suppress the Ku-Klux at once."[54] Further, he called for vengeance upon white supremacists. "When [the black sheriff] got in sight of the place where the Ku-Klux were," Morris proclaimed, "there would be none there. If he saw a black man whom they had hung to a tree, there would be a white man hanging beside him before the morning. That was the way to do it."[55] Morris's calls for vengeance were prescient in their similarities to rhetoric used by other black independents in the 1890s in opposition to lynching.

Undeterred by dissenters, as the election approached, Boston's black Republicans organized a grand convention of black voters from throughout Massachusetts and New England.[56] The organizers, including George Ruffin, Charles Remond, and Lewis Hayden, called the convention to demonstrate the unity and commitment of African American voters in the region to Grant and the Republican Party. Unlike the previous meetings, which were comprised of local and state audiences, this convention hoped to attract attendees from around New England and the nation. In doing so, political leaders linked their debates to national questions of political inclusion. "Many of us," the organizers exclaimed in the address announcing the convention, "will for the first time be called upon to exercise, in a national election, the highest right of freeman . . . a right secured by the thirteenth, fourteenth, and fifteenth amendments."[57]

The Republican Party, in their view, was responsible for the greatest advancements in African American civil rights, the Thirteenth, Fourteenth, and Fifteenth Amendments, and therefore black voters had a responsibility to keep it in power and prevent Democratic ascendency. "[The amendments] will only be continued to us by the Republican Party, which originated and adopted those amendments despite the utmost efforts of their opponents; the party now opposing us . . . would use every exertion to abridge or annul those rights, as the past history of the Democratic Party fully proves."[58] For Republican supporters, continued Republican dominance was all that would guarantee future African American progress and prevent the entrenchment of white supremacy.

When the meeting convened in September 1872 in Faneuil Hall, men from across New England joined with national leaders such as Frederick Douglass and John Langston to express their unified support for Grant. The speakers reiterated the sentiments in their call declaring that the Republican Party was the only protection for African American rights. Grant, George Ruffin argued as he opened the meeting, was a true and consistent ally of African Americans, as compared to the "vacillations and inconsistencies of Greeley."[59] As Ruffin closed, he urged listeners to think of the legacy of the Civil War and look to the election of Grant as a continuation of those successes.

National leaders also spoke out against the Democratic Party. Frederick Douglass, in his first Faneuil Hall appearance since the Civil War, affirmed African American support of the Republican Party and called on black voters to look closely at the past record of the parties and not be swayed by promises and platforms for the future. "There was nothing in the antecedents of the Democratic Party," Douglass explained, "that gave the least hope or encouragement to the colored man that his rights would be maintained by that party."[60] The Republican Party, he proclaimed, had always been consistent in its maintenance of African American rights. John Langston, former inspector general for the Freedmen's Bureau and dean of Howard University Law School, echoed Douglass and urged the audience to "support the Republican and utterly demolish the Democratic Party."[61] For former antislavery activists such as Douglass and Langston, support for Democrats was a betrayal of their victories, and they vigorously condemned black endorsement of Greeley.[62]

Among the officers of the convention were also those such as George Downing, a wealthy caterer and hotel owner from Rhode Island, who advocated political independence. Downing, along with others like Edwin Walker, would lead a decades-long struggle against black loyalty to the Republican Party. He was born to former slaves in 1819 in New York and became an active member of that city's antislavery society. In the 1840s, he moved to Rhode Island where he opened a successful restaurant, hotel, and catering business. While in Rhode Island, Downing actively fought for the integration of the state's public schools. After the Civil War he joined Frederick Douglass in lobbying for black rights in Washington, D.C., and became a close relation of Charles Sumner.[63] Although Downing lived in Rhode Island he spent much of his time in Boston and was a central figure in the city's black political life.

Downing would be a major advocate for African Americans leaving the Republican Party in later decades. In 1872, however, he endorsed Grant and Wilson. He made his sentiments publicly known in a letter published in the *New York Times*. "Hoping for the time when colored men may consistently divide among parties," Downing wrote, "I shall not only cast my vote for the Republican nominees, but with my voice and pen endeavor to persuade my fellow countrymen . . . to do likewise."[64] His support of the Republican ticket despite his advocacy of political independence is indicative of the general sentiment of many black leaders in Boston. Although some expressed disapproval and disappointment with the Grant administration, most were unwilling to cast their votes for the Democrat.[65] This Republican loyalty, however, would diminish in the coming decades.

On Election Day, black voters filled the ward room at the Phillips School House on Anderson and Pinckney Streets to cast their ballots. Grant successfully won the election by a large majority, with over 69 percent of the vote.[66] In Ward Six, more than 1,300 of nearly 1,600 voters cast a ballot for the incumbent president.[67] The *Daily Globe* reported that black residents in the Sixth Ward "turned out in full force, and made a day of it."[68] Despite Grant's overwhelming victory, in Massachusetts over 10 percent of Republicans defected from the party to support Greeley, the largest percentage in the Northeast.[69] While Grant emerged victorious and most black Bostonians celebrated his election, the damage to the Republican Party had been done, and the increasing shift away from the ideological support for black equality would have lasting influence on black Bostonian politics in the next decade.

This election exposed the conflicts within the black community. It demonstrated that some African Americans were willing to oppose the Republicans, and Greeley's campaign only heightened the debate over party affiliation. Indeed, as historian Richard Abbott argues, "The Liberal Republican movements, if they achieved nothing else, did encourage voters to exercise more independence in casting their ballot."[70] Further, the pronounced loyalty that some black Bostonians showed for Republicans in 1872 would exacerbate African Americans' feelings of betrayal as the party began to draw away from a civil rights agenda in the late 1870s. Over the next decade, support of the Republican Party would come under increased fire, and some tenuous Grant supporters, such as Edwin Garrison Walker and George Downing, would become some of the most critical opponents of the party.

African Americans such as Walker and Downing fashioned their own brand of independent politics, one that sought loyalty to ideas of political equality and uplift of African American citizens. While white Republican reformers sought to reduce political patronage, African Americans courted these positions as important entry points and footholds in local, state, and federal government. The white Republican shift toward organizational politics may have eclipsed some of the ideological underpinnings of Reconstruction, but for many of the party's African American members, they wanted a renewed dedication to ideology combined with substantive material gains and meaningful advances in their civil rights agenda. While remaining confident in electoral and partisan politics as a vehicle for black progress, black activists became increasingly convinced that the Republican Party was no longer their only choice. Failure by Republicans to make black interests a priority caused former black supporters to seek other options. By the end of the decade, many of Grant's former supporters would abandon the Republican Party in favor of a man who in 1872 was an archenemy of liberal and establishment Republicans alike, Benjamin Butler.

*Part II*
# No Longer Pliant Tools

On August 18, 1882, an editorial in the *Boston Daily Globe* declared that "the negro is the most pliant tool in the hands of the Republican Party. Ignorant and superstitious, a few paid leaders guide the flock with the ease that a shepherd dog guides a flock of sheep."[1] The statement provoked an immediate outcry from segments of Boston's African American community.[2] Howard L. Smith, black Bostonian and advocate for independent politics, countered the *Globe*'s "gross misrepresentation of our status" in a letter to the editor published two days later. Countering allegations of blind party loyalty and political ignorance, Smith replied, "That the Negro is a pliant tool is but one of the many misstatements made by factions inimical to the welfare of the Negro." "We have lived long on promises," Smith continued, "But that is past. We have awakened from our lethargy to a sense of our condition, and the annals of future history . . . will record for the colored race of today and futurity a brilliant record, that will be second to none of any nationality."[3]

During the late 1870s and 1880s, cracks in the foundation of black Republican loyalty began to widen. With the backsliding away from Reconstruction by the national Republican Party, black voters, some once faithful to the party of Lincoln, sought other electoral options. It became clear to many that attempts to pressure Republicans to prioritize the protection of black rights and lives through electoral and moral pressure was ineffective. There was an increasing perception that the party took black votes for granted and was confident that despite criticisms, African American voters, left with few alternatives, would ultimately support Republican candidates. An emerging cohort of black activists attempted to create an alternative electoral avenue for black politics through the declaration of their political independence. They publicly denounced Republicans and urged black voters to support other candidates, even Democrats. Their strategy was twofold: they hoped that a black exodus from the Republicans would convince that party's leaders that they could not take black support for granted and highlight to Democratic operatives the electoral advantage that could be gained from courting black votes through support of pro–civil rights platforms and patronage positions.

This strategy, however, pivoted on the willingness of both parties to be receptive to this pressure and reject the growing white supremacist politics infecting both groups. Despite concerns, black activists remained convinced that electoral and party politics could still be a primary weapon in the black freedom struggle. Attempted alliances with new candidates and constituencies ultimately exposed the incoherence and inadequacy of independent politics and tested faith in structures of American politics during the 1880s, leading some to choose extrapartisan political alternatives.

## CHAPTER FOUR

# You Will Find the Colored Voters
# on the Butler Ship This Fall

## Urban Politics and Conflicts over
## African American Partisanship

In late September 1879, a *Boston Daily Globe* reporter interviewed black activist John Ruffin about the political sentiment of African American voters in the West End in the final weeks of the gubernatorial campaign. Ruffin praised the political judgment of African Americans, who, he suggested, had great instincts when it came to choosing the best candidates. "[African American voters] have the welfare of the state and the nation at heart," Ruffin explained, "and if any white man is in doubt . . . let him watch the black man and he will not go astray."[1] With this judgment, Ruffin told the reporters that black voters in the West End had chosen Benjamin Butler, who had recently returned to state politics as a Democrat, as their preferred candidate. "I tell you," Ruffin declared, "you will find the colored voters on the Butler ship this fall, and under God's guidance she will reach the harbor a long ways ahead of her competitors."[2]

Like Ruffin, a growing portion of the black electorate in Boston refused to be blindly loyal to Republicans and engaged in heated debates over which candidates and which party, if any, deserved black votes. The exchange reached a fever pitch following Benjamin Butler's campaign as a candidate for Massachusetts governor, which culminated in his successful election in 1882 over Republican Robert R. Bishop. During this period African American voters challenged one another. Some declared their support for Butler and denounced the Republican Party's inaction on civil rights, while others argued that opposing Republicans meant supporting a white supremacist Democratic Party and spelled doom for racial progress.

Heated debate during his initial campaign turned into an inferno approaching Butler's attempt at reelection in 1883 against Republican George D. Robinson. Butler's black Bostonian supporters and opponents both reacted strongly and looked to the coming campaign with either optimism or trepidation. For his supporters, the election meant that their strategy of independent politics had worked, and they were optimistic that they could succeed again the following year. This was a chance to again prove their power in the state and send a further message to both political parties that the black vote could not be taken for granted.

For black Republican loyalists, Butler had to be stopped at all costs. They not only feared Democratic ascendency in the state, but also predicted Butler's ascension to national office, perhaps the presidency, if he was again victorious. If that happened, they worried that nothing would stop southern white Democrats from rolling back the already diminishing gains of Reconstruction. The election of a Democrat as governor was a sign of the growing strength of the party nationally, and they feared a southern white supremacist agenda spreading nationwide. They argued that black independents were treading a perilous path behind Butler. The best way forward was to work within the Republican Party and continue their attempts to advance national civil rights goals within its networks.

The 1883 campaign was a turning point in black Bostonian politics. Republican denunciation of Butler and his black supporters further widened the gulf between the Republican Party and black independents. The failure of the Republican-dominated executive council to confirm Butler's nomination of Edwin Walker to a judgeship reinforced independents' belief that Republicans placed political expediency ahead of black interests. The rejection of Walker and the campaign also exposed the personal and professional consequences of voting against the status quo and highlighted stark political divisions within Boston's black political leadership. Rather than dampening independents' enthusiasm, however, Butler's eventual defeat for reelection hardened their resolve and mobilized them toward pursuing an increasingly national agenda. In the aftermath, they formed new organizations dedicated to withholding black support, locally and nationally, until both parties had proved their dedication to future civil rights struggles.

## The Return of the "Beast" and Growth of a Political Independent Movement

Despite the tensions in the early 1870s, most African Americans remained loyal Republicans. By the end of the decade, however, political conditions at the national and local levels made some black voters openly question their unbending support for the party of Lincoln. Criticism of the Republican Party became considerably more pointed following the so-called congressional compromise in the disputed Hayes-Tilden election in 1877. The consequent acceptance of the policy of redemption advocated by the Hayes administration, which removed federal military occupation from southern states, only

Vol. XVIII.—No. 902.]   NEW YORK, SATURDAY, APRIL 11, 1874.   [WITH A SUPPLEMENT.
PRICE TEN CENTS.

Entered according to Act of Congress, in the Year 1874, by Harper & Brothers, in the Office of the Librarian of Congress, at Washington.

THE CRADLE OF LIBERTY IN DANGER.
"Fee-Fi-Fo-Fum!" The Genie of Massachusetts smells Blue Blood.

*The Cradle of Liberty in Danger, Harper's Weekly*, April 11, 1874.
(Courtesy of Library of Congress.)

heightened black criticism. Such policies underscored the precarious political position of African American civil rights. As one critic explained, "The North is willing, for the sake of peace and commerce, to sacrifice the rights of the colored man. . . . The church and state, the press and public men are silent and dare not lift up their voice against Hayes's policy."[3] Additionally, black critics pointed to growing factions within the Republican Party that placed greater priority on issues of economic development, tariff reduction, civil service reform, internal improvements, national education, and reform of the Internal Revenue Service than on the protection of African Americans' rights.[4]

In Massachusetts, mirroring national trends, members of the state Republican Party increased their focus on issues other than the cause of black freedom, and black Bostonians continued to face daily racism, especially in the city's public accommodations.[5] For African Americans, the apparent rising indifference of Republicans to their plight was a stark departure from the party's focus on antislavery and civil rights only a decade earlier. With memories of this activism fresh in their minds, black critics of the party felt betrayed and refused to let Republicans claim black votes based on past deeds they now seemed less concerned with expanding upon. As black disillusionment with Republicans rose among a cohort of black Bostonians, they cast about for more reliable allies. They found their man again in former Civil War general and U.S. congressman Benjamin Butler.

Like when Butler first ran for Massachusetts governor in 1871, his wartime service and postwar advocacy again endeared him to black voters. Looking past his earlier defeat, Butler's standing in the black community remained high, and many who supported him in his early campaigns joined him again when he contested the governor's seat in the late 1870s. A letter inviting Butler to speak in Boston reflected a broad spectrum of black supporters. Republican George Ruffin and independents Robert Morris, James Trotter, and Edwin Walker praised Butler's work "to secure legal guarantee and efficient protection of our race and rights, and admitted the sagacity and rare foresight [he had] shown in watching the plots against us and the peace of the Union."[6] There was general praise for Butler across party lines for his part in the passage of federal civil rights legislation. This changed when Butler began his campaign for governor in the late 1870s, and black voters divided between those who would remain loyal to the party of Lincoln and those who would follow Butler out of the Republican fold.

After several years in the House of Representatives, culminating in his support of the Civil Rights Act of 1875, Butler ran again for Massachusetts governor in 1878 and 1879. Rejecting the Republican Party, he ran as an independent candidate, calling himself a "Jacksonian Democrat" as he denounced corruption and attacked Republican monied interests and "blue bloods."[7] During these campaigns, Butler forged a coalition of Irish immigrants and white workers. A growing number of black Bostonians joined these groups in support.

In addition to holding well-attended public rallies, political leaders reached out to the African American constituency through the pages of Boston's newspapers. Letters of support declared, "Since he has espoused the cause of the colored man [Butler] has been a consistent friend. . . . [Unlike] all the great army of Republicans who have used and abused the colored man . . . Benjamin Butler is one of the few who has not wavered."[8] Pro-Butler activists called on African American leaders to show political courage and support Butler, even if that meant alienation from Republicans. "The great trouble with the colored people," supporter George Patterson wrote, "is that they have too many men (leaders) on the fence. . . . They talk loud and long about their rights, but they seem to forget that it is only he who votes and speaks as his conscience dictates, without fear or favor, who truly exercises the right of suffrage."[9] Supporters' comments demonstrate the political schism in the African American community and further show the conflicts around independent politics. While there were some who still remained hopeful about the progress that could be achieved within the apparatus of the Republican Party, there were those who saw African Americans as destined for second-class status within the party. The only way for black voters to receive recognition within the major political parties, they argued, would be to cast their ballots with discretion and force the parties to compete for their vote.

Despite the growing endorsements among the state's more disadvantaged groups, Butler lost both elections. Black support for a non-Republican candidate, however, increased significantly in these campaigns. For example, in Ward Nine's third precinct, which was home to many black residents, Butler earned 43 percent of the vote in 1878 and 40 percent in 1879.[10] Although he did not win the majority, these numbers were a marked increase over elections without Butler's candidacy and point to his power to sway black voters.[11]

## Consequences of Independent Support

Butler's black supporters faced stiff opposition for their choice, and these elections made clear the consequences of voting against the Republican Party. Although support for Democrats was growing, the party continued to be a minority in the city. Challenging the majority party often meant severe personal and professional costs for choosing to go against the establishment. Republican business owners, for example, attempted to pressure their black employees into voting for Republicans, and black voters often faced termination if they refused.

Following his loss, Butler compared the intimidation of voters in Boston to that faced by African Americans in the South. He contended that in the 1878 election, the Boston poll was as badly "bulldozed" as those in South Carolina, and that although it lacked the "shotgun-style" intimidation of southern elections, it was equally as effective and "led to as important changes in the public expression of popular opinion as the use of an armed force would have done."[12] While they did not resort to violence, wealthy members of the Republican Party were able to use their control over the employment and livelihood of voters to influence their decisions. For an African American electorate already facing limited economic circumstances, the potential loss of employment was a powerful inducement.

This form of intimidation, some alleged, was just as effective, if not more so, as violence. A display of "arrogant force" in the form of armed intimidation, newspapers argued, could have been met openly and directly opposed, whereas the power exerted by employers was more insidious and more difficult to organize against. "The moneyed men of [Massachusetts]," the *Boston Daily Globe* suggested, "knew a better way of manipulating the voters of humbler standing, and acting upon their knowledge, they instituted a terrorism that from the quiet tone it was impossible to defy, and extremely difficult in most cases to meet openly."[13] These cases of voter intimidation particularly targeted black voters who chose to defy Republican leadership.

One victim of voter intimidation in the 1878 election was Elijah McIntire, who had worked as assistant janitor at the Boston post office for five years. McIntire was working alongside his white supervisor, who asked which candidate McIntire planned on voting for in the coming election. McIntire replied that he was planning on voting for Benjamin Butler, explaining that he thought he had "a right to do so as General Butler has done more for the men of his color than any other man." According to McIntire's account, the supervisor ceased discussion, but his expression was "decidedly unpleasant."[14] Soon after, the post office terminated McIntire's employment.

Other cases of voter suppression were more direct. On Election Day in Precinct Three of Ward Nine, a black voter named Mr. Green came to the ward room to cast a ballot for Benjamin Butler. At the polls that day was Green's employer, R. M. Thompson, a prominent member of the "Young Republican" political club. According to affidavits from the precinct inspectors, he marked off the name of each voter as he made his choice. Thompson confronted Green as he left, and with an "upraised finger," informed Green, "you need not work for me anymore." The *Boston Daily Globe* argued that Thompson's actions "could not fail to frighten off other voters, similarly situated."[15]

The events surrounding the political choices of voters such as Elijah Mc-Intire and Mr. Green demonstrate that by choosing to vote for candidates other than Republican, black voters risked their jobs and reputations. To support Butler was a political decision that extended beyond the rhetorical arguments of prominent leaders and had very real consequences for African Americans who put independent politics into action. Despite threats and acts of retaliation, however, African American voters continued to support candidates outside the Republican Party in future elections, and many would suffer similar consequences for their political independence.

## A Growing Independent Insurgency

In the face of political opposition, following Butler's defeat in 1878, African American independents remained steadfast and increased as a political force in the city and state. As their resistance to Republicans increased, so, too, did the reactions from Republican loyalists. From 1878 through Butler's successful election in 1883, independents and Republicans tested the limits of black political unity. While they came together to advocate for increased civil rights, they were sharply divided over which political party would best help them achieve this goal.

Among the growing number of independents were new vocal opponents of the Republican Party. John Ruffin, for example, was among this new group of leaders. He was a proud advocate of Benjamin Butler and vehemently denounced those who chose to remain with the Republican Party. Ruffin openly targeted prominent African American leaders who, he argued, only supported Republicans to gain political positions and favors. Like independent advocates of earlier years, Ruffin suggested these leaders were too taken in by the Republican Party leadership to join the rising independent movement. He explained, "We don't expect that the colored men in the state-house and custom house will vote for [Benjamin Butler], but I believe that if they could get away from the ring-rule that each and every one of them would support him at the polls."[16] Ruffin and other Butler supporters saw the Republican Party leadership in the state as serving only its own self-interests, whereas they trusted Benjamin Butler to look out for the interests of the people of the state.

While the growing independent insurgency declared their opposition in the pages of the press, community meetings increasingly became the site of battles over preferred party affiliation. For example, the September 1879 meeting of the African American organized Bay State League, the first large public meeting of the organization, was a site of contestation over which party and candidates the organization would advocate. Supporters of all candidates recognized the political influence and force of the league, and each side publicly declared that it spoke for the sentiments of a majority of the league's members. Newspaper coverage of the meeting also shows the political bias of the press in how the same event was reported in different ways. The *Boston Daily Advertiser*, as a supporter of Republican candidates, reported a mass meeting of "Colored Republicans."[17] The *Advertiser*, in its coverage, made scant mention of the African American independents in the crowd, while the *Boston Daily Globe* highlighted the participation of "a large and respectable Butler element."[18]

Among those who supported the Republican John Davis Long for governor were A. B. Lattimore, a former Republican representative to the general court, and James W. Pope, the current candidate for the legislature. Speaking on behalf of the Republican cohort was famous white Civil War commander Colonel Thomas Wentworth Higginson, who, while invoking the memory of prominent antislavery figures, claimed "that the nation had been saved by the moral sentiment and moral courage of the North, which was embodied in the Republican Party."[19] Higginson's statement is representative of a common rhetorical tactic of Republican supporters, who used the memory of and public reverence for antislavery and the triumph of the Union in the Civil War to encourage black voters to support Republican candidates. Higginson concluded by declaring that by the end of the year, all those who opposed the election of the Republican candidate would "see that they had made the most egregious blunder they had ever been guilty of."[20] Not all in the audience agreed.

Black opponents of Long and strong advocates of Butler confronted the Republican speakers. Although the *Boston Daily Globe* recognized that the rally had been advertised as "A Grand Republican Mass Meeting," the reporter highlighted the large number of Butler supporters at the gathering. The newspaper reported that many Butler supporters took notes of the speeches to use in later campaign events. Having records of the speeches from these rallies allowed black politicians to craft rhetoric that either reinforced the party platform or targeted statements made by supporters of the other side.

Among Butler's supporters were those who were voting against the Republican Party for the first time joining those who had a more fundamental opposition to the party. An anonymous attendee of the meeting emphasized the political fluidity of black Bostonians when he declared, "I am a Republican; but I'm going to vote for Benjamin Butler." For others, the very founding principles of the Bay State League were based in political independence and support for the general. Henry W. Johnson, who had made an unsuccessful bid for the common council a year earlier, explained that the league was formed by a group of men from Ward Nine who were dissatisfied with the political situation of the area. Rejecting the labeling of the meeting as "Republican," he not only declared his own opposition to the Republican Party, but also argued that the explicit purpose of the Bay State League was the unseating of Republican leadership. He had "come to the conclusion that the time had fully come for the breaking up of the ring which so long had ruled the ward."[21] Confrontation over partisan affiliation went beyond personal loyalties to define the political identity of the Boston black community at large.

After his second consecutive defeat in 1879 Butler took a hiatus, but returned to the campaign trail in 1882, this time as a candidate for the Democratic Party. With Butler on the ticket, black voters again cast ballots against their traditional Republican allies and supported a Democrat. As in the earlier elections, support for Butler increased the number of non-Republican voters in the black precincts of the Ninth Ward. In the 1882 election, for instance, support for the Democrat in Precinct Three jumped from 16 percent to nearly 38 percent with Butler on the ballot.[22] Unlike in his earlier challenges, however, voters, including African Americans, succeeded in defeating Republican candidate Robert Bishop and electing Butler to the governor's office.

During the 1882 campaign, independents shaped the campaign for Butler into an assault on the Republican Party, targeting its inaction on issues of civil rights. Unlike in the case of the Bay State League, no longer would there be confusion about the loyalty of black political organizations. Across the city, "Colored Butler clubs" and black independents gathered to galvanize support and educate black voters about the candidate. In meeting halls and church sanctuaries, African American political leaders made rousing speeches decrying the Republican Party and openly advocating Butler as their choice. One critic explained the frustration: "The great trouble with the Republican party is that they have treated the colored men as their chattels. They freed them from bodily slavery only to enthrall them in a political slavery . . . but the colored men have determined to throw off this yoke and establish for themselves an independent party."[23] Others defended support for Benjamin Butler, citing his military service and move away from the Republican Party. In justifying Butler's recent party affiliation, they reminded the voters that respected

statesman and advocate of black rights Charles Sumner had distanced himself from the Republican Party toward the end of his life, and thus Butler was
in good company.[24] Sumner's former allies in the antislavery movement,
however, were frustrated by the increase in black political independence.

Former abolitionists in Boston were adamant that voting for the Democratic candidate betrayed the movement's legacy. Others felt that African
Americans owed their loyalty to the political party that fought to end slavery
and afterward promoted civil rights. Newspapers printed letters from prominent former abolitionists condemning support for Butler and warning that
support for the Democratic candidate was political suicide.[25] The *Boston
Daily Advertiser* included letters from William Lloyd Garrison Jr. and Maria
Weston Chapman that vigorously denounced Butler for his support of the
Democratic Party before the war, which was tantamount to a proslavery endorsement. While acknowledging Butler's service during the Civil War,
Garrison wrote, "the darkness of his background brought him into vivid
distinction." "No personal excellence," Garrison continued, "could atone for
bad principles."[26] This contestation suggests how valuable Republicans thought
the black vote was, and the significant inroads political independence had
made into the black electorate.

Entering the governorship and reelection campaign in 1883 as a champion
of Massachusetts's ethnic and economically disadvantaged populations, Butler quickly attempted to transmit his commitment to such groups through
appointments and legislative reform. For Boston's black population, many of
whom were among the laboring class, Butler's advocacy of labor reform and
workers' protections most likely would have been very appealing. But they
inflamed tensions with the state's Republican establishment. Butler, using his
veto power, attempted to push bills through the Republican-dominated executive council and legislature. He supported abolishing the poll tax and advocated woman suffrage, the ten-hour workday, and the protection of women
and children in the workplace. He also pressed the legislature for a reform of
Massachusetts's prisons and poorhouses. Republican officials, however, sty-
mied much of his proposed reforms and legislation.[27] Like tensions within
the white political establishment, Butler's election and gubernatorial campaign expanded fractures within Boston's black electorate.

## The *Hub* and Black Republican Opposition

Despite Butler's legislative efforts and long-term advocacy of African Americans' civil rights, reaction in Boston's black community to Butler's governorship

and reform efforts was mixed. Loyal African American Republicans, many of whom had held government posts, advocated civil and political rights, as did black independents. But they saw the best opportunity for expanded rights protections and racial progress through continued black allegiance to the Republican platform. In the pages of the press and in public forums, they urged Massachusetts's African American voters to remain loyal the Republican Party as they decried "the growing tendency of some of us to advocate the immediate and unconditional severance of our membership with the Republican Party."[28] The acknowledgment of this "growing tendency" reflected a fear that black support for Democrats would strengthen the national party, which led the rollback of civil rights gains made since the Civil War. For black Republican leaders, Butler's Democratic affiliation nullified his past good deeds on behalf of the race, and they dedicated themselves to preventing Butler's reelection in 1883.

Just months after Butler's election, leading black Republicans in Boston organized a black partisan newspaper explicitly committed to making Butler a one-term governor. In doing so, black Bostonians utilized the newspaper, a major tool in urban partisan politics, as it united important constituencies in support of candidates, publicized political meetings, and provided a public forum for attacks on opponents.[29] In July 1883, attorneys Archibald Grimké and Butler R. Wilson joined with other black Republicans to found the *Hub*. That they could organize the paper is evidence of not only the sophistication of their political machinery, but also their access to resources. As the "first, second, and last organ of the colored race," the paper positioned itself as the official voice of black Boston.[30] Other black leaders in the city praised the foundation of the paper and hoped it would lead to a greater organization of African Americans. Attorney J. H. Wolff, for example, called for an organization "as powerful as any . . . that was ever conceived." "The *Hub*," he wrote confidently, "will have that organizing power and influence that will sooner or later make the colored people one of the greatest factors in American politics."[31] Black Republicans organized the *Hub* to mobilize black voters in support of Republican candidates and voice criticism of Butler and his supporters. The paper also listed the names of unregistered voters and encouraged them to go to the polls.

Explicitly conceiving of the paper as a partisan press, its founders and editors allied with black Republican organizations in the city and sought the endorsements of prominent white Republican leaders.[32] *Hub* editors pledged to be outspoken in politics and "advocate the men and principles best suited to the welfare of the people." They also insisted that the paper would "oppose the men or measures thought to be detrimental without stint or favor."[33] For the *Hub* editors, these "men and measures" meant the Democratic Party, Butler, and his black supporters.

The *Hub* editors pointed to the Democratic Party as the party of white supremacy and the primary advocate for slavery and opponent of Reconstruction. Given this legacy, black advocacy of the Democratic Butler was particularly outrageous, and the *Hub* targeted these supporters especially. The editors announced one purpose of the paper was "to save its race from the folly of going over to the Democratic Party until that party has shown its friendship in some tangible and indisputable fact—not once, but many times repeated."[34] "The man who votes for Butler," they declared, "votes to reinstate the Democratic Party, and such an event would be the greatest calamity which could ever befall the race."[35] Naming the Democrats their "worst enemy," they issued a call to action. "The fall election will be of great importance to the colored men of Massachusetts. . . . Now is the time to combine gratitude [to the Republican Party] and duty to the best interests of the race and rebuke the man and party so dangerous to those interests."[36]

They argued that by declaring their political independence, Butler's supporters were giving the white supremacist Democrats just what they wanted. "If they can isolate and alienate us from the Republican Party, and destroy the identity of our interest with that great party," the *Hub* argued, "our ancient enemies think that the remnant of our rights can then easily be throttled."[37] The *Hub* editors, however, remained optimistic that although many voted for Butler in the previous election, they would return to the Republican fold during the present campaign.[38]

Articles and letters in the *Hub* placed the coming election in the context of the long struggle for emancipation and African American citizenship. In doing so, they made this local election part of a much broader struggle for freedom and equality. Writers celebrated the Republican Party and claimed that African Americans in the 1880s continued to owe the Republican Party thanks for its antislavery position before and during the Civil War and its work for black rights during Reconstruction. Loyalty to the Republicans, the editors insisted, was the true legacy of the antislavery movement and represented the authentic spirit of Massachusetts's distinguished history of abolitionist activism.[39]

Support for Democrats betrayed this noble past, and Republican leaders commanded black Bostonians to honor the Republican Party by voting against Butler. "The old Bay State," the editors wrote, "has been foremost in securing for the colored people their rights all over the country."[40] "Now is the chance," they announced, "to combine gratitude and duty to the best interests of the race and rebuke the man and party so dangerous to those interests."[41]

Black Republicans went so far as to refute Butler's past actions on behalf of African Americans. They rejected the assertion of Butler's supporters that the governor, as Civil War general, had been the first to declare enslaved people fleeing to Union lines as "contrabands of war" and therefore free. Republicans declared that it was in fact Lewis Hayden, the celebrated black Bostonian antislavery leader and outspoken Republican, who first used the term.[42] By undermining the mythos of Butler's support of black freedom, Republicans sought to reduce his role in the African American freedom struggle and paint him as a political opportunist not deeply loyal to black interests.

Lewis Hayden penned articles and letters in the *Hub* endorsing the Republican Party and condemning Democrats. Hayden, who was also the general agent for the paper, declared the Republicans "the grand old party of freedom" containing "the best class of the citizens of the North."[43] He argued that "up to the present day the Democratic Party has not in either state or national legislature enacted a single law embodying the equal rights of *all* the nation's citizens." Hayden condemned "honest, but misguided colored men who speak and vote for the Democratic Party."[44] Declaring that a Democratic supporter is "like a baby entrusted with a razor," Hayden wrote, "he is much more dangerous than the babe for he not only cuts himself, but cuts a race."[45] For aging antislavery advocates such as Hayden, African Americans voting for Benjamin Butler and the Democrats not only compromised Republican political power, but also threatened to undermine the freedom they had fought so hard to secure.

The editors of the *Hub* particularly condemned Butler for his role in removing black officials from their previously appointed positions during his early months as governor, as part of a reduction in government size and purge of Republican loyalists.[46] They pointed to Butler's removal of Captain Charles Francis from a clerkship in the executive department, attorney James W. Wolff from the adjunct general's office, and George Lowther from the office of Boston's inspector of weights and measures.[47] It was not just the *Hub* that called attention to Butler's actions. The white, Republican-leaning *Boston Herald* similarly highlighted the way that Butler's partisan actions called into question his commitment to black Bostonians. These dismissals, the *Boston Herald* insisted sarcastically, constituted "a fair sample of the way the Democrats show their affection for the colored man after election."[48]

The *Hub* editors questioned the general's commitment to black Bostonians, arguing that his actions resulted not just from partisanship, but also, and more forebodingly, from his racism and duplicity. Butler's reform efforts in office, they implied, merely masked his limited commitment to Massachusetts's African American citizens and his complicity with the white supremacist elements in the Democratic Party. If removals of black men from office were inspired by regular partisanship, the *Hub* asked, then why did Butler not replace some of the dismissed officials with new African American appointees?[49]

The removals were not just a financial loss for black families, but also undermined the public image of pride, responsibility, and civic inclusion projected by their positions among the community and the wider populous. "If his office is filled by another colored man, all things being equal, the loss is wholly individual," the editors explained, "but if the position is filled by a man or woman not identified with the race, or the office is abolished, then the loss flows over the individual and his family and becomes an injury to the colored portion of the community of commonwealth where the removal was effected."[50] By declaring the removals not only partisan but also racially motivated, black Republicans hoped to sully Butler's reputation as a supporter of black struggles for equality and present his election as a harbinger of future wrongs if African Americans in Boston continued to cross party lines and vote for Democratic candidates.

Butler's supporters quickly responded to the *Hub*'s criticism in letters to the paper lauding the governor's actions on behalf of black people and presenting their reasons for leaving the Republican Party and supporting the governor. African Americans, Butler advocates argued, should freely associate with any party they wish and not feel obligated to support the Republican Party based on past deeds. For example, African American independent James T. Still penned a letter to the *Hub* defending his position. "I feel to be an independent American," he declared, "and although I well remember all of the evils of the Democratic Party, I am also cognizant of the neglects and omissions of the Republican Party."[51]

Still viewed African American partisanship in gendered terms. He declared Republican pursuit of patronage and the elevation of office holding over other vocations to be single-minded and unmanly. Conversely, he elevated his nonpartisan position as manifesting unselfish and industrious manhood. He advocated self-sufficiency and argued that "our laborers, strong armed, unselfish, industrious men, are our only and truly valuable representatives of manhood. All other useful men among us are powerless, for they are buried beneath envy and selfish degradation."[52] "The time has come," he declared, "for [black men] to watch for ourselves; that we must let no party write the music. . . . We must compose and sing and play our own independent tunes, made from our own observations and remembrances."[53] For Butler supporters like Still, independent manhood translated into independent action in the realm of electoral politics. In contrast, continued loyalty to Republicans sacrificed manly independence at the altar of partisanship.

For black Republicans, their support reflected not necessarily an abandonment of manly independence, but a dedication to use the best tools available to protect black freedom. Advocating Republican candidates was the pragmatic choice between a known ally of African American civil rights and a party increasingly known at the national level, and in the South especially, for its dedication to the degradation of black citizens. For Butler's opponents, political independence posed a risk they were not willing to take.

## Cooperation and Dissent

During the 1883 campaign, both Republicans and independents looked to electoral politics to achieve similar goals of political, civil, and educational equality. While especially engaged with local political happenings, black Bostonians were deeply concerned about the condition of black rights nationally. They met in local and statewide meetings and conferences to come to consensus on the most pressing issues of the day, and representatives from Massachusetts were important attendees at national conventions of black leaders. Through this organizing, they sought remedy to the rising tide of disenfranchisement in the South, expanded access to education, and the prevention of racial discrimination in public accommodation across the country. Their mutual agreement on goals, however, crashed headlong into conflicts over partisanship.

These tensions were on particular display in September 1883 as both sides joined together at a statewide conference in order to "consider the best method of attaining all our rights, civil and political, in the state and country."[54] They met, the *Hub* announced, to "form a larger personal acquaintance among the representative men of the race in the Commonwealth, with a view to intelligent and harmonious action in the future."[55] Republicans including Archibald Grimké, Butler Wilson, Lewis Hayden, and George Washington Williams, along with independents including Edwin Walker and James Monroe Trotter, served as officers of the convention. They hoped to forge greater racial unity and the basis for a formal political organization.

The conference members looked to electoral politics as a central strategy in their fight for justice. Participants observed a rapid increase in the African American population and hoped to form an organization out of the convention that would protect black citizenship rights and "make our vote influential."[56] The attendees sought to unify the black electorate to magnify its power. "The time has come," the published address from the meeting read, "when a more perfect union of the colored people of this commonwealth and country is of vital importance in maintaining the rights we now enjoy and in attaining those which, by prejudice, fraud or violence, we are now deprived."[57] However, divisions between black Republicans and independents erupted when participants discussed which political party should receive these influential votes.

While convention participants agreed on the goals of improving black civil rights and educational opportunities, they disagreed vehemently about the role of partisan politics in achieving these goals. Republicans praised their party and worried about growing independent political sentiment. George Washington Williams, a prominent black historian and activist, pledged his continued loyalty to the party. While acknowledging that the party had not done all it could, Williams thought it still the best option. He declared, "I would have it go over the entire country and world that I do not believe the Republican Party has outlived its usefulness."[58] The convention's official address echoed Williams's sentiment.

Written by a committee of mostly Republican stalwarts, the address acknowledged black abandonment of the Republican Party in Boston. "While we deem it our duty first and last to our race, rather than party," it read, "we cannot view without uneasiness the growing tendency of some of us to advocate the immediate and unconditional severance of our membership with the Republican Party."[59] Rather than abandon the party and its historical commitment to black rights, the authors urged black Republicans to reform the party from within. The address read, "With the colored vote organized and acting in concert, the Republican Party will furnish us a place to stand on to remove every obstacle to the complete enfranchisement and citizenship of our race. It is a means not an end."[60] Republicans argued that until African Americans became politically organized nationally, the party provided them an effective platform from which to wage attacks on disenfranchisement and limits on civil rights. "To break away from the Republican Party before we are organized," they argued, "would be an act of political suicide. We therefore say stick, until by new movement we are ready for the new departure."[61] The Democratic Party, they asserted, would "absorb our power and leave us nothing but the carcass of empty promises and professions."[62]

Black independent James Monroe Trotter, who was part of the independent minority on the committee, directly challenged fellow convention participants' ongoing support for the Republican Party. In the 1880s, Trotter joined Edwin Walker as one of the city's most forceful advocates for political independence. Trotter was born enslaved to his white owner and enslaved mother in Mississippi in 1842. His mother, having either escaped or having been freed, moved James and his siblings to Cincinnati, Ohio, in the 1850s. During the Civil War, he joined the Massachusetts Fifty-Fifth Regiment, where he achieved the rank of second lieutenant and fought for the equal treatment of black soldiers. Following the war, he moved to Boston, where Republican officials appointed him clerk and head of the registered letter division in the post office. In addition to his political activism, he started a successful real estate business to help African Americans purchase property in the Boston area's segregated housing market. Trotter's son, William Monroe Trotter, continued the real estate business and founded the *Boston Guardian* newspaper. The junior Trotter became a radical leader in the twentieth century, continuing his father's legacy.[63]

Continuing his calls for political independence, during the 1883 meeting, Trotter denounced the position taken by the committee and announced he "did not agree with the entire address or the Republican Party." Despite Trotter's vigorous protestation, however, convention participants determined to send Republicans George Ruffin and George Washington Williams to the National Convention of Colored Men in Louisville, Kentucky, where they joined black leaders from around the country in a spirited debate over the condition of African Americans and political affiliation of black voters nationally.[64]

The Massachusetts statewide convention's choice of staunch Republicans to represent Boston at the National Convention of Colored Men outraged the independent attendees. Independents, emboldened by the election of Butler, argued that political independence, meaning the rejection of loyalty to either major party, was a viable national strategy of increasing black political power and should be advocated at the national convention. With Butler's election by black independents as evidence, they argued that Ruffin and Williams did not best represent Boston's black political community.

Trotter reiterated in the press that the conference did not speak for all African Americans in Massachusetts. "Let it be understood," Trotter declared in a statement published in the Boston press and reprinted in the independent-leaning black newspaper the *New York Globe*, "that this conference (not delegated body) has no right to claim itself as representative of the 6000 colored voters of Massachusetts."[65] Criticizing conference organizers for misusing the convention for partisan ends, he denounced the choice of " 'thick and thin' Republican partisans." The selection of the attendees, Trotter asserted, was made either by men who held offices under Republicans or "by those who are desperately seeking small offices at the 'stingy' hands of white Republican masters."[66] Black Republicans, he argued, placed personal ambition over the welfare of the race.

Now was the time, independents such as Trotter declared, for African Americans to shape their own political destiny. He connected current questions of partisanship to past struggles against bondage. Blind loyalty to Republicans "enslaved" African American voters to the positions of the white party leadership, which he argued did not reflect the interests of black people. He called for a "new emancipation" of black voters from single-party dominance and argued that political independence was central to African American declarations of freedom and full integration into the national body politic. Trotter asserted that "the question of where the emancipated colored voter is to go is now of only secondary importance. The first work is to get him free . . . [so] that the color line in politics will be forever broken up, until a man's party shall no longer be known by the color of his face."[67]

Other independents agreed. At a large rally in late September, prominent Butler supporters connected the conference to the immediate election. In formal resolutions they announced that no matter what the convention had decided, "such declarations do not voice our sentiments as independent men and citizens."[68] They further pointed to the long interval since the past actions of the party and promoted independent politics as the best way forward. "The Republican Party of Massachusetts of today," the resolutions explained, "is drifting into coolness and indifference to our interests as colored men[;] we deem it wise to take a decided and independent stand. . . . We believe in General Butler and will vote for him this fall, and also use our untiring zeal to persuade others to do the same."[69]

The debates that animated the statewide convention revealed intraracial disagreements over political strategy and partisanship. Both groups agreed that the protection of their current rights and future progress required greater unity and mobilization, and they saw opportunity in the electoral progress. They remained divided, however, over whether to fight for a stronger voice in the Republican Party or to branch off as independents, even if that meant supporting Democratic candidates. The partisan debate continued to rage as Butler's attempt to appoint the first black judge in Massachusetts history became the battleground over party loyalty, patronage, and racial inclusion.

## The Nomination of Edwin Walker

As tensions flared over black partisanship and choice of delegates to the Kentucky convention, attendees at the September conference also celebrated

Butler's attempt to appoint Edwin Walker to a Charlestown District Court judgeship left empty by the death of judge and former mayor of Charlestown, George Washington Warren.[70] The possibility of an African American judge was a clear sign of racial progress in the state. Black Republicans who had initially decried Butler's removal of black officials and his appointment of white officers in their places found common cause with many of the governor's black supporters over Walker's potential appointment, whom they described as a "very reputable and well-read lawyer."[71]

Although supported by black Republicans and independents alike, Walker's nomination was eventually defeated by the state's all-white majority Republican executive council, widening the rift between the two groups. The rejection supported black independents' opinion that the Republican Party was interested in black votes only, not in meaningful racial progress. It became a turning point in the development of independent politics in Boston and hardened the faith of independents in a political path outside of the Republican Party.

Edwin Walker was not Butler's first choice for the judgeship, but his eventual nomination confirmed to black voters who championed Butler in 1883 that they had indeed supported the right candidate. In the months prior to his September nomination of Walker, Butler had nominated two white men, James O'Brien and Joseph Cotton, for the position, but the executive council had rejected those choices.[72] African American commenters, including some independents, criticized Butler for not nominating Walker sooner, and some threatened to abandon the governor as their preferred candidate if he sought reelection in 1883.[73] However, when the press circulated the names of Walker and Republican George Ruffin as possible nominees, J. D. Powell, the Boston correspondent for the *New York Globe* who had earlier criticized the governor for not nominating Walker initially, suggested that "a great political point would be gained in [Butler's] favor."[74] Boston's black independents had long agitated for the political appointment of black men to positions such as the Charlestown judgeship, and they joined with Republicans in celebrating a significant milestone in racial progress in Massachusetts.

On September 13, 1883, Butler met with the state executive council and officially nominated Walker.[75] The nomination carried a wide range of endorsements from Boston's white and black legal community and was praised by black independents and Republican leaders alike.[76] Black Republicans argued that the appointment transcended partisanship, even as they used the moment to again criticize Butler. Black *Hub* editor Lewis Hayden, for example, hoped the appointment could be celebrated without partisanship. "I do not think that there is a single colored resident in the state who would oppose the confirmation of Mr. Walker," he wrote, "I regard it as a very important step in the material progress of the race, and trust that the matter will not be viewed at all as a political question."[77]

The editors of the *Hub*, however, placed politics at the center of the decision and accepted credit for Walker's nomination. Arguing that the *Hub's* editorials had shamed the reluctant governor into acting, *Hub* editors concluded, "We do not believe that a colored man would have been selected to so high a position in the Commonwealth had there been no organ of the colored people.... [Butler] had not the strength enough without the support of the colored citizen. He could no longer delay nor deny us the appointment, so loudly did the *Hub* thunder."[78] By placing responsibility for the appointment with the black Republican press and not the Democratic governor, the *Hub* sought to divert any increase in support of Butler back to the Republican Party.

Still, other black Republicans pointed to the potential negative consequence of the Walker nomination for the Republican Party in Boston when they acknowledged that Butler was using the nomination to court black voters. George Ruffin, for instance, supported Walker's appointment, but confessed, "it will have some political influence." Ruffin explained, "This act will tend to confirm [African Americans'] good opinion of him, and its influence will probably be felt more in distant parts of the country than here at home."[79] Republicans feared that Walker's appointment would improve Butler's and the Democratic Party's standing nationally and could lead to increased Democratic strength going into the 1884 presidential election.

As Republicans opined about the impact of Walker's potential appointment, Butler's pessimistic black supporters were mindful that Republicans sought to discourage black support of the governor and were skeptical that the Republican-controlled state government would confirm his nomination. Continued Republican electoral dominance in the state meant that Butler was the Democratic head of a state government ruled by Republicans. Republicans controlled both houses of the legislature and the executive council; the lieutenant governor was also a Republican. Before Walker could successfully take his seat as judge, his nomination had to be confirmed by the executive council. Thus, the confirmation of Walker, an outspoken opponent of the Republican Party during Butler's campaign, could fail.[80] The *Boston Globe* suggested that "an attempt is being made among certain of the blue blood Republicans and the dudes in that party to bring about the rejection of Mr. Edwin Garrison Walker."[81] As the *Boston Globe* continued, these so-called blue

blood Republicans "dislike exceedingly to have a Democratic governor secure the credit of being the first to honor a colored man by appointment to
high position."[82]

While it did not immediately reject the appointment, the Republican-
dominated executive council did indeed delay Walker's confirmation. Black
independents viewed this as a strategy to prevent the confirmation until after
the upcoming 1883 gubernatorial election had occurred. Butler was seeking
reelection and faced stiff competition from Republicans. The Republican
Party needed black votes and could not risk the African American support
for Butler that might follow Walker's appointment.[83]

Of further concern to Butler's black supporters were the personal attacks
against Walker's character. These attacks signaled to independents that Republican opposition would willingly defame African Americans rather than
see one appointed to high office by a Democrat. Articles in the press played
upon common stereotypes of black men as lazy and corrupt as they criticized
Walker for poor personal character and questionable integrity. For example,
the *Boston Daily Globe* described how the white, Republican-leaning *Boston
Evening Post* published an article declaring that Walker had been arrested in
Charlestown in 1875 for being drunk and disturbing the peace. The *Post* also
attacked Walker's supposed poor financial judgment, claiming that he had
been forced to leave two downtown offices for failure to pay the rent.[84]

Walker's supporters denounced these published reports as false, and a
Republican Party ploy to block Walker's nomination.[85] Walker himself sued
the *Post* for 10,000 dollars, and in the pages of the *Boston Daily Globe*, which supported Butler, publicly refuted the allegations.[86] The attacks on Walker were
further evidence of the costs to personal reputation that could follow opposition to Republicans, and the lengths Butler's opposition would go to get elected.

Despite attempts to discredit him, African Americans across party lines celebrated the announcement of Walker's nomination as the first African American
judge in Massachusetts, and his confirmation was generally expected to be
easy. Walker's supporters' optimism toward his nomination continued during
the final meeting of the executive council on October 5, 1883. Leaders from
both sides made last-minute speeches of endorsement.[87] Republicans such as
John J. Smith joined independents such as James Trotter, who addressed the
council with the promise that its members had "the power to make Massachusetts the first State which had ever dared to place a black man in a high
and honorable position."[88]

Other speakers, like Trotter, appealed to the committee's partisan interest
in making their arguments, by urging the Republican-controlled executive

council to use Walker's confirmation as a means of demonstrating that the Republican Party was indeed looking after the interests of African Americans. Black citizens of the whole nation, they asserted, were "waiting to see whether [the council] would stand by the repeated assurances of Republicanism, or prove, in the hour of trial, that when they said they were friends of the colored man they did not mean what they said."[89] Here was a test of whether the party would live up to its rhetoric of equality and support for black rights.

Those awaiting the response of the council predicted that the result would have great influence on the future political support of African Americans for the Republican Party. "It was intimated," a reporter for the *Boston Globe* explained, "that upon the action of this Council would depend to a great extent the future political course of many colored citizens of the Commonwealth."[90] Walker's advocates placed the Republicans in the curious position of maintaining black support through the approval of a Democratic nominee. This was an opportunity, they argued, for Republicans to show that they could elevate the interests of African Americans over their own partisan position. Success meant that Republican claims of loyalty to African Americans were authentic, while Walker's rejection could further the belief that black voters had grossly misplaced their trust in Republicans and should look for allies elsewhere.

In spite of the last-minute appeals and the general optimism of his supporters, the executive committee, on a tie vote, refused to confirm Edwin Walker as a judge.[91] African American spokespeople, including black Republicans, immediately responded with harsh words about the committee and the Republican Party. Lewis Hayden, a loyal Republican, lamented that after having done everything in his power to help Walker's nomination, he "felt keenly the slight put upon his race by the rejection."[92] The *Hub* refuted allegations that the rejection was race based and argued it should not reflect poorly on the Republican Party. Black Republicans attempted to salvage the reputation of the party by arguing that Walker's nomination was part of a Democratic ploy to place Republicans in the awkward partisan position of supporting their nominee, and Republican loyalty to African Americans remained strong as ever.

Republican voices were joined by members of local organizations and out-of-state commentators. The African American Debate Society and the Garrison Lyceum issued resolutions against the actions of the committee and called all African Americans to "resent the insult to our race as it richly deserves."[93] Attention to the decision also came from outside the state. *New York Globe* editor and outspoken black independent T. Thomas Fortune expressed frustration and condemned the council's decision "made in their insane fear of Benjamin Butler."[94]

Like Fortune, Boston independents viewed Walker's rejection as confirmation that the time of black Republican loyalty had passed. For years they had argued that the party would compromise racial progress for political expediency, and here was hard evidence. James T. Still, who shortly after Butler's election as governor in November 1882 had written to the *Hub* justifying political independence, once again used the *Hub* in the aftermath of Walker's rejection to call for black rejection of the Republican Party. As he exclaimed, "The Republican Party has been for years promising the colored voters recognition, but the moment an occasion occurs for a practical demonstration of their faithfulness to their promise, they desert [it]." "I sincerely look," he concluded, "for a fitting rebuke by the colored voters of Massachusetts, and the exposure of Republican hypocrisy."[95] Howard L. Smith, a correspondent to the pro-Butler *Boston Daily Globe*, similarly demanded black independence from the Republican Party. "As for myself," he declared, "the rejection of Mr. Walker has made me an enthusiastic Butler man."[96] Declaring himself a "Butler Man" allowed Smith to maintain political independence by rejecting the Republican Party without fully giving over his allegiance to the Democrats.

Even loyal Republicans who had never voted for a Democrat abandoned the Republican ticket. As one formerly stalwart Republican who fit this profile wrote to the *Boston Globe*, "The colored men have a duty now to perform and that is to work for the reelection of Governor Butler. . . . The action of the council does not affect solely one man, but all the colored people of the State."[97] In the pages of the *New York Globe*, Edwin Walker himself added fuel to anger directed at the Republicans when he blamed the Republican Party for opposing his nomination "because they did not want to give [Butler] the credit of doing more in nine months than [the Republican Party] had done in twenty years of Republican rule." Butler, Walker declared, was "the best friend the colored people had in this commonwealth."[98]

Walker's rejection marked a transitional moment in African American politics in Boston. Since the 1870s, a substantial minority of black leaders in the city had alleged that the Republican Party consistently made false promises to the city's black voters and took the vote of African Americans for granted. Now they had proof. With Walker's rejection, a noticeable sector of once loyal African American Republicans increasingly questioned their loyalty to the party. Moreover, black independents finally had a specific and prominent example of the Republican Party's not acting on its rhetoric of civil and political uplift for African Americans to back up their assertion that the Republican Party did not support black interests.

## The Election of 1883 and a Test of Independent Power

The failure of Walker's nomination cast a shadow over the final months of the 1883 gubernatorial contest. It confirmed black independents' suspicions that the Republican Party was more interested in securing electoral victory than supporting African Americans. In the aftermath of Walker's defeat, Boston's independent movement solidified in opposition to the Republican Party. They believed that the Republican-controlled executive committee's rejection of Walker had given independents a distinct advantage over their Republican opponents.

Republicans, however, returned to the campaign stalwart in their opposition to Butler and support of Republican candidate George Robinson. They cautioned voters against bolting from the party just because of a failed nomination. George Washington Williams led the way. Williams, who in the September statewide conference had endorsed a pro-Republican platform, strongly advocated Butler's defeat and cautioned black voters against straying from the Republican ticket. He warned them of becoming "too independent" and stated that he "could exercise all the independence he wanted" as a member of the Republican Party.[99] For Republicans such as Williams, a unified black electorate could maintain autonomy and pressure the party best from within its ranks.

Williams also sought to shift the blame for Walker's rejection from the executive committee to Walker himself. He argued that there was more to his rejection than partisanship. Williams explained that he knew reasons for the rejection that had never been shared in public and challenged Walker to "meet him on any stump" and discuss the question.[100] By placing the focus on Walker, Williams hoped to prevent black voters from bolting the party and supporting Butler.

Other black Republican voices joined Williams in the pages of the *Hub* in cautioning voters against supporting the governor. They invoked references to the Republican Party's antislavery past as well as Republican longevity in Massachusetts. As the *Hub* warned its Republican readership in the run-up to the election, "You will not, you dare not sell your birthright, the birthright of citizens of the noblest Commonwealth in the Union, for such a contemptible satisfaction . . . of avenging past offences and neglects upon the Republican Party."[101] "In the present struggle, colored men," they announced, "there is no doubt as to the issue. You are either for Massachusetts or you are against her."[102]

They cautioned black voters against being enticed by Butler's recent record on black equality and his advocacy of their rights. Even if portions of his deeds should be celebrated, they reminded readers that he was still a member of the Democratic Party and therefore represented proslavery and anti–civil rights forces. They also warned that Butler's success in 1883 might serve to propel him to national prominence and help him capture the Democratic nomination for president the next year. This, they feared, would lead to national Democratic supremacy and ultimately the reversal of post–Civil War gains.[103]

In the final weeks before the election, black independents voiced support for Butler and attempted to counter Republican claims of support for black rights. In public meetings they asserted that the period of Republican commitment to ideologies of black equality had passed. For example, at a large rally in late October 1883 just days before the election, a large crowd of both black and white men, as well as many women, filled Parker Memorial Hall to proclaim their political independence and show their support for Butler. Prominent speakers included Edwin Garrison Walker and Rhode Islander and longtime advocate of political independence George T. Downing.

Downing, Walker, and other independents acknowledged that at one time, the Republican Party had stood for African American rights, but they lamented that it had been transformed since its creation. "Between the past and present Republican Party," one speaker proclaimed, "there is a chasm so vast that the conscientious cannot span it."[104] The Republican Party had once been a valuable ally, but perceived inaction on black advancement was cause for African Americans to place their political support elsewhere. They demanded a new electoral style and tradition among black Bostonian voters that rejected party loyalty. "We are to start," Downing told the diverse crowd, "a new departure of the colored people from the Republican to a better party."[105]

Dissatisfaction with the Republican Party, however, did not mean wholesale support for the Democrats. "I come here," Downing told the meeting, "as a Republican, but one who has dared to criticize the party. . . . I doubt not that I shall be charged with going over to the Democratic Party."[106] Downing advocated supporting candidates in the best interests of African American rights, partisan labels notwithstanding. He continued, "If sustaining those measures which are best calculated to advance my race, and voting for men who advocate those measures is Democracy, then I am willing to admit I am a Democrat."[107] Political independence for Downing meant a willingness to break from the Republican Party, but did not automatically make one a Democrat. In fact, as Downing explained, a powerful black independent electorate could force Democrats to change their policies to attract more voters. "I rejoice to say," he told the crowd, "we do not need to go over to the Democratic Party, for it is coming to us."[108]

Like Downing, Walker spoke of his former loyalty to the Republican Party and condemned Republican attacks on Benjamin Butler. He celebrated Butler's work on African Americans' behalf and argued that if Republicans really believed in the goal of racial equality, they would support Butler too. As Walker explained, "I have heretofore acted with the Republican Party, for I believed it to be the best organization for the interests of the colored people, but that party now declares that the only issue . . . is how and in what manner we can best kill Benjamin Butler." Walker recounted Butler's past deeds benefitting African Americans, including the Civil Rights Act of 1875, which prohibited race-based discrimination in public accommodations. Walker declared, "No man . . . has done so much for its advancement of the black man in the last twenty years as General Butler."[109]

As they celebrated the work of Butler, the speakers, like Republicans, invoked the memory of the Civil War. Unlike the authors of the *Hub*, however, Downing did so not to celebrate Republican magnanimity; rather, he criticized the history of the Republican Party's loyalty to African Americans in order to, as he noted sarcastically, "see how much gratitude is due from us."[110] Questioning the sincerity of Republican advocates of emancipation, Downing declared, "When the North went to war it was to preserve the Union, not with any idea of setting the slaves free. . . . Then after the war who but the blacks have held the balance of power so that the Republicans could maintain their control of the government. . . . It seems to me the gratitude should be the other way."[111] Republicans owed African Americans for victory during the war and electoral triumph in its aftermath; therefore, the Republican Party should be held accountable to those who preserved its power.

As the event closed, Walker issued a final call to action. Walker's statements combined his personal disappointment at the way he was treated by the governor's committee and black Republican leaders into an appeal for broad support of Benjamin Butler. "The work of the next few days is most important," Walker declared, "Go work in Boston. . . . Take hold of this work and show on the 6th of November that you feel the insult offered to your race, and the attempt to back it up by fraud, lies, and perjury, and show that you are men enough to resent it."[112]

Meanwhile, black Republicans made a final appeal to voters against Butler and in support of Republican candidate Robinson. In the pages of the *Hub*, they published the names and addresses of unregistered voters in the Ninth Ward, the home to Boston's largest black population, and urged them to go to the ward headquarters and register.[113] "We are on the eve of a great decision," the paper announced the Saturday before the election. "The time for argument has nearly expired, and the day of action is at hand."[114]

Although some Republicans had celebrated the nomination of Walker, they refused to let that drive their support away from the Republican Party. They argued that Butler was no longer a friend of the race and decried black voters who were "hoodwinked" by the governor. In an open letter to Butler that was published in the *Hub* for any wavering Republican readers to see, *Hub* editors declared, "We do not believe you care for us; it is our vote that you want. And our vote your excellency cannot have." In forceful language that associated black electoral votes with manhood and protection, the authors announced, "We throw it against you; we cast it for Massachusetts; you are her enemy, she is our mother. Touch her not again. . . . We vindicate Massachusetts and we reject you and yours!"[115] As Election Day approached, both sides were optimistic about their candidates' success. Regardless of the outcome, black independents celebrated the activism of African Americans in Boston and the evidence that the political parties had begun to value the black vote.[116]

On November 3, black Republicans celebrated Butler's defeat. Butler lost by more than 10,000 votes statewide.[117] In Boston, however, he triumphed with 55 percent of the vote. In Ward Nine, home to most of the city's black voters, he lost by 458 votes.[118] In Precinct Three he still received 38 percent of votes.[119] "Victory!" the *Hub* proclaimed. "The great battle has terminated in the complete triumph of the Republican ticket. . . . Massachusetts has been vindicated. . . . We venture to say that no other class of Massachusetts citizens were so united and loyal to the State and the Republican Party as were these devoted and tried descendants of the slave."[120] They argued that the black vote in the state held the balance of power, and perhaps not surprisingly, the newspaper's editors claimed responsibility for organizing the electorate on behalf of the Republicans.[121]

Republican victory, however, also came with the expectation among their black supporters that the party would once and for all refute allegations of indifference and neglect toward black Bostonians. As the *Hub* editors made clear, "Let no blunders in the treatment of the Negro vote in Massachusetts be perpetuated now. . . . You now enjoy the triumph which they helped you to pluck. Forget not their stalwart hand, albeit black."[122] In the midst of celebrating, Boston's black Republicans appealed to Butler's black supporters and called for reconciliation. Black independents, however, had other ideas.

In the weeks following the election, black independent leaders salvaged what they could from the campaign. J. D. Powell Jr. announced in his *New*

*York Globe* column, "That we are an important factor in politics is a fact that our prominent white politicians will admit."[123] James Monroe Trotter, in a letter to the same paper, explained his encouragement and excitement about the organization of independent voters over the past year. "Although it cannot be fairly claimed that the color 'break' from the so-called Republican Party has been general," Trotter acknowledged, "it has been of proportions so large as to occasion surprise and delight, and to be without parallel in any of the States."[124] As historian Richard Harmond writes about white supporters, Butler's election and year in office inspired disadvantaged groups to see independent politics as a viable strategy. According to Harmond, "Butler helped show [ethnic and economically disadvantaged groups] the power they possessed when they voted as a unit and gave them a new political self-consciousness. . . . It gave his underdog followers a genuine sense of participation in government."[125] Like Butler's white advocates, Trotter and other black independents declared that the ranks of like-minded supporters would continue to grow, and they remained committed to an independent status in all coming political contests.

## A Final Act

Butler made one final act on behalf of Boston's black community prior to officially leaving office. Just days after the election, he successfully appointed George Ruffin to the judicial position in Charlestown that had previously been denied to Edwin Garrison Walker.[126] Although celebrated by the black community generally, Butler's nomination of Ruffin confirmed independents' suspicions that the failure of Walker's nomination had been highly partisan and the result of Republican intransigence. Ruffin, who had been outspoken in his support for the Republican ticket, seemed likely to be confirmed. Indeed, on the evening of the election, the Republican state committee received Ruffin with rousing applause for his contributions to the campaign.[127] "Fortunately for Judge Ruffin," the *Boston Daily Globe* recognized, "he possesses not only ability and character, but, what is vastly more important to the gentlemen composing the present council, [he] is a member of the Republican Party."[128]

Boston's African American community uniformly greeted Ruffin's appointment with great congratulations, but his Republican supporters were especially excited. The *Hub* praised the appointment as evidence of the egalitarianism of Massachusetts in "recognizing a man upon his merits, without regard to his color."[129] Ruffin's appointment, they asserted, demonstrated

HON. JUDGE GEORGE L. RUFFIN.

Hon. Judge George L. Ruffin, P. Thomas Stanford, *Tragedy of the Negro in America* (Cambridge, MA, 1897). (Manuscripts, Archives, and Rare Books Division, Schomburg Center for Research in Black Culture, New York Public Library, Astor, Lenox, and Tilden Foundations.)

that the executive council was not racist, as many independents had claimed during the Walker appointment controversy. "The stupid talk about color-phobia on the part of the council," *Hub* editors wrote, "has been thoroughly silenced."[130] On November 22, George Washington Williams organized a celebratory dinner at Young's Hotel. Many among Boston's prominent black leaders were in attendance, including Archibald Grimké, Charles L. Mitchell, William H. Dupree, John J. Smith, John H. Wolff, Julius C. Chappelle, George W. Lowther, and Lewis Hayden. "The appointment of Mr. Ruffin to the municipal bench was an important move on behalf of the colored people," Williams proclaimed. "It is not only an honor for one man but for the whole colored race."[131]

Despite Williams's calls for unanimous celebration, noticeably absent from the dinner were Edwin Walker, George Downing, James Trotter, and other black independents. Butler's supporters praised the governor's decision as proof of his dedication to African American progress and regarded it as vindication that they had supported the right candidate in the election.[132] Although proud of the first African American judge in Massachusetts, the state's black independents criticized Republican support of Ruffin's confirmation, arguing that if men such as Ruffin were willing to accept the political favors of Butler, they should have voted for him.[133] They continued to argue that the Republican Party of the state liked African Americans well enough as voters, but not enough to confer political positions upon them. They called upon African Americans to withhold votes from the Republican Party until the party had proven that it was going to serve the interests of African Americans and, like Butler, appoint them to significant positions.

Black independents manifested this sentiment in a new organization. Only weeks after Butler's defeat they met to form the Sumner National Independent League, later the Sumner National Political League. Disappointed following the defeat of Butler for reelection as governor, Boston's black independents, many of whom, like founder Edwin Garrison Walker, were active Butler supporters, hardened their resolve to defeat Republican candidates.[134] "We create this independent political organization because we believe the great political parties have not been true. . . . We believe that a broad and independent movement for the general good may emanate from the poor and humble of the land."[135] In organizing, they looked beyond the borders of the Bay State and sought to inspire a national movement.

The members of the league transcended the boundaries of local and state politics as they spoke of organizing a national movement. "We desire," they concluded, "a correspondence be commenced all through the land, to give force and efficacy to the determination to henceforth pursue a more independent policy as to political parties."[136] Rather than defining themselves as simply a Massachusetts or an African American institution, the Sumner National Independent League planned to reach an audience beyond the streets of Boston and to influence politics at the highest levels of government and in all regions of the nation. Although they failed to bring about a partisan transformation in Massachusetts, they remained optimistic that their strategy could still work, and league members and other black independents quickly embraced the chance to influence national politics during the 1884 election and the first term of Democrat president Grover Cleveland. Yet, the failure of Walker's appointment and the ultimate defeat of Butler for reelection highlighted the limits of independent politics and reminded many of the pitfalls of placing too much emphasis and faith in electoral and partisan politics as a tool for black progress.

## CHAPTER FIVE

# A Recognized and Respected Part of the Body Politic

## Grover Cleveland and Pursuit of Patronage

In February 1886, members of the Sumner National Independent League (SNIL) gathered at 27 Cornhill Street, the former headquarters of the anti-slavery newspaper the *Liberator*, to declare their support for the administration of President Grover Cleveland. At the conclusion of the meeting, the attendees, led by league president Edwin Garrison Walker, penned a letter to the Democratic president. The letter, "respectful, and at the same time, manly and dignified," explained why this group of black Bostonians supported the president and requested that they be rewarded for their dedication.[1] Their message expressed "the hope and further the belief that your administration will advance in the direction of properly acknowledging the colored people as a . . . recognized and respected part of the body politic."[2]

Members of the SNIL, like other black independents, believed that the Republican Party took African American support for granted and refused to appoint black men to government offices, as it did for its white supporters. These offices not only provided a local political foothold, but also were a wider symbol of African American advancement and a public manifestation of full citizenship and equality. The refusal to appoint African Americans to prominent government offices, the league explained to Cleveland, "deprives him of the advantages of enjoying the respect that goes along with recognition and the possession of respectful offices, [and] it keeps him from becoming practically educated in the management of the government." Such appointments, the league argued, would influence more African Americans to embrace political independence and support other Democratic candidates. Further, the league members declared that political appointments would go a long way toward increasing the status of African Americans nationally. "[Political appointments] would," the league argued, "have a happy influence in reconciling the whites of all sections . . . regarding merit in the management of public affairs in preference to other nonessential distinctions." "It would," they concluded, "be a simple act of justice toward those who have been so unjustly treated."[3] For Cleveland's supporters, political appointments would help African Americans gain access to government offices that were otherwise unattainable.

Central to presidential patronage was the relationship between local and national politics. Black independents in Boston were emboldened by their successful organizing during the gubernatorial campaigns of Benjamin Butler, despite his failed reelection, and they hoped to organize on a much broader scale in national campaigns. New organizations, the SNIL especially, had a national focus and hoped to shape national public opinion through local activism. They hoped that by publicly demonstrating support for the moderate Democrat Cleveland, African Americans in other regions would join in dividing the black vote. They hoped that as the northern branch of the party adopted a more progressive platform in order to secure the votes of African Americans, the southern branch would either moderate their position on civil rights or split off from the national Democratic Party, thereby weakening their position nationally. For black independents, political activism at the state level in local campaigns was part of a strategy that sought to shift the dynamics of national party politics.[4]

The pursuit of federal appointments also brought a new national visibility to Boston's black independents. After a protracted and frustrating nomination process that resulted in the rejection of Cleveland's first choice, New Yorker James Matthews, Bostonian independent James Monroe Trotter was successfully appointed to replace Frederick Douglass as recorder of deeds for the District of Columbia. The controversy surrounding the nomination process placed African Americans at the center of heated debates over civil rights, patronage, and the power of a centralized federal government. The opposition of Republicans to Matthews's and Trotter's confirmations confirmed the fears of independent black Bostonians that indeed, the Republican Party was willing to put its own interests before those of African Americans. In this way, they saw on a national level what they had witnessed in the failed appointments of black candidates to state and local offices.

The shifting strategy of the Democratic Party created significant openings for strategies of African American politics apart from, and sometimes in opposition to, the goals of the party leadership. Black pursuit of political appointments went beyond personal ambition. For African American politicians, the appointments of a few men would assist the uplift of the entire race. However, the failure or difficulty in gaining appointments revealed that despite local personal and community success in reputation or education, African American candidates were still hampered by national conditions of race relations. The experiences of black independents seeking appointed office and the debates over party loyalties contributed to disillusionment with both parties and had a direct effect on the strategies and political ideas espoused by civil rights organizations in the last decade of the nineteenth century.

## Boston's Independents Regroup

Disappointed following the defeat of Butler for reelection as governor, Boston's black independents hardened their resolve to defeat Republican candidates. One of the central vehicles of this nationalization of the local movement was their new political organization, the SNIL. Founded immediately after Butler's defeat, the new organization expressed its rejection of unwavering loyalty to the Republican Party. "The undersigned believe," the league affirmed in its founding resolutions, "it is just and timely to affirm that it is their interest to no longer ally themselves with any political party that is manifestly disposed to not treat them with due consideration. . . . Our primary consideration is to have increased respect for our rights."[5]

The formation of the new organization outraged black Republicans in the city, many of whom hoped the defeat of Butler had crushed the independent movement. "We thought negro-Independentism dead," editors of the *Hub* declared.[6] They feared a black independent resurgence and the ramifications that continued black opposition to the Republicans would have for the 1884 election. They called the SNIL a political Trojan horse, which they were "determined shall not be carried over the walls to 1884, to defeat the Republican Party and imperil the rights and liberties of the colored people of the Union."[7]

The adoption of Charles Sumner's name by the independents was particularly egregious. "Independent," the editors of the Boston *Hub* exclaimed, "is certainly one of the most repulsive epithets in our political nomenclature."[8] They argued that naming the organization after Sumner was a "political decoy" that disguised the sinister effects of black independent politics behind a title appealing to African Americans' gratitude, patriotism, and pride.[9] "What must be the character of the game which requires such high quality sauce to worry it down?" As Boston's black Republicans were finding out, Butler's defeat did little to weaken independent sentiment, and the members of the newly formed league organized to extend their influence.

In newspapers, like the *Boston Daily Globe*, the members of the SNIL explicitly announced their outrage at the Republican Party and declared their support for the Democrats. "The Republican Party has not been consistent and true to its colored ally," they announced. "We believe that the Democratic Party, which antagonized us so bitterly from policy, is beginning to see that it is politic to change its course."[10] The league members called for African Americans across the nation to organize and become a powerful independent bloc. "We desire," they concluded, "a correspondence be commenced all through the land, to give force and efficacy to the determination to henceforth pursue a more independent policy as to political parties."[11] It was hoped that by denying any party the permanent affiliation of black people, their vote would not be taken for granted, and their interests would be attained and their rights respected.

The SNIL enumerated their demands and expectations for the enforcement of equal protection laws and for the recognition of black political allegiance with appointed positions. These were central causes for black voters' shifting loyalties in the late 1870s and early 1880s and would continue to influence black Republicans to support Democratic candidates. "We ask for nothing that is unreasonable," the league explained; "We demand the protection of our civil or public rights under the laws protective of all citizens regardless of color, race, nativity, or faith."[12] Further, they declared, "We have the ambitions and aspirations of other true Americans. . . . We are not willing to be passed by . . . because of our color, or in any manner discriminated against on that account when honors and offices are being bestowed."[13] League members acknowledged the importance of official positions as a symbol of progress. In their view, the lack of political positions depressed the conditions of African Americans as much as the harm caused by civil rights violations had. The league asserted that governmental appointments would go a long way toward "creating respect for a class despised and treated with contempt, which contempt depresses in many ways not thought of by those not thus situated."[14]

The members of the SNIL hoped that it could appeal to the sympathy of the Democratic Party toward American workers. "A better feeling is growing daily, between the colored man and the rest of the laboring class," they explained. "It will attract to it a further representation of the moral sentiment of the land through being just toward those who, though poor and of the laboring class, are struggling to command respect."[15] League members recognized that the Democratic Party was hoping to make further inroads into northern states, and by claiming that it was "politic" to support African American interests, they hoped to tap into this new strategy. Further, its members, many of whom were active in independent politics during Benjamin Butler's gubernatorial campaigns, turned their sights toward the coming presidential election and hoped to unite a national black independent coalition. "We issue this brief appeal to the colored people," the league concluded, "with hope that others in other parts, like us, will organize and become a power in the coming presidential campaign and until our rights are recognized."[16] By unifying black voters across the nation, the SNIL hoped to demonstrate the power of the black electorate as a swing vote in national elections.

## President Cleveland and New Independents

In the pursuit of the presidency in 1884, the Democratic Party leadership attempted to downplay sectional differences and distance the party from its history of white supremacy and opposition to Reconstruction. The Democratic Party asserted in its 1884 platform "the equality of all men before the law.... We hold that it is the duty of the Government ... to mete out equal and exact justice to all citizens of whatever nativity, race, color, or persuasion."[17] Equality before the law, however, did not mean aggressive federal enforcement of rights. The Democrats celebrated the end of federal military protection of polling places as "conclusive proof that a Democratic administration will preserve liberty with order."[18] While the Democratic Party affirmed a dedication to equal rights, it stopped short of calls for federal interference in policies of the states. Grover Cleveland continued the Democrats' policy of noninterference that left much of the party in the hands of southern conservatives.[19]

While the Democratic platform was some cause for concern, Grover Cleveland was a likely presidential candidate to attract black independent voters. Cleveland's black supporters hoped, given his moderate record on race issues, that he might help reform the national party or cause the white supremacist faction to splinter off. As governor of New York, Cleveland had signed legislation integrating the public schools in New York City, while preserving black governance of traditionally African American schools.[20] Further, his support of civil service reform and the 1883 Pendleton Act, which required examinations for federal jobs, opened up federal employment for a growing number of African Americans.[21] Yet, despite the indications of Cleveland's amiable stance on black rights, many African Americans were wary of his election.

Black Republicans in Boston, in particular, fought vehemently against Cleveland. In the pages of the *Hub*, they openly endorsed Republican candidates James Blaine and John Logan and denounced black support of Cleveland. "There is but one way at present ... for the political emancipation of the negro in the South, and that is a vote by every colored man in the North for Blaine and Logan."[22] They argued that black voters in the North were a powerful weapon against white supremacy and were the difference in election outcomes. "The growing power of the colored vote in the North has attracted the attention of all parties," black Republicans noted. "No presidential election can now be carried by the Republican Party without the cordial and united support of colored men in half a dozen great states in the North."[23] This power should be used to remedy the condition of African Americans in the South, and they argued that this could only be done through the support of Republican candidates.

Prominent black Republican leaders, while acknowledging that the party deserved much criticism, remained committed to Blaine and Logan, thinking the alternative too dire. They hoped that Republicans' recognition of black voting power in the North would make them more aggressive on the welfare of southern African Americans. Republican members of the Wendell Phillips Club penned a letter to the *Hub* expressing this view.[24] They wrote, "While we see much in the Republican Party, in state and nation, to criticize and condemn . . . with all of its shortcomings and unfaithfulness, we believe it to be the best instrument which now exists by which our rights may be obtained and our wrongs redressed."[25] Despite these calls and Blaine's narrow victory in Massachusetts, voters nationally elected Cleveland the twenty-second president of the United States, and the first Democrat since the Civil War.

Cleveland won the national election with 49 percent of the popular vote. In Massachusetts he lost to Blaine's 48 percent plurality, with 40 percent of the votes.[26] In Boston, however, Cleveland defeated Blaine by almost 18,000 votes.[27] Notably, in this election Benjamin Butler had run as a Greenback Party candidate, winning 8 percent of Massachusetts's votes, which likely siphoned some votes away from the Democratic candidate. Voters in Ward Nine, with the highest concentration of black voters, went for the Democrat Cleveland by a slim margin over Blaine.[28]

In the aftermath of Cleveland's inauguration, some African Americans remained skeptical of the Democratic president. There was fear among African Americans that the rise of a Democratic president would usher in a new era of white supremacy.[29] An anonymous "Cautious Democrat" from New York wrote to Cleveland that "the impression prevails . . . among the Negroes that it is within your power and that you intend to make slaves of them again."[30] Frightened voters also faced white southerners who were anxious that Cleveland's election would provoke violent black resistance or the emigration of African Americans from the South.[31] Boston's black Republicans lamented Blaine's defeat, but remained committed to working for racial progress. "Friends," the *Hub*'s editors wrote, "lend us your shoulder to the wheels of our car held in the mire of caste prejudice and political slavery. . . . Parties come and parties go . . . but the cause of man shall remain forever."[32] The *Hub*, however, would not remain much longer—it closed due to lack of funds in January 1885, less than two months after Cleveland's election.[33]

Cleveland's black Bostonian supporters were jubilant and sought to quash concerns about the Democratic president. Nearly simultaneously with the demise of the *Hub*, black independents started the *Boston Advocate*. The *Boston Globe* identified the *Advocate* as "the only weekly paper in New England devoted to the wants and interests of the colored race."[34] In the paper, regular contributors such as William Bonaparte assuaged fears of Cleveland. As Bonaparte explained, "The colored people have at last seen that the election of Mr. Cleveland has in no way affected them either North or South. . . . Colored men are growing liberal and independent each day; and in no better time than now."[35]

Bonaparte made an effective advocate for independent politics, given his former allegiance to the Republican Party. As he recalled, in 1883, on the eve of Butler's failed reelection, he was offered the opportunity to lead a group of black voters from Ward Eleven in support of Butler. However, as Bonaparte explained, "I declined, as I was a believer in the Republican principles and party, and although I thought that General Butler has been our friend, it was un-Republican to support him as a Democrat and candidate of the Democracy of Massachusetts. . . . Since that time the whole thing has turned around."[36]

The election of Cleveland had a significant effect on convincing black Bostonians to support Democratic candidates. As Bonaparte continued, black voters had "some fear last year, that the election of a Democratic president would change their condition for the worse, but now they find that everything goes along just the same even with the head of the government Democratic, they see now that it will be best for them now to go to the Democratic Party."[37] "This," Bonaparte concluded, using the popular term for those who bolted the Republican Party to support Cleveland, "is unquestionably the mugwump year for the colored voters."[38]

The election of Cleveland, a northern moderate, convinced some that perhaps the animosity of Democrats toward black civil rights could be assuaged. This optimism encouraged others to join the independents in support for the president. The victory of independent politics at the national level, together with the perceived failure of the local Republican leadership, attracted former Republicans away from the party. Black residents of Ward Eleven, for example, formed the Citizen's Club of Ward Eleven just previous to the presidential election to support Cleveland. With a membership of approximately 200, the Citizen's Club, the *Boston Daily Globe* explained, demonstrated the politics of a new generation of black Bostonians. "The young men of the race," the *Globe* explained, "who have been educated in the public schools and are a thinking class, have followed the Republican party heretofore for the reason that they had been taught by the Republican leaders that it was for their interest so to do."[39] This new generation was breaking away from their former political allegiances, recognizing "that the promises made to them have been made only to be broken, and although they helped to elect Republican candidates they received nothing in return."[40]

William Bonaparte affirmed the claims of the new political generation of black Bostonians and their search for better treatment outside the Republican Party. As he explained, "There has been a movement among the colored men, particularly among the younger and more intelligent class, to form independent clubs in the interests of the colored race."[41] He celebrated the formation of independent political clubs in the South and West Ends, as well as in Cambridge. The rise in the creation of independent organizations was evidence to Bonaparte of the declining confidence in the Republican candidates and in support of the Republican Party as a strategy for black political progress.

Bonaparte, like other detractors of the Republicans, pointed to the public recognition African Americans had received under local and state-level Democratic officials. For example, Bonaparte reminded readers of Frederick O. Prince, the current Democratic candidate for governor, who as mayor of Boston in 1875 appointed African American Rev. Andrew Chamberlin to read the Declaration of Independence at a July Fourth celebration before local and visiting dignitaries. In Bonaparte's opinion, "There has never been anything done by the Republicans to offset this."[42]

Other prominent Bostonians such as attorney James H. Wolff also expressed their frustrations with the Republican Party. Wolff had previously campaigned for Republican candidates, including Governor Robinson, and was among the authors of a letter to the *Hub* endorsing Blaine. In personal correspondence and in the press, this year however, he lamented that despite black support, Republicans had done little to appoint African Americans to government office. He explained that African Americans had been an important constituency in Robinson's campaign, and that "the colored man had considerable to do with his election."[43] However, with regret, he explained Robinson's "false promises." In a confidential letter to former governor and current U.S. congressman John D. Long in 1884, Wolff explained that while Democratic New England governors had appointed black men to prominent office, Robinson and other Republicans had not. Wolff warned Long that without concessions from Republicans, more might bolt the party and join the independents. "Colored people," Wolff wrote, "are growing restless and dissatisfied with the Republican Party and its weaknesses and contemptible policy towards them."[44] Wolff hoped that Long might encourage Robinson to meet his black supporters' demands.

Wolff, as part of a delegation of black Bostonians who visited the governor, requested that he appoint black men to fill several vacancies, including master in chancery. Robinson, according to Wolff, "gave us to feel that there was not a man among the colored people that was adequate or capable of filling that position.... Things that he has done towards us and not done for us make the men almost to a unit against him.... Robinson may be a man of brains, but he is not a man of heart."[45] The failure of the Republican to recognize black voters with patronage convinced Republicans such as Wolff to follow independents out of the party.

The election of Cleveland, coupled with the perceived inaction on the part of Robinson, led other former Republican supporters to speak out against the Republican Party. Holmes Hill, for example, whom the press described as "one of the staunchest of the Republican Workers, heretofore," declared his allegiance to Prince, the Democratic candidate. In particular, it was Prince's appointment of African American men to offices that convinced him to switch his support. "I am for Prince every time," Hill explained. "He has done ... what the Republicans have failed to do for us, appointed to public office and to posts of honor colored men."[46] Further, Hill reiterated the sentiment that Republican leaders were taking African American votes for granted and felt no obligation to work on their behalf once elected. "[Republicans] think that we will come up to the polls at every election and vote the straight Republican ticket just because they say we must do so," he continued. "They talk about the 'good they have done for us' and how the Democrats are our natural born enemies." Again reminding readers of the changes in African American politics, Hill explained, "This talk would do very well in years gone past, but now there are a different class of men growing up. They have been educated and they read the papers. They are able to think for themselves, and when they tell us what we know to be untrue, we know it."[47]

The optimism surrounding the election of Grover Cleveland gave former Republicans the confidence that some Democratic candidates could be trusted to support African American interests, and that the election of such officials would not lead to an immediate restoration of white supremacist racist policies. As black Bostonians became convinced that Democratic support could be a viable political strategy, more Republicans renounced their allegiances and joined the independent cause. As an editorial in the *Boston Globe* recognized, "Republicans continue to desert the ship. . . . The colored men are now breaking away."[48]

Despite their support of Democratic candidates, Bonaparte and other supporters of Prince were careful to explain that while they might cast their ballots occasionally for Democrats, they were not dedicated supporters of either party. "We have come here together," Bonaparte said of the October 26 meeting, "not as a Democratic club . . . but as free and independent citizens to express (with open doors) our minds concerning the present contest."[49] The Citizen's Club of Ward Eleven endorsed similar statements with a resolution. "We no longer cling to the rotten hulk of the Republican craft, nor pledge allegiance to any other party, but intend to remain independent in politics until a better and more thorough understanding is had between the colored man as a voter and citizen and the different parties in the country."[50] Just as they rejected blind allegiance to the Republican Party, these black independents made sure that neither party could count on their vote without concession.

Although deeply engaged in local elections, Boston independents understood themselves to be part of a broader national strategy in black politics to divide black voters between the parties and force the national platforms to make concessions to African American interests in order to garner black support.[51] As Bonaparte explained, "The sun will shine on a brighter day when the colored voter throughout this country will divide himself in politics and be an object of concern to all parties in the government of the United States."[52]

The expansion of the independent ranks and calls for a national independent movement culminated when members of the SNIL joined with other Cleveland supporters to form the Massachusetts Colored League in December 1885. New and old supporters of Cleveland hoped to expand the local Boston independent mobilization into a national movement. Prominent advocates including John L. Ruffin, William H. Bonaparte, J. D. Powell Jr., and Edwin Garrison Walker led the new organization. It also attracted leaders from outside of Massachusetts such as New York newspaper editor T. Thomas Fortune and George T. Downing.[53] The Colored League sought to unite independent voices not only from throughout the state, but from all over the country. In his opening statement, Ruffin, the chairman of the meeting, addressed the expanded scope of the organization. "The first object of this League was simply a State affair," he explained, "but meeting with so much encouragement from abroad, we intend to make it a national one."[54] The league, "having withdrawn from all party affiliations and determined to labor in the interest of the colored race of the State and Country," declared that they were "desirous of having the opinions of our ablest exponents of Negro Political Independence," and had decided "to endorse President Cleveland in his wise administration and fairness towards the Negro."[55]

When the Massachusetts Colored League held its first meeting at Faneuil Hall, some of the most prominent black independents from all over Massachusetts attended. In addition, there were men from Rhode Island and New York, including prominent black independent and newspaper editor T. Thomas Fortune. John Boyle O'Reilly, the Irish poet and newspaper editor, also attended and served as a vice president of the organization. The organizers also invited Massachusetts congressman John F. Andrew.[56] League members supposed that the current Democratic Party had transcended its racist past and was becoming an ally of black civil rights. "We are gratified at noticing," the league resolved, "[that] as contrasting with the past . . . the disposition on the part of the present Democracy is more equitable and just in its relation to the colored people at large."[57]

League members supported the Democratic Party and the Cleveland administration, hoping this support would yield appointed positions. The league argued that such appointments would not only help African American political advancement, but also benefit the Democratic Party by encouraging more black supporters. "We entertain the hope," the organization declared, "that the Democratic administration now in power, with its resolute chief, Grover Cleveland, will accord the colored man through a fair and just recognition of his rights and merits, to be elevated generally in the esteem of his fellow citizens, which hope is fostered because it is plainly evident that it will not only be just, but politic to do so; it will surely be appreciated by the colored people of this country."[58] In addition to these resolutions, and declarations at community, state, and national meetings, black Bostonians and their allies contacted Cleveland and other leaders in the Democratic Party in the hope of gaining appointed offices.

## "To Break Up the 'Color Line' in Office Holding"

In the immediate aftermath of Cleveland's election, his supporters urged him to appoint African Americans to prominent positions in the government. They argued that doing so would help the Democratic Party make important inroads among northern black communities and would help refute Republican allegations of racism. C. L. Smith, an African Methodist Episcopal Church bishop from Bloomington, Illinois, wrote to the Cleveland administration that "it is highly advisable for the president to break up the 'color line' in office holding."[59] "The Republican Party in the North," he observed, "will not yield any portion of the colored vote without a struggle. . . . As a matter of party concern the political managers of the administration should see that some colored [man] of political experience . . . is given a position where he can be of service in endeavoring to make friends for the administration among the colored people."[60] Cleveland supporters such as Smith argued that by securing large portions of the black vote in the North, the Democratic Party could swing state and local elections in its favor. "The colored vote," Smith concluded, "must be encouraged, watched and nursed, in the states where it is the most influential."[61] Political patronage of African Americans would encourage support in the northern states as it gave black citizens a foothold in the halls of government.

Cleveland supporters in Boston urged the president to appoint prominent African Americans to office. In particular, they suggested George Downing as their preferred nominee. Since the 1870s, Downing had become a vocal proponent of independent politics, a fact that the SNIL brought to Cleveland's attention. A political appointment was due Downing, the league argued, "because of his pioneership in the independent movement among the colored people, because of his long and favorable service in the cause of equity and his people and because he is capable, worthy, and a responsible member of his community."[62] The appointment of Downing would send a message to the national black electorate that Cleveland recognized their support and they would be rewarded for their work and sacrifice.

Letters from supporters joined Downing's many requests to Cleveland offering his services.[63] Downing sent letters to the president searching for an appointment and hoping to use the electoral power of black independents to influence Cleveland's and the Democratic Party's position on racial equality and civil rights. His letters show the strength of the belief in strategies of independent politics and the faith in the Cleveland administration to advocate progressive racial policies. The correspondence also exposes the opposition that Downing faced and the personal sacrifice involved in his support of Cleveland. The failure of Cleveland to award Downing any appointment demonstrates the misplaced optimism that a Cleveland presidency would bring with it a new black political ascendency.

In his letters, Downing called upon the president to make decisions that would encourage African American voters to support Democrats and not the Republican Party. He took vocal exception to Cleveland's actions that he thought would damage calls for partisan independence and give fuel to Downing's Republican opposition. For example, in 1887 Downing wrote to Cleveland urging him to recall an order evicting African Americans from the

"Arlington Reservation" at Fort Meyer just outside of Washington, D.C., in Virginia. Also known as "Freedman's Village," it was home to a large shanty-town of African American residents who first moved there as refugees during the Civil War.[64] Downing informed Cleveland that the eviction would be used by the Republican Party to undermine African American Democratic loyalty. "It will be used and I fear seriously by the enemy," Downing explained. "It will erase the efforts of such of us as are striving to destroy the colored man's 'blind' adhesion to the Republican Party."[65] Although the direct impact of the correspondence is unknown, the secretary of war suspended the evictions on December 12, 1887, just days after Downing wrote his letter.[66]

In another case, Downing urged Cleveland not to remove the African American tax collector for the District of Columbia, John F. Cook. The removal, Downing argued, "will cause considerable comment among the colored people, especially by those who oppose our movement for a division of the colored vote."[67] He urged Cleveland and his administration, regardless of motive, to be mindful of the way their decisions regarding African Americans would be perceived in the press and how those reports would be used to discourage African Americans from supporting Democratic candidates.

In addition to affecting direct presidential decisions, Downing's and Cleveland's other supporters sought to shape the platform of the Democratic Party in the hopes of dividing the African American vote and encouraging black support of Democrats. "Those colored men," Downing wrote in a May 1888 letter, "who are laboring to break the blind adhesion of the colored vote to the Republican Party, will in the presidential contest be greatly assisted by the National Democratic Convention."[68] He proposed an addition to the Democratic platform. "The party," Downing proposed, "happily recognizes that involuntary servitude, except for crimes for which the party has been duly convicted, does not exist in the United States; that equality before the law for all American citizens is an affirmed principle; and that all citizens may, through merit, hope for equal consideration; it affirms in the line thereof, and in conformity with the democratic principles, its adhesion thereto."[69] Adopting such a platform, Downing argued, would generate confidence in the Democratic Party among both black and white voters. Further, it would contradict attempts by the Republican Party to portray Democrats as against racial equality or African American civil rights.

Downing sought the opportunity to advise Cleveland about the state of African Americans and recommend the best tactics to secure them as Democratic voters. Following a short interview in February 1887, he hoped to secure a longer meeting with the president to discuss "the enlightenment of colored men about the best policy as to political parties [and] how colored people may be reached and affected . . . and how [their ideas] may be brought into sympathy and cooperation with your conception of duty and right policy."[70] In another letter, to Secretary of the Navy William C. Whitney, Downing described his ideas about African American partisan loyalty and how to overcome it. "Their blind adhesion to one party," he explained, "is much like the adhesion to faith or sect that is so observable in most cases; they adhere to their faith because it was their parents' faith; reason has not much to do in the matter."[71]

The appointment of a recognizable African American official to a prominent position, Downing argued, would make black voters take notice and support the Democratic Party. "The attention of the colored vote [would] be arrested, as it would be by the appointment of a worthy colored man, one who is nationally known to some prominent federal position of honor and trust away from Washington, in the North, say in the New England States. The sentiment of the section is ready for it, of this I am assured."[72] The appointment of such a candidate, he concluded, would "be favorable to the party. . . . It would assist the hope we entertain of carrying four of the New England States in the presidential election."[73] Downing hoped to convince the Cleveland administration to address African American concerns in exchange for black votes at the polls.

In addition to calling on the Cleveland administration to transform the Democratic platform and make public attempts to court black voters, Downing looked to the president for government positions as recognition for his service in the campaign. Early in Cleveland's first term, Downing wrote letters to the president requesting positions in the government for himself and other African American supporters. "There are worthy aspiring colored men," he wrote, "who would appreciate a position of honor and trust in the North; not only for personal reasons but that they might render a state good service, and because of its beneficial effect on their class, hitherto passed by in the section."[74]

These sentiments echoed those of *Boston Advocate* editor J. D. Powell, who declared the importance of nominating an African American man to office in New England. Cleveland's supporters argued they had sacrificed much by supporting the Democratic Party and therefore sought recognition. "The time has come," Powell told Cleveland, "when you can do much for the class of men many of whom have stood up and been ostracized not only in social but political circles."[75] Powell argued that black independents were distinct from white voters who had left the Republican Party. "There are many things," he explained, "to be considered in a colored man who is an independent voter that aren't thought of when a white man leaves his party [including] . . . the non-support of his people who think he is an enemy to his race if he becomes a Democrat. He becomes a martyr so to speak."[76] "If you have the interest of the colored people at heart," Powell concluded, "we sincerely trust that . . . the colored men of New England may be recognized not by mere promises but by appointments."[77] Powell joined Downing in advocating positions in the government for African American men so that they would be public examples of black political acumen, contradicting allegations that they were unworthy or ill-suited for positions of prominence in the government.

Downing argued that if the president made African American appointments it would bolster black support for the Democratic Party in African American communities and could lead to significant Democratic gains in the North. "It is the interest of the party," he wrote, "to encourage political independence among colored men."[78] "It would be an act that would be attractive," he continued, "to appoint . . . say two or three colored men to positions of honor and trust in the North. . . . It would serve the party and probably benefit me."[79] While Downing advocated appointing African Americans to office generally, he offered himself as a viable and attractive candidate.

With the support of northerners such as those in the SNIL, Downing sought a government position both as personal recognition for his service to Cleveland and as a symbol of the Democratic president's support for African Americans.[80] "A number of gentlemen of standing," he wrote to Cleveland, "have very kindly said to me that it would in their judgment be no more than my due, that it would be politic as well as in the line of justice for me to secure recognition."[81] Among the positions that he requested were "postmastership, collector of port . . . marshalships, commissionerships, and the like."[82]

Downing sought a prominent appointment, which he argued would lead directly to electoral gains and help secure the president's reelection. He sought a position "in which my standing and dignity would not be compromised."[83] Such an appointment, he attempted to convince Cleveland, would "attract favorable attention and cause the colored people to grow in confidence and regard toward the [Democratic] Party; to hasten the day when being a colored citizen will not be regarded as decisive as to his selection of the political parties."[84] Downing also hoped his appointment would "have a happy reconciling effect on the more liberally disposed whites of the South."[85]

Since the Democratic Party would be able to gain easier access to offices in the South, Cleveland's appointment of Downing would do more to convince southerners of the worthiness of black men for offices than did appointments from the Republican Party. "I am concerned," he wrote to Cleveland, "to have a Democratic administration with Grover Cleveland as its head, succeed itself, rather than have a Republican administration that might be as good."[86] The Democratic Party needed the opportunity to demonstrate that it was no longer the party of white supremacy and slavery. Cleveland's reelection, Downing argued, "would give the Democratic party the opportunity it should have to grow."[87] In particular, he argued that the Democratic appointment of black officials would help mollify southern antipathy against African American office holding. "It would ease contracted minds," Downing argued, "that have been educated in the idea that one half of the people are not capable, and loyal as to hold office; it would exercise an influence in the South, no present Republican administration could."[88]

Cleveland's supporters, such as Downing, argued that they were instrumental in leading black voters to the Democrats, and they sought recognition for this service. For example, in 1887, following the victory of Democrat John W. Davis as governor of Rhode Island, Downing wrote to D. S. Lamont expressing the importance of black voters in Democratic success at the polls. "I am proud of the conspicuous part colored voters played in bringing about the result," he exclaimed; "there is hope for Massachusetts in the same direction."[89] Future victories, Downing argued, could be secured by Cleveland's appointment of him to a prominent position in Rhode Island. "The old aversion to the Democratic Party, naturally existing among the colored people, will be overcome by kindness and recognition."[90] Downing hoped to fill a vacancy in the custom service at Providence, or "some position at Washington or elsewhere."[91]

Prominent northern white Democrats supported Downing's pursuit of a position. For example, he received endorsements from the Democratic State Committee of Rhode Island as well as from the Democratic caucus in the city of Newport, where he was nominated for election to the general assembly.[92] Rhode Island governor Davis, state officers, and officials from Newport signed a letter endorsing Downing and urging Cleveland to make the appointment. "It is a just appreciation of character," the Rhode Islanders wrote, "and a recognition of patriotic efforts of a broad and liberal nature for us, as we do, to refer to George T. Downing . . . as being worthy to be recognized, and as being competent."[93] Further, they explained, "a recognition of the gentleman by his being appointed to some worthy national position of trust would be in several respects a politic move."[94] These recommendations, Downing told Cleveland, were "because I had worked to convince the colored people that it was their interest to look toward the Democratic Party with more hopeful feelings."[95] Although Downing garnered significant support among white Democrats and black independents, he faced resistance from Republican Party opposition.

In his letters to Cleveland, Downing often complained of the attacks he faced from black and white advocates of the Republican Party. There were African Americans, he argued, who opposed his advocacy of independent politics. "I am severely antagonized," Downing wrote to Cleveland, "by the leading colored men because of my liberal policy. I am proud to say some of them are cutting the scales off their eyes."[96] He urged the president to reject this opposition. In a letter to D. S. Lamont, Cleveland's personal secretary, Downing urged the president to ignore "any adverse representation that may be made from jealousy, for personal ends, or through the lingering of the old prejudice."[97] Downing's letters expose the personal damage that independents endured for their positions. These attacks were exacerbated by the failure of the Cleveland administration to reward black supporters for their sacrifice.

Black independent organizations wrote to Cleveland to defend Downing. In February 1886, the SNIL wrote to Cleveland decrying the attacks. "We hasten to assure [Cleveland]," they declared, "that in every state in the Union where our deputies have been [Downing] is held in high regard as a most worthy representative of the race among the foremost to encourage and indorse the independent position taken by the colored people."[98] The success of local independent politics was closely connected to the federal appointment of leaders such as Downing. Federal recognition, they argued, would expand the ranks of black independents, while rejection could push black voters firmly back into the Republican fold.

Despite his many requests and letters of support, Cleveland did not appoint Downing to any desired position. "I feel some concern as to my relation to the Administration," he wrote to Lamont in June 1887.[99] He had faced much opposition and abuse for his allegiance to Cleveland, and even as the president lost reelection, Downing continued to press for a position. "For advocating a policy that crossed the unenlightened convictions of the body of the colored people," he wrote to Cleveland, "I have encountered jeers, misrepresentation, yes, abuse.... I ask that you give me some recognition . . . it would be an acknowledgement of services favorable to the party."[100] African American supporters such as Downing hoped that with the coming of the Cleveland administration their independent stance would be rewarded, but as his frustrated attempts show, this optimism did not always transfer into physical benefits.[101]

## A Delayed Victory for Independent Politics

While Downing was unsuccessful at gaining an appointment, the Cleveland administration did not totally ignore its African American constituents. In the controversy over the appointment of a black replacement for Frederick Douglass as recorder of deeds for the District of Columbia, black Boston's independents were placed at the center of a national discussion over black rights, political appointments, and federal authority. As historian Lawrence Grossman observes, "The fate of this appointment would transcend the bounds of mere patronage, becoming a focus of racial politics. . . . It would demonstrate at the national level the divergent attitudes toward political recognition of [African Americans] held by Northern Democrats and many of their more prejudiced colleagues from Southern and Border States."[102] The eventual selection of James Monroe Trotter demonstrated a significant victory for black independent politics. This success, however, contrasted with the diminishing conditions of African Americans nationally, and in the South especially, and showed starkly the limits of independent mobilization.

Cleveland, like many of his predecessors, appointed African Americans to positions typically allotted to black officials. Among these were the recorder of deeds for the District of Columbia and ministers to Liberia, Haiti, and Santo Domingo.[103] Although many black federal employees lost their jobs following the change in department leadership, Cleveland's administration attempted to preserve black members of the federal bureaucracy.[104] The position of recorder of deeds for the District of Columbia was particularly important. Because it had been held by Frederick Douglass and was located in the nation's capital, the office held great physical and symbolic meaning as an example of African American progress and national inclusion. Although Downing did not receive the nomination, Cleveland sought to replace Douglass with another black candidate loyal to the Democratic Party.[105]

While most of Cleveland's appointments of African Americans caused little controversy, the choice to replace Frederick Douglass with another black man drew northern Democratic racial moderates into conflict with the southern arm of the party.[106] The president's nomination of a black man to this office was a test of the influence of black independent politics. Black journalist William Bonaparte wrote to New York senator William M. Evarts questioning the viability of such a nomination. "May we ask," Bonaparte wrote, "if in your judgment the President should nominate some colored man for Recorder of Deeds . . . would the Senate confirm him? And is a colored man objectionable because of his alliance with the Democratic Party?"[107]

Bonaparte's questions addressed the central controversy. Cleveland's decision to nominate a black candidate enraged white Democrats in Washington who opposed black officials. This racism was disguised in discussions over local control of nominations and federal intervention. Opponents decried the president's black nominees as "carpetbaggers" who infringed on the sovereignty of the city's white leadership.[108] The nomination also forced the Republican Party to confront black political independence and decide whether to allow Cleveland the credit for prominent African American appointments. As James Trotter was eventually appointed to the office, it placed black Bostonians at the center of a controversy about local rights and the place of African Americans in the Democratic Party.

When Fredrick Douglass retired as recorder of deeds in January 1886, Cleveland's first choice to replace Douglass was James C. Matthews, a black attorney and former campaign worker from Cleveland's home state of New York.[109] Matthews endorsed dividing the African American vote and actively campaigned for Democratic candidates in New York. He had a long relationship with the New York Democratic Party, making him a likely candidate to replace Douglass.[110] Democrats in Washington, D.C., however, were angry that Cleveland would appoint an African American official and insisted that they maintain local control over the appointment. Here opponents masked the racial issue with a question of residency.[111] As Matthews's nomination went before the Senate, both parties had to weigh ideas and campaign promises against voters advocating white supremacy and local autonomy.

The appointment of an African American man to so prominent an office caused conflict within the two parties. In the Democratic Party, Matthews's supporters had to count on the endorsement of northern Democrats and hope that some representatives from southern states would support an African American nominee out of loyalty to the administration. For the Republican Party, members had to balance their legacy as the standard bearers of racial equality with the threat that Cleveland's appointment of a black recorder would convince more African Americans to leave the Republican Party. This was exactly the strategy Downing advocated in his letters to the president, and the Republican reaction to Matthews shows that there was some basis for his faith in dividing the black vote.

Arguing on the grounds of Matthews's nonresidency in the capital, twenty-nine Republican senators and eight Democrats voted to reject Matthews's nomination. All four northern Democrats, nine border and southern Democrats, and one Republican supported Cleveland's decision. Although Cleveland used a recess appointment and made Matthews recorder of deeds in spite of the Senate's rejection, the largely Republican opposition of Matthews further convinced black independents that their trust in the Republican Party was misplaced, and that perhaps their future lay with Cleveland and Democrats.[112] Calvin Chase, the editor of the African American–owned *Washing-*

*ton Bee*, remarked, "The Republican Party doesn't realize it yet, but the action of the Senate . . . has alienated the negro from its ranks. . . . There will be no more negroes who will vote the Republican ticket."[113] Cleveland attempted to capitalize on this rising discord and again nominated Matthews when the Senate reconvened. The Senate, however, renewed its objection to Matthews's nomination, this time seventeen to thirty-one.[114]

While prominent Democrats argued that Cleveland, having gained the advantage over Republicans, should drop the race issue and nominate a white recorder, Cleveland refused, and at the urging of the *Boston Globe* and Massachusetts independents, instead nominated James Trotter to the office.[115] The choice of Trotter, a Civil War veteran, a prominent advocate of independent politics, and a supporter of Benjamin Butler for governor and Cleveland for president, would please northern Democrats and again dare Republicans to reject the president's nomination of a black recorder and face further African American discontent.

George F. Hoar, the Republican senator from Massachusetts, urged Trotter's confirmation due to the number of recommendations from constituents.[116] Letters supporting Trotter reflected the diverse support the nominee received.[117] For example, among the endorsements were letters from black Republican Lewis Hayden and also John Warren, editor of the *Irish Republican and Freelance*.[118] Warren, in particular, spoke of Trotter's support for Irish independence and argued that his nomination could help bridge the gap between black and Irish. "Lieutenant Trotter," Warren wrote, "is a friend of mine and closely identified with the National Irish American element. . . . In connection with his confirmation on behalf of the class with whom I affiliate and myself I earnestly recommend him . . . and hope that you will help to remove a prevailing impression that our party is opposed to the removal of the colored line."[119] The support from Hoar and others was successful, and although the Senate District of Columbia Committee rejected it, the Senate confirmed Trotter's appointment by a vote of thirty to eleven.[120]

In Boston, African Americans of both parties praised the decision. In a letter to Cleveland, William Bonaparte expressed the gratitude of black Bostonians. "Accept the grateful acknowledgements," he wrote, "of the thousands of Massachusetts colored citizens irrespective of party ties for the just and fitting recognition."[121] The *Boston Daily Globe* reported that Lewis Hayden, the famous antislavery advocate and Republican leader, conferred with Senator Hoar regarding Trotter's nomination. Following his confirmation, Hayden told the *Globe*, "for the sake of the race I am forced to rejoice that we still hold the lucrative office in which Mr. Trotter has just been confirmed."[122]

James Monroe Trotter, William J. Simmons, *Men of Mark: Eminent, Progressive, and Rising* (Cleveland, OH: G. M. Rewell and Co., 1887). (Schomburg Center for Research in Black Culture, Jean Blackwell Hutson Research and Reference Division, New York Public Library, Astor, Lenox, and Tilden Foundations.)

JAMES M. TROTTER.

Julius C. Chappelle, a Republican and former representative to the general court, celebrated Trotter's appointment and recognized Cleveland's political strategy. "The President," Chappelle told a *Boston Globe* reporter, "couldn't have made a better selection among independent colored voters.... Of course, Mr. Trotter and myself differ on general political questions. I believe the appointment is a shrewd political one."[123] William O. Armstrong, the current African American member of the Massachusetts General Court, remarked that "while perhaps some of us would have preferred a Republican, still we are grateful to President Cleveland that he should have recognized the colored race by the appointment of a colored man, and we look upon it in that light rather than from the standpoint of Mr. Trotter's politics."[124] Trotter's independent supporters also agreed to put aside partisan differences and celebrate the victory for all African Americans.

At a reception hosted by SNIL and the Republican-dominated Wendell Phillips Club, Edwin Garrison Walker, the chairman of the occasion, expressed the nonpartisan gratitude for the appointment. "I congratulate you," Walker told the audience, "on the thought that in the future you will be able to say that you were among the first of the colored people of New England who met to do honor to the first colored American belonging to Massachusetts ever selected . . . to fill an honorable and responsible position at the capital."[125] The chairman urged attendees to put aside partisan differences for the time being. "We are not here for the purpose of discussing politics or congratulating one another on the success or defeat of any political organization," he announced. "That is something we may deem proper to do on some other and different occasion."[126] While Walker agreed to set aside his opposition to the Republican Party, he did not declare an end to African American partisan independence.

Trotter, like Walker, hoped that his appointment would convince black voters to support, regardless of party, candidates who endorsed civil rights. "My hope is that the colored voter will grow into the feeling that now and hereafter the color question is no longer in politics," Trotter told voters. "I shall be satisfied," he continued, "if I can feel that the colored people are voting as their judgment dictates. I feel that they have got into a second slavery, and if they can shake off the shackles that bind them to a party they will be truly free."[127] Trotter, like other black independents, hoped that the contentious debate around his nomination would cause African American voters to recognize the utility of dividing black political allegiances.

Indeed, the controversy over the Matthews and Trotter appointments was evidence of the Republican Party's increasing willingness to compromise African American advancement for the sake of political expediency, and a sign of the potential success of partisan independence. As historian Lawrence Grossman concludes, "Trotter's confirmation symbolized the black electorate's potential power, when freed from the straitjacket of party, to further the interests of the race, a lesson that some Northern [African Americans] had already learned in state and local politics."[128] Trotter's appointment demonstrated the result that threats to support Democrats could have on Republican officials.

While African Americans in Boston praised the appointment, Cleveland's administration failed to bring the expected groundswell of further government positions. Although the Trotter and Matthews affair encouraged black support of Democrats, these successes did not mask the continued hardships and the deteriorating political status of African Americans in the South. With the exception of some federal appointments, Cleveland continued the Democratic Party's position of southern state sovereignty and federal noninterference. This policy of nonintervention in southern affairs kept open the door to the rise in racial discrimination, disenfranchisement, and the violence of the coming decade. Indeed, white supremacy and southern radicalism reemerged as the driving force behind the Democratic Party. African Americans in Boston, however, did not fully reject Democrats and rush back into the Republican fold. Although opportunities for advancement in the national Democratic Party diminished, in Boston, black independents drew upon alliances among an unlikely group, the city's Irish population. In uniting with the Boston Irish, they urged coalitions rooted not only in partisanship, but also in struggles for equal rights and independence in both the United States and Ireland.

## CHAPTER SIX

# For Ireland's Cause

## Black and Irish Political Coalition Building

On the bright but chilly morning of November 14, 1888, a grand procession moved toward the Boston Common.[1] African American Civil War veterans and an armed drill squad in full uniform led the parade.[2] In addition to the soldiers, the display also included prominent leaders from both the Democratic and Republican parties and from Boston's Irish and African American leadership. In particular, Boston's first Irish-born mayor Hugh O'Brien joined the participants.

Along the edge of the Common, the crowd stopped in front of a veiled monolith. William H. Dupree, a black community leader and the chairman of the arrangement committee, opened the dedication. "In the occurrence which we commemorate," Dupree began, "the colored race has a profound interest, for one of that race was a principal figure in it."[3] Amid deafening cries and applause, Governor Oliver Ames joined nine-year-old Lillian Chappelle, the daughter of the general court's only African American member, Julius Chappelle. Together they pulled the cord that released the covering on the monument to Crispus Attucks and other victims of the Boston Massacre.

Following brief statements from Governor Ames and Mayor O'Brien, the procession reformed and made its way down State Street toward Faneuil Hall for continued celebrations. Ex-Louisiana lieutenant governor P. B. S. Pinchback, who had traveled north for the dedication, remarked about the interracial cooperation reflected in the event. "Would to God I could present this picture to the people of [Louisiana]," he declared. "No spectacle seems so grand as that I see before me, the ruler of the State here, of the city here, Anglo Saxons both, and your black chairman between them—perfect equality of the races."[4]

While Pinchback characterized the governor and the mayor as "Anglo Saxons both," he neglected to remark on Mayor O'Brien's Irish heritage. As O'Brien and Dupree stood to commemorate the victims of the Boston Massacre, they demonstrated over a decade of political coalition building between the city's black and Irish immigrant populations. In Boston during the 1880s, black and Irish residents forged political alliances that combined ideas about citizenship rights with notions of ethnic nationalism. In their sympathy for the

Crispus Attucks statue, Boston Common. (Photograph, 1888, Boston Pictorial Archive, Print Division, Courtesy of the Trustees of the Boston Public Library.)

cause of Irish independence and their appeals for Irish support of African American civil rights struggles, members of Boston's black community united calls for local, state, and national civil rights protection with broader transnational independence movements. In their activity during the political campaigns of Irish leaders, black activists manipulated machine politics and used their support for Irish and Democratic candidates as leverage against Republican leadership.

African Americans and Irish immigrants built successful coalitions in three primary areas. First, in their support of Irish nationalist organizations including the Irish Land League and Charles Parnell's Home Rule movement, black journalists and spokespeople drew parallels between the plight of African Americans in the United States and the oppression of the Irish in the British Empire.[5] By appealing to a shared history of oppression, black and Irish leaders argued that the two groups should be allies in struggles for independence and civil rights. Next, as some black voters rejected the Republican Party, they united with Irish supporters of Democratic candidates such as Boston's first Irish-born mayor, Hugh O'Brien.

Boston's black and Irish coalition emerged as the political landscape of the city was changing. For decades, the city had been dominated by older Republican leadership. By the late 1870s and 1880s, however, an increasing number of voters, black and white, were drawn to the Democratic Party. During the 1880s, the Democratic Party was the party of the political insurgency pushing against the Republican establishment. In that way, Irish supporters joined with disillusioned African American Republicans in the support of Democratic candidates in city elections. In particular, the Irish nationalist political leadership found valuable allies in the party, which became a valuable advocate for working-class rights. Undoubtedly, since many black Bostonians were also laborers, Democratic advocacy on behalf of workers also encouraged black support.

Finally, both electoral politics and shared sympathies came together in a successful proposal for the construction of a monument to Crispus Attucks and the other victims of the 1770 Boston Massacre. The figure of Crispus Attucks and the events of the Boston Massacre were given a meaning that appealed to African Americans as an example of involvement in the founding of the nation, and to Irish supporters as an example of resistance to British colonial rule. When leaders of Irish Boston, such as newspaper editor and poet John Boyle O'Reilly and Mayor O'Brien, stood alongside black leaders in commemoration of the event, they presented a visible example of political cooperation and cultural sympathy. By the end of the decade, however, the circumstances holding together these alliances had grown more tenuous, and ultimately the coalition proved to be short-lived, dashing hopes of a broad interracial struggle and indicating to black independents that they could count on few allies in the long run as they turned further inward to organizing beyond traditional electoral political structures. Cooperation with Irish nationalists, though brief, provided another example of the power of racial or ethnic solidarity as an organizing paradigm, and pushed many to reject partisanship in favor of race-based organizations. Finding few faithful allies elsewhere, black activists increasingly looked within for political strength.

## "Be a Power That Will Be Irresistible for the Right"

The black and Irish alliance on display on Boston Common in the late 1880s had its origins in earlier moments of mutual support, and events abroad strongly influenced black and Irish relations in Boston. In Ireland, nationalists challenged British authority by forging independence and Home Rule movements. At the end of the 1870s, Ireland plunged into a food shortage reminiscent of the horrors of the famine of the 1840s. In response, men and women of Irish descent on both sides of the Atlantic organized land leagues to protect Ireland's peasant class and resist government policies that favored British landholders.[6] The land leagues used nonviolent techniques including boycotts and rent strikes combined with occasional acts of violence.[7] These overt acts of resistance bolstered the movement for Irish Home Rule championed by famed leader Charles Parnell. Demands for Home Rule moderated calls for full independence. According to the Home Rule plan, Ireland would have an independent legislature, which would control all affairs not specifically reserved for the imperial parliament.[8] In order to achieve these goals, Parnell depended on money from abroad to bolster the campaign coffers of parliamentary candidates. Reports of Irish poverty and starvation engendered significant sympathy and financial support from Americans. American land leagues held meetings in cities across the nation and raised money for both famine relief and Land League activity in Ireland.[9]

African Americans in Boston joined their Irish neighbors in advocating land league agitation. For example, in March 1881, at a rally at Monument Hall in Charlestown, Edwin Garrison Walker, who counted on Irish support during his election to the legislature in the 1860s, spoke in favor of the league. In his speech, he invoked the memory of Daniel O'Connell and used the history of African American resistance to slavery to inspire league members. Walker recalled reading of the antislavery activism of O'Connell and others in the pages of the *Liberator* as a boy, and "often wished that there could be some colored man as strong intellectually as Daniel O'Connell, who could come out and strike such blows as he had done for the liberation of the Irish people."[10] Inspired by O'Connell's activism, he drew parallels between the cause of Irish independence and the African American struggle for equality. As he concluded, Walker compared the liberation of African Americans from bondage to the emerging independence of the Irish: "Thirty years ago, and who would have believed that the colored race would be occupying the position it now occupies? The time," he urged, "would surely come when the Irish nation would shake off the English yoke."[11] These hopes for an independent Ireland would continue and gain prominence among African Americans as Charles Parnell's Home Rule movement in Ireland increased in popularity.

Black Bostonians were part of a national trend of black support for Irish independence. In 1883, delegates at the Colored National Convention in Louisville, Kentucky, passed a resolution supporting Ireland.[12] Correspondents to the *Newport Daily News* commented on the resolution. "It is gratifying to notice the exhibition of this liberality on the part of the colored people," they recognized, "for certainly they have been the subjects of persecution at the hands of those towards whom they have magnanimously extended the olive branch of peace and good feeling." "We hope," they concluded, "that the result will be greater harmony, enlarged ideas, and a broader conception on all sides of what belongs to good citizenship."[13] There was optimism among black advocates of Irish independence that cooperation between the two groups would overcome previous animosity and conflict. Many hoped that the Irish and Irish Americans would appreciate black support and endorse claims of African Americans for full equality. As the black correspondents in Newport suggested, the uniting of African American and Irish interests "will be a power that will be irresistible for the right."[14]

These sentiments echoed through the first meeting of the Massachusetts Colored League in December 1885. Black independents organized the league to support local and national candidates and to push for "civil freedom for the black man."[15] The Irish editor of the *Boston Pilot*, John Boyle O'Reilly, joined the black leadership cadre as a vice president. Although the central cause of the meeting was the expression of political independence in America, the league explicitly recognized support for Charles Parnell and Irish Home Rule. "The 8,000,000 of the colored Americans of the United States," a resolution read, "who know what it is to be oppressed, send a hearty greeting to the Irish people in Ireland who are struggling to be free from the oppressive policy of the English government. . . . 'Go on in your noble career that victory will surely attend your efforts.' "[16] O'Reilly, who had escaped to Boston from an Australian penal colony, celebrated and declared his support for the cause of black political independence and civil rights. "When questions of right or wrong are concerned, of suffering, injustice, degradation, or exclusion," he declared, "there ought to be and there are no races or classes."[17] In a letter to George Downing several days after the meeting, O'Reilly reaffirmed his views. "I felt only one thing in speaking to the colored men," O'Reilly wrote. "Surely that is one of the world's great races—a blessing to America."[18] O'Reilly encouraged African Americans to look within themselves for uplift and reject modeling themselves after whites.

Advocates of a black-Irish alliance urged African Americans to support Irish independence regardless of Irish reciprocity. For example, soon after the Massachusetts Colored League meeting, New York newspaper editor T. Thomas Fortune addressed critics of the league who questioned what Charles Parnell and Irish nationalists had done for African Americans to deserve their support. Fortune, who was invited to the meeting but could not attend, affirmed that the Massachusetts Colored League had done the right thing, even without broad-based Irish support for the black freedom struggle. Fortune declared that regardless of what they would get in return, African Americans should stand up against injustice. "The colored people know what oppression is, for they have been, they are now, oppressed," Fortune declared. "It is manifestly right and proper, therefore, that they should sympathize with oppressed people under whatever government such may be found."[19]

Fortune echoed the sentiments of the Massachusetts Colored League organizers, who blended support for Irish struggles with continued advocacy of political independence. He condemned what he perceived as political passivity on the part of black Republicans and insisted that they take inspiration from the radical political traditions of the Irish. "The difference between an Irishman and a colored man is this," Fortune explained. "You strike an Irishman and he yells and strikes you back; you strike a colored man and he yells and runs like a deer . . . and pins his hopes to some slimy, oily, tricky white man for leadership."[20]

Black supporters of Irish independence argued that through political unity, both groups could overcome political marginality and force issues of Irish nationalism and black civil rights to the forefront. George Downing, in a letter to the *New York Freeman*, revealed himself as the author of the Massachusetts Colored League resolution supporting Irish Home Rule and rejected any criticism of the cause.[21] Downing recalled the story of Daniel O'Connell and Irish support for the abolition of slavery. This support, he concluded, required that African Americans similarly assist, however they could, in the cause of Irish resistance to British oppression. He argued that it is "politic always for the despised black man of the United States to invariably make friends rather than enemies." During such a politically shifting and volatile period as the 1880s, Downing, like other black leaders, recognized that a political coalition between the two groups could be invaluable in furthering the interests of Irish independence and African American equality.

In their calls for unity, African American advocates accounted for the history of animosity and conflict between Irish immigrants and black residents. Rather than placing blame for this tension on the attitudes of Irish immigrants, Downing and other critics blamed native-born white Americans for instilling feelings of hatred and bigotry among the new arrivals. "I remember," Downing explained, "how [the Irish] generous nature became perverted by contact with America. . . . I remember that our fellow countrymen, the white native American . . . set him the example. . . . He was even there taught to antagonize us as an obstacle to his success in his new field of labor; as crossing his pursuit of happiness; that the black man was a revolting, degraded being despised by all men."[22]

Downing perceived that racism on the part of Irish immigrants was a learned behavior. Therefore, Irish Americans could unlearn these tendencies. "The Irishman in America," Downing continued, "is breaking away from the teachings once taught him by Native Americans; is exhibiting a disposition to be friendly and to affiliate with those he was once taught to despise; he is beginning to realize that it is the duty of as well as the interest of the two oppressed classes to sustain harmonizing relations."[23] This opinion was supported by Boston's African American newspaper, the *Advocate*.

The *Boston Advocate*, in addition to pushing independent politics, was the primary organ for black support of Irish independence and Home Rule. The editors, William Grandison, J. D. Powell Jr., and William H. Bonaparte, central figures in the Massachusetts Colored League meeting that resolved to support Parnell and Irish Home Rule, refuted the idea that there was any inherent animosity between African Americans and Irish immigrants. Rather, they argued, any such conflict grew out of the lack of education of both the black and Irish lower classes. "There lies in the bosom of both races, among the lower, poorer, and unlearned part . . . a feeling of unfriendliness." Like Downing, the editors of the *Advocate* pointed to native white Americans as the cause of such ill will. "The Irishman," the editors explained, "knows no man by his color or religion until he is 'collared' by mean, selfish, white Americans whose first aim is to teach the Irishman that his color alone . . . entitles him to a superiority."[24] The editors continued, "The Negro is persuaded, on the other hand, by designing politicians and unscrupulous Negroes to believe that an Irish man is inferior to him and should not claim an equal share or anything on this side of the water with him."[25]

The *Advocate* argued that the more educated African American and Irish classes recognized the similar paths of both groups toward citizenship. "As education wends its way into the ranks of both races," the editors hoped, "the clouds of prejudice and distinction must melt and dispel."[26] For Downing and the editors of the *Advocate*, if African Americans and Irish immigrants could overcome their misconceptions about one another, they could form a powerful force against oppression and for Irish self-rule and African American equality.

Black supporters of Irish independence also encouraged Irish nationalists to take inspiration from African American resistance to slavery. For example, Edwin Walker issued a similar statement before a crowd commemorating the 108th anniversary of the death of Irish nationalist and rebel leader Robert Emmet at Faneuil Hall.[27] In his speech, Walker compared the current situation of the Irish to the status of Irishmen and African Americans just before the Civil War. "Ireland is as near free today as the negro was when John Brown struck at Harper's Ferry," he declared. "The freedom of Ireland may tarry awhile longer, but it will come; peaceable, if possible, but it will come."[28] Walker invoked the language of the Irish Land League, which advocated large-scale rent strikes among Irish tenant farmers. "The Irish people have a firm hold of the hammer," he announced, "and the word should be, Strike!, Strike!, Strike!"[29] Several days later, on March 9, 1886, the Sumner National Independent League reaffirmed support of the Irish struggle, saying that "they should not forget that 'he who would be free must himself strike the blow.'"[30]

In addition to advocating physical resistance, black supporters, including the editors of the *Advocate*, joined with Boston's Irish leadership in a transatlantic effort to raise funds directly in support of Charles Parnell's Home Rule movement.[31] In February 1886, Boston's Irish leadership organized a committee, led by recently elected mayor Hugh O'Brien, to raise money to assist Parnell in his campaign for Irish Home Rule. "To the native and adopted citizen alike," the committee appealed, "that free New England's tribute to struggling old Ireland will be such that its example will be followed in other sections of the country."[32] Leaders of Boston's Irish nationalist movement valued African American support and invited them to take part in the movement.[33] The editors of the *Advocate* were confident in the cooperation of the leaders of Boston's Irish community such as Patrick Maguire, Hugh O'Brien, and John Boyle O'Reilly. "The *Boston Advocate* is ready in this noble cause to take the first step," the editors declared. "If we do our part, the distinguished sons of Ireland will be only too glad to meet us 'half-way' to carry the project to success."[34]

African Americans, who were fighting for civil rights protections in the United States, asserted the importance of equal participation in democracy for Irish citizens. They made explicit reference to the service of Irish soldiers on behalf of the Union in the Civil War and argued that African Americans should stand up for any group "deprived of the rights of self-government." "The Irishmen fought side by side with the negro soldier for the Union and for freedom," the editors of the *Advocate* explained. "It is a pleasant duty for us to perform whenever we can, for Ireland and the restoration of the proper rights of citizenship to Irishmen."[35]

Black supporters held a large benefit concert in March 1886, which displayed the multitude of black cultural talent, but also demonstrated in a large-scale, public way the interest of black Bostonians in the welfare of the Irish people. The organizers proposed that support should come from Boston, "where the first sound of freedom was heard, and where there has ever been kind and feeling responses to aid the down trodden."[36] The *Boston Advocate* displayed a quarter-page advertisement for the event, announcing, "For Ireland's Cause. A Grand Concert Will Be Given by the Young Colored Citizens of Boston in Aid of the Five Dollar Parnell Parliamentary Fund."[37]

On March 30, 1885, a large audience braved a cold and steady rain as they waited to fill Boston's Tremont Temple.[38] Tickets for the concert ranged from fifty to seventy-five cents, and among the invited attendees were leading members of Boston's Irish community, as well as African American supporters of Irish independence.[39] Formal committees made up of black Bostonians made the concert arrangements. Organizers also named an honorary committee that included sympathetic black leaders from New York City, Washington, D.C., and Savannah, Georgia. The audience listened as black sopranos Marie Selika and Nellie Brown Mitchell sang popular Irish ballads such as "Kathleen Mavourneen" and "Come Back to Erin," along with pieces such as "Ave Maria," "Echo Song," "Home Sweet Home," and an aria from "Il Trovatore."[40]

The reviews of the concert were generally positive, and after paying the artists and fees, the organizers raised $125 for Parnell's fund.[41] The editors of the *Boston Pilot* expressed their appreciation for the donation. "Good-will," the editors explained, "cannot be bought with money, but money is often a token of good-will. We hail with pleasure the growing reciprocity between Irish Americans and Colored Americans."[42] On April 15, the Five Dollar Parliamentary Fund held a reception for the organizers where representatives from the black community presented leader John E. Fitzgerald with the proceeds.[43]

"For Ireland's Cause," *Boston Advocate,* March 13, 1886. (Courtesy of Boston Public Library.)

Black support of Irish Home Rule was extended not merely out of moral altruism; it was expected to produce significant political outcomes. One of the central purposes of the concert was to build a broad transatlantic coalition in opposition to British oppression and for the cause of African American equality. "We see a way at present for the uplifting of the two races," the

*Advocate* editors recognized, "and that is the Negro and Irish copartnership in the great struggle for equal rights and privileges before the laws of America and England. . . . In this effort we hope to gain much by the way of assistance from our Irish American fellow citizens."[44] The organizers hoped that Irish Americans, upon seeing the black support for the cause of the Irish homeland, would in return support African Americans in their struggle for full equality. "Let us aid Ireland," they concluded, "and when the fruits of our labors shall be seen, we, in common with the Irish, may rejoice at the sight of free flags waving over the heads of the Irish in Ireland, and the Negro in America."[45] African American supporters of Irish independence advocated interracial and interethnic unity, which they anticipated would lead to greater political power in Boston for both Irish and black residents. Both African Americans and Irish Americans put this plan into action during the mayoral campaigns of Hugh O'Brien.

## Hugh O'Brien for Mayor

In addition to calls for unity around Irish nationalism and African American civil rights, the mutual support for partisan independence also was central to the proposed political cooperation between black Bostonians and Irish Americans. As the editors of the *Boston Advocate* recognized, "We can but hope for a reconciliation of the two races, and one thing that is doing the greatest part towards that end is the political independence to which the American Negro is now inclining."[46] While some of this politically independent spirit functioned at the statewide and national levels, there was also significant cooperation between black Bostonians and the emerging Irish Democratic political machine in Boston municipal politics.

Spurred on by the increased strength of the Democratic Party around the gubernatorial election of Benjamin Butler in 1883, African Americans, disillusioned with the Republican Party, sought alliances with Irish supporters and candidates. Many of the most vocal boomers of support for Irish nationalism were also the most fervent advocates of the election of Irish Democratic candidates. During an 1883 rally, independent leader John Ruffin recognized the changes in the political environment. "We are now joining a new move," he announced, "and let us espouse the cause of the Irish, who are struggling to break the chains which hold them down, that they may in time aid us." At this same rally, Patrick McGuire, the leader and chief strategist of Boston's Irish Democrats, delivered an address encouraging the union of Irish immigrants and African Americans and calling both groups to fight their cause politically.[47]

The attendance of McGuire at this meeting is significant. As the chief strate-gist of the Boston Democratic Party, he recognized the potential strength re-sulting from black support of Democratic candidates. Despite their small population, African Americans were a vital interest to Boston's emerging Irish political machine.

Following the defeat of Butler for reelection in 1884, African American in-dependents continued their support for Democratic candidates for city office. This was particularly true in their support for Hugh O'Brien. O'Brien came to the United States from Ireland at age five and attended public school in Boston until he became an apprentice at the *Boston Courier*. O'Brien continued to be successful in business, and in 1875 he was elected to the city's board of alder-men.[48] After failing to win the mayoralty in 1883, he succeeded in being elected the following year with a 3,100 vote plurality; he won nearly 40 percent of the vote in Ward Nine.[49] In addition to his success in city government, O'Brien also served as head of the executive committee of Boston's Five Dollar Parliamen-tary Fund, which supported Charles Parnell's efforts to secure Home Rule for Ireland.[50] In this way, he gained African American support both as a popular Democratic candidate and as an active voice for Irish independence.

While it was the Irish vote that was principally influential in O'Brien's as-cent to power, he also garnered support from vocal black independents. One of O'Brien's central attractions was his appointment of African American men to positions within the city government. Patronage could be a valuable tool for encouraging political support, and black independents argued that the Demo-cratic Party deserved their support because of its willingness to appoint African Americans to city positions. For example, as a member of the city's board of aldermen, O'Brien favored the appointment of black officers to the police and fire departments, which was then overruled by the board's Republican majori-ty. As mayor, he went on to secure appointments successfully for a black offi-cer at police headquarters and in the Office of Weights and Measures.[51] George Downing, in an interview with the *Boston Daily Globe*, summarized the impor-tance of patronage in encouraging black support for O'Brien. "I think the colored voters should cast their votes solidly for Mayor O'Brien," Downing de-clared. "He has acted more consistently in recognizing the colored man as a member of the body politic than any of his predecessors."[52]

In addition to celebrating O'Brien's successes, his black supporters argued that the Republican Party had made a significant political blunder when the Republican governor George D. Robinson did not appoint an African Ameri-can to replace black judge George L. Ruffin, who died in 1886.[53] Despite the partisan controversy over the appointment, this judgeship had represented victory for African Americans in Massachusetts when Democratic governor Benjamin Butler appointed Ruffin in 1883. Black Bostonians, whose loyalty to Republicans was already wavering, saw the failure of Governor Robinson to appoint an African American successor as a serious betrayal. As one observer noted, "It looks as if [the Governor] did not wish to allow the question to be discussed of whether the colored people of the State . . . would have a decent recognition in the state."[54] In contrast, John Boyle O'Reilly expressed his deep sympathy following Ruffin's death, and Josephine St. Pierre Ruffin requested that O'Reilly be a pallbearer at her husband's funeral.[55]

Voters reelected O'Brien in 1885 and 1886, but he again faced a tough Republican challenger in 1887. Once again, his black supporters rallied to his side and condemned the lack of recognition from the Republican Party. According to J. Gordon Street, a vocal supporter of Irish nationalism, Boston correspondent to the *New York Freeman*, and lead organizer of the West End O'Brien movement, there was a general feeling among the speakers that the Republican Party had used black voters as political "stepping stones."[56] Once elected, Street argued, they did not feel obliged to appoint black men to positions of significance. Street declared that African American citizens desired "places of dignity and worth," such as clerkships. However, when they applied for such positions, state officials told them "they had men running elevators, washing windows, working in the restaurant, and in the barbershop, and this was all that is due them."[57] Black voters demanded respected positions within state government and were determined to hold the lack of significant patronage against the Republican Party.

Complaints against the Republican Party on the state level had direct implications for black support of city election candidates. A meeting of black citizens in the South End, for example, resolved, "The colored citizens have been faithful and zealous in their support of the Republican Party in the past, but having received such cold and indifferent recognition after election . . . we deem it our duty to look well to our interest in the coming city election."[58] This frustration increased the black support for O'Brien, and African American observers predicted a large number of Republicans would vote Democrat in the coming election.

The *Boston Daily Globe* counted African American voters as one of the constituencies from which O'Brien had gained unexpected strength. The paper recognized an "independent O'Brien movement" in the West End.[59] "According to several colored men," the *Globe* reported, "it appears that the white Republicans, who are counting on a solid colored vote for their candidate, will find that they are greatly mistaken."[60] J. Gordon Street affirmed the *Globe's* observation. "The colored people," he attested, "will receive as much, if not more, recognition at the hands of Mr. O'Brien than they will from . . . [any] Republican that may be elected Mayor of the city." In wards across the city, according to Street, there were "many colored O'Brienites."[61]

In addition to a lack of patronage, some black Republican voters claimed that they were not getting fair representation and participation at the Republican ward caucuses. For example, in Ward Eight, black voters decried the denial of the "right of suffrage and free speech in said caucus" by the ward's white Republican leadership.[62] In light of these outrages, the ward's black Republican voters held their own caucus meeting, nominated their own candidate for common council, and vowed to "use every effort to defeat the nominations . . . of the Republican Party and pledge ourselves to secure the election of Hon. Hugh O'Brien, a gentleman whom we believe to be the friend of the colored people of Boston."[63] African American voters organized and worked within the apparatus of urban machine politics to assert their strength as voters and force candidates to respect the interests of black Bostonians.

On the eve of the election, across the city raucous meetings shook meeting halls and ward rooms as supporters on both sides boomed for their candidates. For Boston's black community it was no different. O'Brien supporters held a meeting at the Phillips School on the corner of Anderson and Pinckney streets. According to newspaper coverage, about 400 people attended, "including a mere sprinkling of white people."[64] The evening's speakers recognized the diverse crowd and advocated unity among the black and white working classes. For example, Stewart E. Hoyt and Joseph King spoke as "laboring men" and addressed the relationship between African Americans and white workers in the Democratic Party. "No men here are bankers; no men here are merchants," Hoyt declared. "We are, all of us, allied with the workingmen." Hoyt went on to compare the opposition to Irish candidates to the challenges black politicians faced. "Two-thirds of the opposition to Mayor O'Brien is because he is Irish and a Catholic," Hoyt continued. "When you run for office you will be opposed because you are black."[65]

J. Gordon Street, the chairman of the meeting, reminded the audience that although they remained Republicans, they endorsed O'Brien over Republican candidates. He celebrated the loyalty O'Brien had shown to black Bostonians and reminded the audience how the mayor, in addition to appointing candidates, had fought segregated pews in Boston's churches and was one of the few white city officials to attend the funeral of Judge Ruffin. In closing, Street declared that O'Brien had supported African Americans' struggles for equal rights out of an authentic spirit, "not, as they say now, to catch the colored vote."[66] Although Street denied the political motives of O'Brien in attending African American community events and standing up for black Bostonians, the discussion of O'Brien's courting of Boston's black vote is further evidence of the importance of black voters in municipal elections in spite of their small population citywide.

O'Brien won reelection in 1887 with barely a 1,500-vote majority; he won barely 30 percent of the Ward Nine vote.[67] Nonetheless, black support for the victory further widened ruptures over partisan affiliation in Boston's black community. Continued support of the mayor by J. Gordon Street and the other so-called colored O'Brienites outraged black Republican leadership in the West End. "The colored leaders at the West End," the *Boston Globe* reported, "swore vengeance on him for daring to divide the colored vote."[68] These men charged Street and the other O'Brien supporters with supporting O'Brien only in exchange for government offices. In response, Street opposed the hypocrisy of Republican African American leaders who, he argued, lamented the lack of political appointments in private, but then "come right out on the streets and in their own newspapers and deny that they ever entertained the idea of wanting offices."[69]

Street recognized that political patronage could be a valuable tool in securing a foothold in the urban political sphere, but argued that African Americans must be willing to fight for and defend these positions. "Black men are no different from white men," Street argued. "They do wish positions, but are not worthy of it unless they stand up and conscientiously avow the fact."[70] Political patronage was a central part of urban politics, and like other groups in the city, African Americans wanted to be rewarded for their support. "The matter might just as well be stated plainly," Street told the *Boston Globe*. "The colored voter wants to be an office holder as well as the men he assists to place in position of honor and emolument."[71] Despite these tensions, Street and the other "O'Brienites" continued to be steadfast in their support. "The fact is just this," Street explained: "in the future colored men will be guided by what a candidate has done for the colored race, whether or not he is in favor of giving the black man recognition, and treating him as he would any other political allies."[72] Black office holding was a marker of "civic status," and men such as Street were willing to vote for whichever candidate moved them closer to that reality.[73]

## A Monument to Crispus Attucks

A result of years of political cooperation between black and Irish Bostonians was on public display on the Boston Common in November 1888 as

representatives from both groups unveiled a grand monument to Crispus Attucks and the other victims of the 1770 Boston Massacre. Before the giant
granite column stood the citizens committee that helped organize the event.
The committee included African Americans William Dupree and Julius Chappelle and Irish representatives such as John Boyle O'Reilly.[74] During the
planning and construction of the monument, both African Americans and Irish
immigrants were forceful advocates for its creation and used the moment to
assert the triumph of patriotism over ethnic and racial animosity. Attucks became more than an African American icon; he symbolically united the struggle for black equality with the Irish independence movement.

African Americans such as Lewis Hayden, Robert Morris, and William
Cooper Nell had advocated the construction of a monument to Attucks since
the 1850s. However, the Boston and Massachusetts governments did not make
significant moves to erect a memorial until the 1880s.[75] Petitioners sought two
methods of remembrance, and the requests went to two different legislative
bodies. The first, which was sent to the Massachusetts General Court, was for
the construction of headstones at the city's Granary burial ground, where,
according to the petitioners, "no stone marks their burial place."[76] The second, sent to Boston's city council, was for a larger monument to be placed at
a central location in the city, near the site of the massacre, or in front of the
former city hall building in Charlestown. Advocates of the larger monument
requested that the cornerstone of the memorial be laid during the first week
of August 1887 so that the veterans of the Fifty-Fourth and Fifty-Fifth Infantry
regiments and the Fifth Massachusetts Cavalry volunteers, who were going to
be in the city for a reunion, might participate. Mayor O'Brien later explicitly
endorsed this request in a letter to Boston's common council and board of
aldermen.[77]

In 1887, both Irish and black Bostonians sent petitions to the general court
for the construction of a monument. Among the petitioners were leaders from
Boston's black and Irish communities. In particular, John Boyle O'Reilly, Patrick Maguire, Patrick A. Collins, and Mayor O'Brien were prominent signatories. Irish support was drawn not only to Attucks, but also to the remembrance
of Irishman Patrick Carr, who was mortally wounded alongside him. Irish city
councilmen explicitly outlined arguments for Irish support in debates at Boston's city council over the allocation of funds for the dedication.

During the common council debate, Ward Eight councilman Thomas F.
Keenan joined with the sole African American councilman, Andrew B. Lattimore, in outlining the historical significance of Attucks and his fallen
comrades. "I might say here that had it not been for Crispus Attucks it is a

question," Lattimore stated, "whether this would ever have been the republic of which we boast so much. . . . It is a disgrace that such a man's memory has not long since been properly commemorated." Further, Lattimore recognized that the resistance to the British during the Boston Massacre was likely to garner Irish support. "I know my friend from Ward Eight has such a great antipathy to England that he will vote for . . . a monument to Crispus Attucks."[78]

Keenan reiterated Lattimore's sentiment and added that the commemoration of the massacre was a reminder of how both African Americans and Irish immigrants stood up to British tyranny. "I desire to speak of the Irishman who stood by his friend Attucks when he went down," Keenan announced, "but we make no social distinction with reference to honoring Crispus Attucks. . . . Of all the Bostonians who have honored Boston in the last century, no man stands higher than Crispus Attucks, although his skin is not the color of mine."[79] For Keenan, too, Attucks was a symbol of resistance to oppression, and he invoked Attucks in order to condemn the Republican rule of the Massachusetts General Court. "I believe," he attested, "if we had a few more men like Crispus Attucks we would not be subjected to the persecution that even the majority in this city are at present undergoing at the hands of the minority through the State legislature. . . . If there were more of such men, and if their history were known, it would be better for the rising generation . . . as regards following in their father's footsteps."[80] In this exchange, the black and Irish councilmen expressed the overlapping meanings ascribed to Crispus Attucks and the Boston Massacre. For Lattimore, the Boston Massacre was evidence of the fundamental part that African Americans played in the founding of the nation. For Keenan, the event was symbolic of the necessity of resistance to perceived unjust rule.

The opposition to the monument among some of Boston's older elites provoked particular ire among Irish and black supporters of the memorial. Irish spokespeople branded these voices "Anglomaniacs" and the "Tory Element," as they drew parallels between the opposition to the monument's construction and the oppression by the British that caused the commemorated event in 1770. Those who opposed the monument declared that the men slain during the Boston Massacre were common street hooligans who should not be honored among Boston's more revered patriots. Councilman Keenan expressed resentment toward this opposition in statements to the city council. "Some of the great men here tonight," he recognized, "represent a great constituency on Beacon Hill, who have characterized Crispus Attucks as a rioter."[81]

The *Boston Advocate* joined with Irish commentators in condemning the opposition to the monument. Responding to an article in the *Marlboro Times* rejecting the Granary burial ground monument, the editors of the *Advocate* accused the authors of basing their opposition on Attucks's race. They argued that Attucks was no more a hooligan or criminal than those who participated in the Boston Tea Party. "Be consistent in one case as another," the editors demanded. "The government and state are one hundred years tardy in their proper duty, in not erecting a monument to Attucks, higher than the Statue of Liberty, considering how his race has been treated ever since. . . . If the State, the government, and the *Marlboro Times* will not build one, let the colored race do it."[82]

The Massachusetts Historical Society, in particular, forcefully opposed the monument, which immediately made them a target of attack in the press. In May 1887, the Massachusetts Historical Society appointed a committee to present to the governor a resolution expressing regret at the action of the state legislature in voting to construct a monument to the victims of the Boston Massacre. Members of the committee contended that the victims of the event were rioters and hoodlums not deserving such recognition. "While greatly applauding the sentiment which erects memorials to the heroes and martyrs of our annals," the committee resolved, "the members of the Society believe that nothing but misapprehension of the event . . . can have led to classifying these persons with those entitled to grateful recognition at public expense."[83]

Such statements drew immediate response from the monument's advocates. The *Boston Pilot* attacked the authors as British sympathizers and "foggy gentlemen" who "muddle up the history which live men have made." "If you want to find American Tories today, search for them in local Historical Societies," the editors of the *Boston Pilot* proclaimed. "The Tory never makes heroic history; but he keeps a dogged and secret hand on the records."[84] The *Pilot* editors argued that "the animus of the attack is evident in the gratuitous insults offered to two elements . . . the Irish-American and the Negro-American—because both were honorably represented among the first martyrs to American Liberty."[85]

The *Pilot* and other Boston newspapers further attacked an editorial written in the *Congregationalist* on behalf of the historical society. The *Congregationalist* condemned the "absurd and mischievous proposition," declaring, in reference to the supporters of the monuments, "there is always a sprinkling of 'cranks' hovering near . . . all of which bear watching, and most which demand throttling, for the public good."[86] The newspaper also chided the black and Irish threats to withhold their votes from the governor if he did not endorse the monument. "We hear it openly threatened," the article read, "that if the colored and the Irish vote be not 'recognized' by the executive endorsement of this bill, his Excellency, should he ever want those votes again, may have to whistle for them in vain."[87]

Based on articles such as these, the *Boston Evening Transcript* went so far as to suggest that opposition to the monument was funded and organized by British operatives. As evidence, the *Transcript* pointed out that the opposition leadership was also coordinating the arrangements for Boston's British residents to honor British Queen Victoria's jubilee.[88] "It is too late," supporters of the monument declared, "for the Massachusetts Historical Society to attempt at this late day to pervert the facts of history.... The Queen's jubilee will not be celebrated in Boston by the triumph of a conspiracy to blacken the names of the martyrs who died on its streets at the hands of English hirelings."[89]

In spite of the opposition, the Republican governor Oliver Ames signed the monument bill, and soon the site was moved from Charlestown to the Boston Common.[90] The memorial committee, made up of Irish, African American, and Yankee supporters, arranged for a grand dedication. The Commonwealth commissioned sculptor Robert Kraus to supervise the design and construction.[91] Organizers placed a subcommittee of prominent black and white Bostonians in charge of organizing the dedication ceremony.[92] In addition, John D. Powell Jr. sent out an invitation to the Massachusetts divisions of the Sons of Veterans requesting their participation in the parade prior to the unveiling ceremony.[93]

During the celebrations dedicating the monument, Irish and African American leaders publicly proclaimed the unity of supporters and declared that the memory of Attucks and the Boston Massacre transcended racial and ethnic difference. Following the unveiling, a crowd filled Faneuil Hall for an event presided over by Governor Ames. Ames first introduced Mayor O'Brien, who specifically addressed the controversy over the monument's construction. "I am aware," he stated, "that the monument to Crispus Attucks and his martyr associates has been the subject of more or less adverse criticism and that by some they are looked upon as rioters who deserved their fate." O'Brien refuted these claims, declaring that it was the Boston Massacre that ignited the American Revolution and prompted the writing of the Declaration of Independence. "I rejoice with you [Mr. Dupree]," the mayor concluded, speaking to the black arrangement committee chairman, "that after a lapse of more than one hundred years the erection of the Attucks monument ... ratifies the words of that declaration, that all men are free and equal, without regard to color, creed, or nationality."[94]

John Boyle O'Reilly, in a poem celebrating the life of Attucks, affirmed calls for racial unity and equality. O'Reilly's poem received warm praise from those who heard the reading, and it was republished widely.[95] "Where shall we seek for a hero, and where shall we find a story?" O'Reilly asked. "We come to the learning of Boston's lesson today / The moral that Crispus Attucks taught in the old heroic way / God made mankind to be one in blood, and one in spirit and thought / And so great a boon by a brave man's death, is never dearly bought."[96]

The optimism about racial equality continued, following the day's events, at a banquet at Parker's Restaurant hosted by the citizens committee. The *Boston Daily Globe* described the diversity of the attendees. "Not an assembly of men has gathered in Boston in many a day that contained more noble representatives of a race now becoming great than this," the *Globe* reported. "There were men ranging all the way from an ex-governor to a depot porter."[97] Julius Chappelle presided over the celebration, and Governor Ames and Mayor O'Brien again gave speeches. O'Brien attested to the cooperation between Irish and African American factions in organizing the monument's construction and called for equality and fellowship between the races. Other guests expressed similar sentiments and declared that the events leading up to the erection of the monument demonstrated the ability of Bostonians to overcome partisan and racial divisions. An elderly Lewis Hayden, who had worked to get a monument to Attucks constructed in the 1850s, rose and declared, "There is not a man who has ever graced city hall who has a larger heart than Mayor O'Brien. Always he has been just, considerate, and painstaking with matters concerning our race. . . . Our Democratic mayor and our Republican Governor are men who are second to none."[98]

However, not all of the advocates of the monument joined in accolades to the transcendence of race. While the official banquet was taking place, the Colored Knights of Pythias, an African American fraternal association, held a separate celebration at the Ebenezer Baptist Church. The hall was filled with members of Knights of Pythias lodges from Worcester and Boston.[99] While the attendees at the official banquet were former or current elected officials and longtime loyal Republicans, the attendees at this celebration were some of the city's outspoken advocates of Irish nationalism and black political independence, including George Downing and Edwin Walker. Their speeches were less focused on interracial unity, and rather celebrated the meaning that memorializing Attucks held for black Bostonians.

Walker delivered the oration and placed Attucks in the context of African American history. "When the ancestors of the colored men of today were first brought to this country as slaves," Walker began, "their captors little dreamed that this country would someday be indebted to the children of those slaves for entering a wedge which was to sunder America from the control of a kingly power." "This fact," he continued, "gives the world a lesson that as time wears on . . . the people whose rights are withheld become uneasy and will never rest until the privileges intended for them by the Creator are possessed."[100] Walker continued, explaining that Attucks was worthy of special honor among the victims of the Boston Massacre because "he himself was not in possession of the rights for which he gave his life in the interests of others."[101]

In both the official public celebrations and the smaller commemoration, black advocates from across the partisan divide came together to celebrate the monument's construction. Their political differences, however, shaped the meaning of the monument. For Republicans and black elected officials, the monument was evidence of the power of historical sacrifice to transcend racial division. For black independents such as Walker and Downing, the memory of Attucks was a reminder of the oppressed status of African Americans and an inspiration for continued agitation.

## The Breakdown of a Coalition

Edwin Walker knew better than most that declarations of racial equality did not translate into political gains. In the months before the dedication, he learned that support for Boston's Democrats and their Irish-born mayor could have severe consequences, making the decision to cross party lines risky. In June 1888, in a four to seven vote, the board of aldermen rejected Mayor O'Brien's nomination of Walker for assessor of the city. Although their exact motives were not clear, Walker supposed it was his refusal to support the Republican Party that led to his defeat. However, he also refused to declare himself loyal to the Democratic Party. Instead, he rejected any partisan affiliation, declaring himself "a *Democrat* within the true meaning of the word."[102] Walker continued, "Intelligent colored people . . . are looking for something real and not visionary, and they are not to be frightened anymore by the cry of 'Democrat,' or be deceived by the enumeration of the word 'Republican.' We are thinking for ourselves; we are looking at men's actions, and we are preparing to strike out with any man or men who offer us real, tangible things, instead of professions and promises that they are constantly breaking."[103]

The Republican defeat of Walker's nomination was part of a resurgence that would remove the Democrats from control of City Hall. In the late 1880s, a cross-section of Boston's Protestant community united in opposition to Catholic parochial schools. The schools controversy ignited religious and ethnic passions more than any cultural issue since the Civil War.[104] The increase in

Protestant mobilization cost O'Brien his reelection in 1888, by roughly 2,700 votes.[105] With this, the Irish Democratic leadership was driven from City Hall, and with it, some of black Boston's most influential Irish allies.

O'Brien was not the only Irish ally whom black Boston lost during this period. In September 1890, a crowd filled Boston's Tremont Temple to mourn the sudden death of John Boyle O'Reilly at only forty-six years old. Members from both the city's black and Irish communities attended.[106] Edwin Walker was among those who stood before the crowd to eulogize O'Reilly. As he spoke, he declared the sympathy of the black community. "I have talked to you today," Walker concluded, "from the standpoint of one who belongs to a race not yet delivered from the clutch of the oppressor." "Men that are oppressed or denied the enjoyment of any of the rights that belong to them," Walker explained, "are apt to feel the hand of the Almighty, when it falls on one who is not of their peculiar kind, if he was their friend and an outspoken defender of their rights."[107] Without O'Reilly as a powerful ally, African Americans in Boston struggled to find a voice among the Irish community to advocate their concerns and call for Irish and black unity.

Several other factors contributed to the breakdown in political cooperation during the 1890s. The death of Charles Parnell and the demise of the 1880s Home Rule movement in Ireland made Irish nationalism less of a pressing issue among Irish Bostonians during the 1890s.[108] Further, as the numbers of Irish-born Irish Americans decreased, local economic and political issues took on a more pressing relevance, and as Irish political strength increased in the city, the need for black votes became less urgent.[109] Finally, as the Democratic Party renewed an overt policy of white supremacy that damaged already tenuous support from black Bostonians, a black and Irish Democratic coalition grew increasingly unlikely.

The ultimately short-lived alliance between Irish and African Americans in Boston during the 1880s grew out of a shared recognition of mutual oppression and a combined need to carve out a space in the American body politic. By uniting around the figure of Crispus Attucks, Irish and African Americans made important claims about resistance to tyranny, and in a column of stone, affirmed their place in the formation of the nation. This period of coalition illustrated how organizing across ethnic lines could effectively transcend the structures of party politics and unite African Americans, not only in a national struggle for equality, but in a global struggle for independence.[110]

As their decade-long alliance with the Irish weakened, by the 1890s black Bostonians looked to themselves to forge a new weapon against oppression and inequality. In forming the Colored National League and other new organizations, black independents and some Republicans sought to use political tactics practiced on a local level and inspired by Irish nationalist movements to attack the national rising tide of antiblack violence and injustice. In doing so, even as they never lost sight of the need for black voters to remain independent and they continued to reject calls to return to the Republican Party, they looked beyond electoral organizing as a way to unite black men and women against oppression.

*Part III*

# To the Negro Alone Politics Shall Bring No Fruit

In fall 1900, the Boston-based Colored Cooperative Company published a new novel, *Contending Forces,* by black author and playwright Pauline Hopkins. In her fictional account of African American life in Boston, she described the debates over partisanship she saw firsthand as a participant in the city's black political life. She was critical of black allegiance to party, and through her characters she celebrated those who placed the interests of African Americans over partisanship. Through William Smith, who emerges as one of the novel's chief protagonists, Hopkins makes clear her disillusionment with partisan politics. For Hopkins, black engagement with political parties as a central strategy had not been successful. While other groups such as the Irish had gained a foothold in local and national political life, white supremacy made such gains for African Americans impossible. As protagonist Smith declares, "To the Negro alone politics shall bring no fruit."[1]

By the time Hopkins wrote her novel, black activists had become increasingly disillusioned with partisan politics as a guiding political strategy. Despite decades of advocating independent politics, by the turn of the twentieth century they had few victories. Although the number of those willing to eschew the Republican Party had grown, independent activists failed to ignite the mass departure they had long hoped for. Further, rather than yielding to black electoral pressure, white supremacy became further entrenched within the two parties as Democrats and Republicans did little to stop, and sometimes advocated, the brutal system of Jim Crow and lynch law.

In the face of rising opposition, black activists channeled the energy formerly focused on independent politics to the creation of new organizations that, while still engaged with electoral politics, looked to extrapartisan solutions. Organizations such as the Colored National League and the Massachusetts Racial Protective Association pressed for the end to lynching and the trampling of black rights across the nation. They held mass rallies, fundraised for national antilynching movements, and hosted victims of southern racial violence. They petitioned national leaders, including the president, directly with calls for federal action and criticized the government for failing to protect black lives and rights.

As the century closed, black activists reflected on their nearly forty years of political action. Many spent the first postwar decade largely working within the Republican Party, hoping for internal reforms. During the 1880s, the independent movement grew stronger as activists pressed for electoral solutions beyond strict partisan allegiance, but still within the bounds of party politics. As they entered the 1890s, a strategy of independent electoral politics evolved into the creation of black-run organizations rejecting white-dominated political institutions for black leadership and an autonomous political movement, legacies of which would continue into the next century.

## CHAPTER SEVEN

# Let Us Grow Strong by Organization and Earnest Cooperation

*Antilynching and Independent Politics in an Era of Mass Organizing*

The same year black Bostonians called for a monument to the fallen heroes of American independence, they gathered to organize the next fight in their current struggle for liberty. In 1887, they formed the Colored National League, forged in the crucible of independent politics, with a mission of advocating black rights and racial equality across the nation. The new organization was a primary channel for black independent politics during the final decade of the nineteenth century as activists turned from mainstream electoral campaigning and political appointment seeking to confront directly the rising tide of racial violence. In this era, activists used the rhetoric of independent politics and political abandonment to admonish the federal government, and Republicans in particular, to defend black men and women from the horrors of lynch law.

Following the defeat of Cleveland for reelection in 1888, black Republicans and even some independents hoped that a Republican return to power with Benjamin Harrison would mean accelerated and meaningful change. However, Republican inaction and the defeat of the 1890 federal election bill, which would have helped secure southern black voting rights, dashed this optimism.[1] Unconvinced of white political loyalty to their cause, and literally facing life or death at the hands of white supremacist mobs across the nation, activists sought strategies that merged grassroots organizing with tools of electoral politics.

Black Bostonians created the Colored National League during a new era of African American civil rights organizing. Typified by T. Thomas Fortune and his Afro-American League, black activists across the nation forged new organizations to respond to deteriorating race relations.[2] Fortune was a close ally to Boston activists. He participated in their mass meetings, and Boston correspondents addressed a national audience in the pages of his New York–based newspapers. The Boston league, however, did not formally join as a branch of the Afro-American League, although they did send delegates to its founding convention.[3] One reason for maintaining autonomy is likely the Bostonians' remaining commitment to using electoral politics as a tool for racial uplift. The Afro-American League eschewed such activity, choosing instead to remain strictly nonpartisan and apolitical.[4] Further, the Colored National League continued to thrive and remained a conduit for black activism even after the Afro-American League declined in the early 1890s. When the Afro-American League was eventually reincarnated as the Afro-American Council at the end of the decade, the Colored National League continued to remain independent and dedicated to electoral politics as an effective weapon in their arsenal against racial injustice.

Although the Colored National League remained the commanding force for civil rights organizing in Boston, black activists organized other groups to uplift the race and address issues of racial violence in particular. Through groups such as the Massachusetts Racial Protective Association and the Woman's Era Club, black men and women continued to link a defense of black lives and liberties to electoral politics and partisanship as expressions of full American citizenship. To be fully free and equal, black interests must be supported in the mainstream political culture, with black citizens a respected part of the electorate. As the decade progressed, however, and violence increased in the face of inaction from both parties, faith in party politics as a strategy was replaced by a growing sense that progress was going to come through black action alone and beyond official partisan structures.

## The Colored National League

On October 11, 1887, prominent leaders of black Boston met in the Charles Street AME Church to found the Colored National League. Advocates of both independent and Republican politics were among its first officers. William Dupree served as president, with Edwin Walker as vice president. Black legislator Julius Chappelle was recording secretary, and Butler R. Wilson, who was also a correspondent to the *New York Age*, served as corresponding secretary. The executive committee also included former Republican legislator and city councilman John J. Smith.[5] By the end of the decade the executive committee also included prominent black women such as Josephine St. Pierre Ruffin and Lillian A. Lewis.[6] Thomas Riley, an Irish attorney, supporter of black rights, and founder of the Irish Land League in America, also publicly supported the new organization and urged African Americans to take inspiration from Irish freedom struggles.[7] Riley joined with black leaders as they mounted a national movement for black equality. He heartily endorsed the league and called on its organizers to put aside their personal differences as they formed a "harmonious organization."[8] In its regular meetings, the league provided a forum for addressing concerns and offered political education with lectures and presentations from local and visiting activists.

League members sought to establish a national organization with separate chapters united by the central Boston league. Edwin Walker, during the first public meeting of the league, affirmed the national position of the organization as "the nucleus around which [African Americans] in New England and the country would rally for the purpose of making a manly stand."[9] The organizers pointed to a lack of unity among African Americans as a cause of their declining rights protections. "We are denied our rights," they argued, "because we are weak. Let us grow strong by organization and earnest cooperation. Let the outrage committed upon the weakest one of us in the remotest corner of the land arouse us with one impulse throughout the nation to determined and intelligent effort to right that wrong and punish its perpetrators."[10] William Dupree urged every black man and woman who could devote one evening a week and one dollar a year to join the organization.[11] A letter sent to prominent African Americans throughout the state concluded with a call to action. "Do not wait for your neighbor, but move yourself at once in the matter and communicate with us, that we may act together."[12]

Members of the league affirmed their commitment to the protection of black equality and the use of the ballot as a weapon for justice. They pledged to "use every effort" to guarantee that African Americans, "secure the full and free enjoyment of the natural, essential, and inalienable rights guaranteed them by the constitution of the United States and several states."[13] They called for "the right of free and fair suffrage; that of equal privileges in all public institutions; that of equal privileges on all railroads, steamboats and other public carriers; that of fair and impartial trials in all the courts of justice; and that of freedom from insult, from odium, and from proscription because of race or color."[14] Members of the league committed to use black electoral strength to achieve their goals. They proclaimed the intention "to wage eternal war on all men in public life who are not in favor of the Negro enjoying said rights," and to defeat "all candidates for public office, irrespective of party affiliations or political belief, who are not in active sympathy with and support the object of this League."[15]

From its foundation, questions of partisanship plagued the new organization and brought a new generation of activists into heated conflict with older leaders. According to the Boston correspondent to the *New York Age*, some critics of the league refused to join the organization because it "had a political flavor," while "others quietly used their influence against it because the man who organized it happened to be an Independent instead of a Republican."[16] A heated exchange in the Boston press between journalist Robert Teamoh and Frederick Douglass showed the willingness of young activists to reject the paths of earlier generations over the question of partisanship. In February 1888, Douglass wrote to the league declining an invitation to address the new organization. In closing, he urged the new organization to use its resources for explicitly partisan ends. "I know of no better use that [the League] can make of their organization than to help place the Republican Party in power by their votes and their influence at the November election of the present year."[17]

Robert Teamoh, a photographer, journalist, future city councilman, and corresponding secretary for the league responded to Douglass.[18] Referring to Douglass as part of a "fogy element" of out-of-touch older leaders, Teamoh took immediate issue with Douglass's call to use the league to support Republican candidates. Attacking Douglass, Teamoh declared, "It seems as if the only advice possible for that gentleman to give the advancing young American colored men is to use their organization for nothing else but to help place the Republican Party in power once more." "Such advice," Teamoh wrote, "is today entirely out of place. . . . It tends towards holding the race back in its onward and irresistible progress. It makes servants instead of masters."[19]

Echoing years of independent political rhetoric, Teamoh condemned calls for black Republican loyalty and was defiant against claims of gratitude to the party of Lincoln. "It is the Republican Party," he wrote, "who should be deeply obligated to the colored people for its continuance in power for nearly a quarter of a century. . . . The race owes that party nothing."[20] Black voters should hold the party accountable and not be afraid to cross party lines to vote for the candidate in their best interest. "Let every individual vote as he pleases," he declared. "If he is benefited by voting the Democratic ticket, let him vote it; call him patriotic, and not a traitor."[21] With the formation of the Colored National League, black Bostonians hoped to break with the past and forge a movement less grounded in the era of emancipation and more dedicated to the current condition of African Americans.

In their struggle, national political parties and the federal government became increasingly unreliable allies, increasing feelings of betrayal and disillusionment. Across the country, but especially in the former Confederate South, as white supremacist governments replaced the interracial legislatures of Reconstruction, African Americans increasingly became victims of both lawful and extralegal restrictions on their right and ability to vote. In response, the Republican-dominated Congress along with newly elected Republican president Harrison sought to use federal power to protect black voters and make sure their votes counted.

In 1889, Massachusetts Republican congressman Henry Cabot Lodge put forward new legislation calling for the supervision of congressional elections by federal inspectors. The hope was that this oversight would prevent racist malfeasance and guarantee free and fair elections.[22] While Democrats overwhelmingly opposed the legislation, the rhetoric of opposition recognized the inroads black activists had made in moderating the tone of the northern wing of the party. As southern Democrats complained of "negro domination" and cast black voting as a threat to white supremacy, many northern Democrats distanced themselves from the racial implications of the bill during the midterm elections, choosing to oppose the legislation as a threat to free elections and local sovereignty.[23] Others downplayed the significance of the election bill in favor of less controversial issues such as the tariff.[24]

Following a Democratic victory in the 1890 elections, when the bill finally came to the floor in Congress, Senate Democrats filibustered, and with the help of some Republicans, denied the election bill a vote.[25] Defeat of the bill enraged black activists and shattered their faith that their persistence could push northern Democrats to moderate their southern colleagues. Attacks on the bill ultimately united northern and southern Democrats more firmly. Further, the lack of a Senate vote showed the unwillingness of Republicans to stand up for black interests. By the early 1890s, a commitment to white supremacy seemed to paper over prior points of division between the two parties, with deadly consequences.[26] Continued betrayal by Republicans and the closing of opportunities for alliance with Democrats pushed African Americans to use the Colored National League as a primary political vehicle.

## Antilynching and Independent Politics

Without the power of the federal government to protect black freedom, Boston's black activists used the Colored National League to resist the increase in antiblack violence. As accounts of southern lynching passed among the Bostonian community, the league increasingly became a hub in the emerging antilynching movement. Journalist and national antilynching activist Ida B. Wells, an important ally, encouraged African Americans in Boston toward more explicit antilynching activism. Wells was particularly effective in bringing the horrors of southern violence to audiences in the Northeast, and Boston was a significant recipient of her writings and became an early supporter of her cause. Wells had early trouble gaining support for her movement and depended on the political and financial support of black communities such as Boston.[27] The league vowed "in conjunction with colored people all over the country to arouse public opinion against lynching; to sustain Miss Ida B. Wells."[28]

During an 1894 rally the diversity of the antilynching movement was on full display. Longtime male and female advocates of African American rights joined with new but vocal activists. Some, such as Edwin Walker and Archibald Grimké, had been active for years, while others, such as Emory T. Morris and Edward E. Brown, were relatively new among black Boston's political activists. Also included were former and current black elected officials such as Julius C. Chappelle, Andrew Lattimore, and Robert T. Teamoh, as well as church leaders such as Bishop Benjamin Tanner and Rev. Dolphin A. Roberts. The meeting also included important African American spokeswomen such as Eliza Gardiner and Frances Ellen Watkins Harper.[29]

Inaction by the federal government continued to be of central concern. Edward E. Brown criticized the use of federal troops to protect mail trains during the Pullman strike in Chicago while refusing to send federal enforcements to southern states to protect the rights and lives of black men and women. He noted, "If President Cleveland could find that there was law enough in this country to protect freight cars at Chicago, there ought to be a law strong enough to protect American citizens."[30]

Brown also laid claim to the place of African Americans in Massachusetts as investigators of southern violence, and, echoing the language of Robert Morris decades earlier, raised over the proceedings the specter of African American extralegal strategies. The Colored National League was dedicated to the protection of African Americans, and if the government could not provide it, they declared that African Americans in the Bay State had both the resources and the intention to mount their own protective campaigns. "There is a movement now going on in this state looking towards a formation of an organization with $10,000 behind it that will stretch out into every state," Brown told listeners. He explained that the purpose of this new movement was to provide protection and vindication for African Americans who were denied such by state or federal governments. "With this money," Brown continued, "it is intended to search out the murderers of black men and women in the south and to see to it that they are brought to justice."[31]

Edwin Walker reiterated Brown's claims and called for African Americans to take responsibility for mounting antilynching campaigns. "We would not be here at this time to hold up the hands of Miss Wells," Walker declared, "if the pulpit of this country was doing its duty on this question of murdering innocent men, women, and children of the South." He attacked the perceived silence and inaction on the part of African American communities. "It is high time," Walker declared, "that the black men of this country took a decided stand upon this question of lynching. As long as they remain quiet it will go on."[32]

The league held regular meetings with renewed calls for political agitation to stop racial violence. Although its members began to call for action outside of official channels, the league was still optimistic of a political solution. It called upon its members who held political office to exert their influence within the major parties. From within the central committees of the Republican, Democratic, and Prohibition parties, they pressed for the platforms of each organization to include explicit antilynching planks. In this way, the Colored National League still hoped that partisan political power achieved at the local level could have a direct influence on the policies of parties outside Boston and outside the state.[33] Their hopes would be tested in the coming years.

## The Massachusetts Racial Protective Association

The Colored National League, though one of the most outspoken and consistent opponents of lynching, was not alone. The other significant political force against racial violence was the Massachusetts Racial Protective Association (MRPA). The MRPA, which gained particular notoriety in the early twentieth century under the leadership of James Trotter's son William Monroe Trotter, was significant in the middle 1890s, along with the Colored National League, as a forum for radical opposition to lynching.[34] In 1895 the MRPA held a meeting at Faneuil Hall that attracted more than 2,000 attendees. Although the meeting was largely dominated by African Americans, the audience included a noticeable number of working-class white Bostonians. According to the *Boston Daily Advertiser*, "[The white attendees] took a hearty interest in the evening's proceedings and stayed with the latest!"[35] Along with members of Boston's white working class were prominent white Bostonians such as Mayor Edwin Curtis, Irish-born Catholic priest Father Thomas Scully, and Captain Nathan Appleton.

The organizers of the meeting were explicit in their antilynching motives and they provided the audience with a clear symbol of their cause. Observers noted that unlike other political meetings where the hall was festooned with banners and pictures of prominent leaders, at this meeting the attendees sat in a hall "devoid of visible decorations." The only ornament was a small American flag to which the organizers had attached illustrations of a recent lynching in Texas.[36] By attaching images of racial violence to the American flag, the organizers were providing a visual image of their rhetorical allegations. As Mayor Curtis declared, "This disregard of law and the right of all accused persons to a free trial is a dark blot on the fair name of this free country." The audience faced an American flag that was literally corrupted and tainted by horrific images of torture and death.[37]

The main subjects of the meeting were charges that the legal system had been usurped by the lynch mob, and calls for independent politics to force the parties to oppose lynching and for the use of armed resistance if other more moderate methods failed. Mayor Curtis invoked the Bostonian history of resistance to oppression as he celebrated the meeting at Faneuil Hall. "It is fitting," the mayor declared, "that the voice of the people of Boston, condemning these crimes, should be proclaimed from the Cradle of Liberty, where the spirit of resistance to English oppression was fostered and there the anti-slavery agitation was aroused."[38] Further, for Curtis, acts of lynching transcended region or race. "As the disgrace of one member of a family brings shame to the household," he explained, "so the crime in any one state brings dishonor to the whole country."[39]

The mayor rejected the defense of the perpetrators that they were merely "anticipating justice." Many lynch mobs, acting on allegations of rape or murder, felt that their acts were justified in the defense of white womanhood or in community protection. However, "They often put innocent men to death." In addition to lamenting the usurpation of judicial procedure, Curtis clearly pointed to the racial motivation of lynching, an allegation that would draw the ire of Texans in the pages of the press in the coming weeks. "Members of one race are especially picked out as victims," the mayor explained. "Justice is represented as blind," he continued, "but lynch justice in certain localities has an eye open and is ready to take vengeance whenever a colored man is even suspected of committing a crime. . . . The bloodthirsty element in man's nature is excited by race prejudice and what is called lynching would . . . be more properly named murder."[40]

While there was general agreement about the usurpation of judicial authority and the heinousness of the actions, there was some disagreement over the preferred strategy to combat lynching in the face of government inaction. Some, such as Irish attorney Thomas Riley, urged political organization and the use of the vote, while others including Edwin Walker, once a strong voice for electoral politics, now advocated more radical solutions. Riley repeated the argument made by black Bostonians in the 1880s that if African American voters could unite, they could use their electoral strength to sway the platforms of the major parties. If the voters could organize, he argued, "they would have both political parties waiting on them. They would have the strength to brain those who did not please them."[41] Riley was clear in his opposition to force as a political strategy. While he supported "braining" opponents electorally, he did not support literally attacking perpetrators.

Unlike Riley, Walker and MRPA president Rev. W. H. Scott urged armed resistance when all other methods failed. "Black men cannot be murdered in the South with impunity," Walker warned. "Let the American people beware. If outrages continue the Negro will look around to form an alliance with some one who will aid in stopping the barbarous treatment."[42] Walker and the other advocates of self-defense looked to armed resistance movements in other countries for inspiration and proposed that African Americans unify with these movements in a global struggle. Scott advocated "something a little stronger than moral suasion." "We are organizing," he said, "and then we shall join with the Irish or the Germans or the Bulgarians and have it out."[43] Activists such as Walker and Scott saw the African American struggle against political marginalization and racial violence as part of an international battle against oppression and envisioned a united transatlantic struggle.

George Downing proposed resolutions, which the attendees of the meeting adopted unanimously. "We condemn without any reservation the lynching, the mutilating, and the roasting alive of American citizens now commonly practiced in parts of our country," the resolutions began. The statements attacked perpetrators of lynching for using allegations of rape as excuses to oppress black political aspirations. Massachusetts, the resolutions declared, "takes no part in the falsehood that the negro race is more immoral than the other races; that they are rapists.... The charge is false.... The real design [is] being concealed, which is to crush the lawful growing aspirations manifesting themselves among black men."[44]

The resolutions concluded with an appeal to the memory of both the moderate and the radical leaders of the antislavery movement, to motivate listeners to action. "We invoke," Downing declared, "the uncompromising spirit of Garrison, of Phillips, of Sumner, of Andrew, and in their names... cry out: 'Stop this brutality which darkens our nation's fair name.'... If it can not be stopped, the impetuous spirit of Crispus Attucks or John Brown, who is still marching on, will in its march haunt into action."[45] These resolutions, in particular, were the target of heated responses from the readers of southern newspapers, which printed a transcript of the proceedings.

## Southern Reactions

The reaction to the Faneuil Hall meeting was swift, as newspapers in regions throughout the country carried coverage of the event. While some northern newspapers praised the protest, newspapers in the South decried the meeting as interfering with the affairs of southern states and threatening to reopen sectional tensions.[46] Mayor Curtis's office received letters from angry Texans who were infuriated at the allegations levied against them by the meeting's speakers. In particular, the letter writers were outraged at the calls for the protection of men whom they viewed as criminals and perpetrators of crimes deserving of lynching. They accused Bostonians of being ignorant of the true nature of black southerners and scolded them for interfering in affairs where they were not welcome.

An editorial in the *Dallas Morning News* condemned the resolutions passed by the meeting. The *Morning News* argued that while "in the heat of passion over the butchery of a defenseless woman by a black brute, some excuse may be found for burning the despoilers of our homes and the murderers of our women. . . . What excuse may be found for the promulgation of such monstrous lies as those contained in the set of resolutions passed in Boston [?]"[47] The newspaper editors argued that, although brutal, lynching was an understandable response in the face of the alleged crimes. They professed that none of those executed was innocent, and that "effete" Bostonians were committing "villainous lies" for stating the opposite. The attendees at the MRPA meeting "may never attend a 'burning' in this world," the Dallas editors ridiculed, "but if they keep up this practice they are warned that they may expect a high temperature in the next."[48] Other letters from southerners exposed the resentment and tension between the regions. They accused the meeting's organizers of inflaming "a sectional hatred of the South." "You know absolutely nothing," an anonymous writer from Fort Worth, Texas, maintained, "about the negro and the relationship in which he stands to the white people of the South. . . . The malignity of their prejudice and the density of their ignorance is apparently all the excuse 3000 Boston people have for making 3000 asses of themselves."[49]

The letter writers suggested that while lynching should not replace the court system, in the case of alleged black-on-white rape or murder it was not only appropriate, but justified. "No intelligent Southern people advocate mob law as a general practice," one writer explained, "but when it comes to dealing with negro rapists you are advised to come South . . . before you preside at any more meetings to arraign Southern people for protecting their families and homes from such in any way they think best and find most effectual."[50] W. C. Crawford from New Orleans explicitly explained that southern lynch mobs were forced to action in order to protect southern white womanhood. "Our women in our Southland are our most holy possession; their persons must be held sacred," Crawford argued. "Any brute who does violence to them shall suffer, and not . . . recline at ease in a well-kept jail . . . and we run the risk of having them break their prison bars and then escape to do their hellish work on more of our women. . . . All the vile croakings from Massachusetts cannot prevent us from protecting our wives, our mothers, our sisters, and our daughters."[51]

An editorial in the New Orleans *Daily Picayune* refuted Bostonian allegations that the perpetrators of lynching used allegations of rape to cover up attacks on black uplift. "The people who proclaim such doctrine," the editors charged, "are worse than those who do the lynching, because they encourage the commission of the atrocious crimes which cause the outbreaks of popular violence."[52] Rather than condemn or show remorse at the use of violent retribution, the editors of the *Picayune* declared lynching to be not only justified, but required for men "who value the honor and purity of their women."[53] These men will "visit with condign violence the masculine outragers of that honor, and they will doubtless continue to do so, in every part of this country."[54] The editors argued that rather than relying on the judicial system to judge the guilt of perpetrators, their method of justice was swifter and more reliable. "There is no punishment," the editors explained, "too severe for any ravisher, whatever his color, race or condition, and the people will not submit to the tedious delays and obstructions which operate so often to cheat justice in such cases."[55]

It is notable that these letter writers addressed Mayor Curtis rather than the MRPA. The authors looked to Curtis as a white man, and therefore more likely to sympathize with lynching. They appealed to Curtis's whiteness and accused him of merely not understanding their position. If Curtis would just come to places such as Texas, the authors argued, he would see that white southerners are not the villains portrayed by organizations such as the MRPA and the Colored National League. Authors called on Curtis to reject the radical stance on civil rights and side with them as white men in defense of white womanhood. "If you have a white man's heart in your breast," one writer asked, "then come South and see for yourself. . . . You will know better how to teach the 'cultured idiots' of Boston to attend to their own business, and will be willing to let John Brown's remains rest in the grave, where the just cinch of the hangman's long ago placed him."[56] Despite the authors' intent for the letters to speak to Mayor Curtis specifically, black Boston was quick to respond.

## Boston Responds

More than 1,000 people crowded into Charles Street AME Church for a Colored National League meeting held on November 19 to respond to the southern insults and defense of lynching. They also celebrated the extent to which their local voices had reached national audiences. President of the league E. T. Morris told the crowd, "The Faneuil Hall meeting last week had thoroughly aroused the state of Texas. . . . The iron is now hot, and now is the time for us to strike."[57] Edward E. Brown echoed these sentiments. "We have got the Texas bull by the horns and he is roaring," he proclaimed. "He will roar more before we are through with this matter." Rev. Walter Gay, a black Baptist minister from Haverhill, recalled that following the failure of the Ku Klux Klan in the 1870s, white southerners "have sought to reach the hearts of northern people by claiming that the colored people of the south were rapists and brutes of the worst kind." Captain Nathan Appleton, a member of a prominent white family, relayed the southern attempts to find sympathy among white Bostonians. "The old southern bourbons, embittered by the results of the war," he explained, "have been circulating and exaggerating everything that is bad about colored people in order to bring us of the north to the same way of thinking that they do."[58]

While white southerners were a prominent target for the meeting's ire, the league also placed blame for the atrocities on the inaction of the federal government. In particular, they focused on the hypocrisy of American foreign and domestic policy decisions. "We have witnessed the leaders of both political parties going up and down the state asking that our flag protect Armenians," Edward Brown explained, "but not one of them, from governor down, had a word to say about the damnable lynchings of American citizens in the South."[59] Brown also criticized President Cleveland for using U.S. troops to put down the Pullman strike in Chicago, "but not a single soldier could he send to protect the lives of the American citizens in the South." Brown urged churches to "call your missionaries back from China and Turkey, and send them down south to convert those southerners to true American patriotism."[60] Other speakers, including Edwin Walker, suggested purely racist motivations behind the refusal of the government to act. "Do you believe that if, in that bloody South, one tenth of the number of white men had been murdered that there have been black men," Walker asked, "the government would have allowed this cursed business to go on?"[61]

As in the earlier discussions at the MRPA meeting, Colored National League members debated confronting lynching through political or legal means versus armed resistance. Captain Appleton urged restraint and advocated raising money and making political appeals. "I advise you," Appleton suggested, "to collect funds to make a test case. . . . Make an appeal to the President of the United States to call out the troops and bring the perpetrators to justice." Some in the crowd, however, were interested in more radical means.

Advocates of violent resistance argued that as long as African Americans remained passive and did not counter white outrages head on, the atrocities would continue with impunity. "We have increased from 4,000,000 to 10,000,000," Edwin Walker declared. "We are flooding this country with educated young men and women, who will not be cornered or exterminated without retaliation." Rev. Dolphin P. Roberts, the pastor of the Charles Street AME Church, argued that by using the press and the churches, African Americans could mobilize against lynching, but there would be limits to nonviolence. "Let the ministers and the press continue to educate," Roberts urged, "for it is by the voice of the people that this must be stopped . . . peaceably if possible,—if not, otherwise."[62] The reverend continued that if his race could not "find redress in the law for outrages . . . then it would be time for revenge on those who were responsible for the murders."[63] Rev. Walter Gay agreed that the time for moderation had passed. "We have preached to our people to desist from retaliation," Gay began. "Now I say to my race, find revenge, if we have to use the torch; find revenge, if we have to cut the throats of those white southerners who rape our women. Retaliate, I say. Take life for life. . . . There is a great duty devolving upon the young people of the north. You must learn to use your right hand in defense of your race."[64]

In addition to arguing for direct action, the league members targeted southern claims of black inferiority and justifications based on the protection of white womanhood. James Logan Gordon argued that lynching was a manifestation of the barbarity and uncivilized nature of white southerners.[65] Gordon declared, "What 1,000 cool and calm citizens in Faneuil Hall think is worth more than what those people in Paris Texas think. . . . If the Negroes in the south should be there 200 years they could not get so low as to burn a man at the stake for twenty minutes." Gordon refuted assertions of the protection of white womanhood. "It is bosh," Gordon proclaimed, "for any southerner to rise and talk about the purity of a white woman. . . . The purity of a woman, white or colored, should be as much respected in one part of the country as another."

Gordon concluded by attacking white southern morality and claims of racial superiority. "If there is anything wrong with the African in the south, it is 50 percent white wrong," Gordon concluded, "due to the fact that they were too familiar with their ancestors." Flipping the narrative of natural black inferiority, he declared that it was the "white" blood in southern blacks that should be blamed for any impurities. George Downing further pointed out the hypocrisy in claims of white virtue and combined it with calls for black self-defense. "The black south," he declared, "is as ready to protect the virtue of women as the white south is. Talk of respect for womanhood when white men will walk into the cabins of black men and ravish their wives and daughters before their eyes. We want a law that will protect all women."[66]

## "A Woman's Place Is Where She Is Needed"

Black women in Boston, however, did not wait for the law or black men to protect them; they were forceful advocates for their rights themselves. By the 1890s, Boston's black women had been engaged in politics for decades as organizers and as voters. These women were party to the contentious discourse surrounding African American partisan affiliation. As members of the Colored National League and other organizations, black women debated political strategies, including independent politics, and challenged white supremacy. In their activism, these women affirmed the integration of the interests of black women with the destiny of all African Americans.

In addition to general activism for equality, African American women engaged in political organizations focusing on electoral politics explicitly. For example, as part of the Massachusetts Woman Suffrage Association black women joined with some of their most important white allies for political instruction. The society hosted a forum called the Boston Political Class that taught regular lessons in parliamentary politics and debated current political events. In December 1890, for instance, Pauline Hopkins, the notable black playwright, journalist, and author, joined the Boston Political Class to discuss the proposed Federal Elections Bill.[67]

In addition to organizing, black women in Boston had exercised their right to vote since 1879, albeit in school elections only. When black men and women across Boston descended on the voting booths on Election Day, 1888, among the voters were a large number of women who were eager to cast a ballot in the school committee election. Women voters were particularly agitated by the controversy surrounding city funding of Catholic parochial schools, and women on both sides of the issue rushed to the polls to defend their perspectives.[68] Further, the school committee elections, as Lisa Materson's work attests, served as local sites for national political discussions.[69] For example, in 1896 the Silver Democrats nominated Josephine St. Pierre Ruffin as their candidate for school committee, prompting a discussion about rejecting affiliations with the Republican Party.[70]

Women also helped staff the polling places and campaigned for their interests. Women canvassers stood in and outside the ward rooms and polling places and converged upon male and female voters in an attempt to sway their opinions toward a particular candidate. A correspondent for the *New York Age* commented on the activity of African American women at the polls. "The women are in earnest," the reporter explained. "At every voting precinct there are women ballot distributors and in many cases they are more intelligent and present claims of their candidates in far more concise and convincing argument.... Their presence and influence in the polling places are in the interest of dignity and clean methods."[71] For witnesses to the election, the presence of women in and outside of the polling place was transforming the nature of urban electoral politics.[72]

African American women were not satisfied with limited access to the ballot during school elections, and they campaigned for broader suffrage rights. Josephine St. Pierre Ruffin, in particular, was a prominent advocate for full voting rights. In an 1894 *Boston Globe* column she observed that women lacked few other rights in Massachusetts, but by excluding women from suffrage, the state effectively limited women's rights in other areas.[73] "I know of no rights denied to women by New England laws 'save the ballot,'" she explained, but "that exception denies them, among other things, the right to be tried by a jury of their peers ... [and] a right to help strengthen by discreet laws their morally weak men folk."[74] There are few rights, Ruffin concluded, "that the use of the ballot could not either directly or indirectly affect."[75] Empowered with access to the ballot and committed to expanding their rights, Boston's black women campaigned against lynching and embraced electoral and independent politics as a tool for change.

During the 1890s, black women's political organizing surged, prompting some commentators to term the decade the "woman's era." Indeed, during this period, black women became important spokespeople on both local and national issues of race and gender rights. Arguably, the most important of their new organizations was the Woman's Era Club. Founded in 1892 by Josephine St. Pierre Ruffin and her daughter Florida Ruffin Ridley, it soon became one of the most vocal and respected organizations among black women in the nation. The leaders of the Woman's Era Club envisioned themselves as national leaders, hoping to unite disparate black women's organizations under one mantle.

Ruffin channeled her decades of activity in Boston's political and social circles into the new organization. A Boston native, she was born in 1842 to a mother from Cornwell, England, and a black father who was the son of French immigrants from Martinique. She began her education in public schools in Salem and Charlestown and later attended the Bowdoin School in Boston. In the 1850s she married George Ruffin. During the Civil War, she worked as a recruiter for the Massachusetts black regiments and joined women's solider and contraband relief associations. After the war, she was actively involved in Boston's club life and was a member of several women's rights organization like the Massachusetts School Suffrage Association. She was also an officer in the Massachusetts State Federation of Women's Clubs in the 1890s, a founding member of the National Association of Colored Women, and later helped found the Boston chapter of the National Association for the Advancement of Colored People (NAACP).[76]

In addition to regular meetings, The Woman's Era Club's publication of the *Woman's Era* newspaper contributed to its prominence. This journal received national circulation and was read by women in similar political movements throughout the nation. The paper included not only instructions on proper housekeeping, health, and child care, but also significant commentary and advocacy on political issues. Correspondents for the newspaper provided news from communities of black women throughout the nation, and the paper's editors offered important commentary regarding local and national events concerning women and African Americans. While the Woman's Era Club supported the independence of local clubs, its leaders hoped that the *Woman's Era* newspaper could unite the organizations. "The especial work of this paper," Florida Ruffin wrote in the first issue, "is the binding together of our women's clubs . . . and bring[ing] the colored women together in a great and powerful organization for the growth and progress of the race."[77]

The leaders of the Woman's Era Club encouraged African American women to become more active outside the home and to take an interest in politics. This sentiment was expressed in a speech given to the club by Laura Omiston Chant, a white supporter from England. "A great deal of the advice given to women about their staying at home," Chant criticized, "is wrong altogether." Clubs were importance sites for education in not only domestic science and child raising, but also political issues. "Clubs," the Englishwoman told the audience, "make women read and think in order that they may not sit like idiots when some bright paper is being read."[78] Further, she deemphasized the role of women as mothers, urging them to look toward independent lives outside the home. "Not all women are intended for mothers. Some of us have not the temperament for family life," Chant declared. "Clubs will make women think seriously of their future lives, and not make girls think their only alternative is to marry."[79]

The presence of white women as speakers at Woman's Era Club events reinforced the sentiment of some members that they should focus on issues affecting not just African American women, but all women, regardless of race. "It is not our desire," Florida Ruffin Ridley explained, "to narrow ourselves to race work, however necessary it is that such work should be done and particularly by colored women." Rather, Ridley and other members of the Woman's Era Club called African American women to unite their struggle with that of women throughout the world. "We the women of the Woman's Era Club," Ridley proclaimed, "enter the field to work hand in hand with women, generally for humanity and humanity's interests, not the Negro alone, but the Chinese, the Hawaiian, the Russian Jew, the oppressed everywhere as subjects for our consideration, not the needs of the colored women, but women everywhere are our interest."[80]

Despite calls for interracial unity, Ridley argued that African American women must take up the cause of black victims of lynching in particular. While she endorsed the work of white women's clubs, she argued that they often neglected the plight of African American women. Indeed, this neglect required African American women to unite in their own organizations. "There are so many questions," she explained, "which in their application to the race, demand special treatment, so many questions which, as colored women, we are called upon to answer, more than this, there was so much danger that numbers of women would be over-looked unless some special appeal was made to them."[81] While the organizers of the Woman's Era Club called upon African American women to work for the uplift of all women, they were concerned that without an organization specifically mobilized for the purpose of protecting black rights, these interests would be ignored.

Through public meetings and their paper, Boston's women were prominent organizers against lynching and helped shape the discourse of antilynching across the city and nation in the 1890s. Additionally, the Woman's Era Club was one of the few early organizations to support antilynching activist

Ida B. Wells. Wells, in letters to the *Woman's Era*, praised the organization and proclaimed that without their early and continued support, her travels abroad and throughout the nation would have been impossible.[82]

In addition to their advocacy of antilynching, the editors of the paper were very interested in the cause of black woman suffrage and published articles on Bostonian suffrage agitation alongside articles from communities throughout the country. The editors of the paper refuted charges that voting would somehow diminish a woman's "womanliness."[83] In particular, in late 1894 the *Woman's Era* publicized the voting activity of black women in Boston, Illinois, and Colorado. In response to an article in the *Virginia Baptist* that declared that a woman's participation in teaching or preaching in the church or voting in elections was an act "contrary to divine authority," the editors of the *Woman's Era* answered, "It is according to law, gospel, history, and common sense that a woman's place is where she is needed and where she fits in. . . . To say that the place will affect her womanliness is bosh."[84] The paper urged readers not to take these criticisms seriously but rather "treat them as the strong womanly woman treat all pin pricks."[85] Although they were able to vote only in elections for school committees, the editors of the *Era* took that position seriously and lamented the difficulty in electing black candidates to the school committee.

Authors published in the *Woman's Era* did not shy away from openly criticizing the Republican Party and male leadership. For example, following the failure of the Republican Party to accept the nomination of two black candidates, the editors of the *Era* wrote, "An able, wide-awake representative on the school board is our due and means more than appears at first blush."[86] Further, they argued that black male political leaders must take woman voters seriously. "In presenting a candidate," the editors of the *Era* urged, "colored men should not be indifferent to the women voters; they hold a tremendous power over school matters."[87] Sentiments of political independence from male political leaders, as well as from party were bolstered by correspondents from other cities.

In particular, Frances Barrier Williams, who was a strong suffrage advocate in Chicago and for the paper's Illinois department, vocally supported political independence.[88] Williams urged that "the importance of suffrage, as a means to complete emancipation from the impositions of prejudice, should be eagerly taught, and brought home to the conscience of our women everywhere."[89] She also echoed the calls for political independence that permeated the rhetoric of black male leaders in Boston, and she used these calls to condemn the perceived blind party loyalty of African American men. She warned that a new bloc of black woman voters would be "satisfactory to the most exacting 'boss'" and be put "in the humiliating position of being loved only for the votes we have."

Williams called black woman voters to use the franchise against candidates who supported the exclusion of black women from places of employment and "the enjoyment of civil privileges." Failure to exert political independence, she warned, would result in "the same folly and neglect of self-interest that have made colored men for the past twenty years vote persistently more for the special interests of white men than for the peculiar interests of the colored race." "There is no good reason," she concluded, "why our women should not be made to feel sufficiently independent not only to make their peculiar interests a motive in the exercise of the franchise, but to array themselves, when possible, on the side of the best, whether that be inside or outside of party lines."[90] In this way, Williams called for women to embrace suffrage as a political strategy only if they were going to use it to hold politicians accountable and pursue African American uplift. Further, by advocating political independence, she was incorporating black women into an electoral discourse that placed the interests of race and ideologies of uplift above party loyalty.

## Continued Partisan Discord

In 1896 black Bostonians met, again under the auspices of the MRPA, to call for a national convention to organize African Americans across the country politically. Although they had hoped for consensus, tensions in the meeting erupted over partisanship and exposed electoral politics to be a barrier against unity. Their goal was to unite African Americans around a particular candidate and demonstrate that through their numbers, black voters could be a significant force in American politics. "The colored voters of the United States," the Boston press explained, "are about to inaugurate a movement which . . . will cause the colored men to assume a very important position in national politics."[91] Prominent African Americans from across the country would endorse candidates for president, vice president, and governor of each state. The convention organizers predicted more than 1,800 attendees and expected more than 1,200 from locations outside Massachusetts. Observers argued that African Americans held the balance of electoral power in the southern border and central states, and that "unless there should be a landslide, the ballots of the colored element could be used to turn the State for either of the two leading candidates."[92]

While the promoters of the convention sought to engage in spirited debate over black political loyalty, they predicted that the convention would ultimately support the Republican William McKinley for president over Democrat William Jennings Bryan. "The movement," Edward E. Brown, one of the Boston promoters, explained, "is of vital importance to the colored man. The convention will discuss the position our race should take politically and whether or not it is advisable to divide our vote or throw it solidly for one party."[93] For organizers such as Brown, the choice between Democrats and Republicans was easy due to the involvement of South Carolina Democratic governor Benjamin Tillman in Bryan's campaign. Tillman had promoted acts of violence against African Americans and endorsed changes to South Carolina's state constitution limiting black men's right to vote.[94] "We are united," Brown explained, "in the feeling that the success of the democratic ticket means the return of Tillman and the Southerners to power, and then the welfare of the black man will be given a bad rap. Anything that savors Tillmanism we want no part in."[95] The rise of leaders such as Tillman was evidence of southern white supremacist political resurgence and the reversal of the gains of Reconstruction. "[Southerners] have never repented since the war and are now acting in a spirit of animosity and revenge."[96]

Conference organizers predicted that the delegates would endorse McKinley despite earlier Republican tensions over the prevention of lynching. "We have for years been trying to get the Republican Party to take a stand on the lynching question," Brown explained, "and now that they have come out frankly, we feel very friendly toward them. We feel somewhat shaky about Bryan . . . but with McKinley we are perfectly satisfied." The organizers of the convention hoped the convention would be large and make a significant impact on the national political stage. "The meeting," Brown predicted optimistically, "is expected to unite the colored people of the country for the future advancement of the race."[97]

As delegates descended on Boston for the August 10 convention, their hopes for unity confronted the reality of divergent opinions regarding political endorsement and partisan affiliation as a political strategy. While Massachusetts delegates made up the majority of the convention, the crowd that filled Ebenezer Baptist Church included representatives from Arkansas, Alabama, Connecticut, the District of Columbia, Louisiana, Mississippi, New Mexico, New Hampshire, Ohio, Rhode Island, South Carolina, Tennessee, and Virginia. Organizers opened the convention with a call to coordinate nationally to confront increasing obstacles to uplift and the present dire conditions facing black men and women. "We have summoned you here," organizers declared, "because we regard this present time as one of the most momentous that has occurred in this country for thirty-six years."[98]

Speakers pointed to four areas that they felt contributed to a weakened state of African Americans and advocated racial self-reliance without the help of white Americans. "Four elements are lacking with us ... the lack of organization, racial pride, confidence, and capacity." By pooling their resources, African Americans could educate black men and women in areas of business, "racial developments," racial pride, religion, morals and education, and industrial trades. Further, by drawing on the legal acumen of the race, African Americans could mount broad legal challenges to prejudice.[99] Conference organizers argued that African Americans could not rely on the support of white allies or political leadership; rather, they must become independent and support African American leaders and organizations. "The negro has been unfortunate in one thing especially," they explained. "He has looked outside of himself for help, which he has learned by bitter experience to be delusive. He must learn to be self-reliant and look within."[100]

The main speaker of the first day of the convention was Harvard Law School graduate, first African American college football player, and Harvard University football coach William H. Lewis. Lewis called on African Americans to unite behind the cause of civil and political liberty. He drew comparisons between African American and immigrant groups in American cities. "The Irish race," Lewis argued, "with far less cause for grievance than we, unite and rule the great metropolitan centers. The Germans, with practically no grievances at all, unite and control the destinies of the mighty states of the northwest. The negro unites today ... simply to demand that he be made in reality what he is in name—an American citizen."[101]

While speaking of racial unity generally, Lewis advocated African American voters' uniting behind the political party that best supported black civil and political rights. "Whatever may be our party affiliation, whatever may be our political beliefs on other matters ... the first question to ask of a political party is, what will you do to secure me in the exercise of my rights as a man and a citizen?"[102] Although Lewis asked listeners to disregard party affiliation, he made it clear that he supported voting the Republican ticket. Lewis ridiculed the Democratic Party platform for supporting "free silver, but not one word about free men."[103] Further, he announced that the Democratic platform "is reeking with anarchy, seeking to overthrow existing institutions, the spirit of the mob, the spirit of lynch law, for lynch law is anarchy."[104] The Republican platform, by contrast, according to Lewis, "[is] regnant with liberty, law, and order." Lewis celebrated the Republican platform for condemning lynching and declared that in the party, "we find not only the gold standard, but the gold standard of manhood."[105]

While Lewis's statements reflected the optimism that the convention would build a consensus around the Republican Party, not all delegates to the convention were so confident in McKinley's candidacy, and while the convention agreed on most issues, decorum broke down over partisan affiliation. Edwin Walker, in particular, declared that the delegates had met to discuss the condition of African Americans and should not use the forum for political endorsements. "I am glad we are getting to this place. . . . The only question proper for us to consider is the negro. . . . We don't want any scheme fixed up here to deliver the colored people over to the party in a gathering like this."[106]

Attempts to get the convention to endorse the Republican candidate continued until the end of the proceedings and resulted in the meeting adjourning in disorder. As the *Boston Globe* reported, "the row was over politics."[107] In the final hours of the convention, Republicans moved that the convention endorse McKinley. This, according to press reports, caused the convention to devolve into confusion before the president declared that the meeting was not political and ruled the motion out of order. Delegates moved to censure Republicans for repeatedly putting supporting motions before the meeting, but the vote was defeated and the convention quickly adjourned.

The end of the meeting, however, did not put an end to the partisan rancor, with Republicans publicly declaring that the defeat of censure was an endorsement of their motion in favor of McKinley and opponents asserting that they had prevented McKinley supporters from taking over the convention. "In their haste to close the convention and their refusal to censure me," a Republican told a *Boston Globe* reporter, "they have tacitly indorsed the republican nominees. . . . In refusing to censure me they admitted that I was right and had the proper remedy."[108] Independents argued that they had not endorsed McKinley, but rather prevented Republican leaders from turning the meeting into a Republican political rally. "We were afraid," explained an anonymous minister, "that some of the local delegates would come in there tonight and sweep the convention clear for McKinley and Hobart. . . . They were just getting ready to carry everything tonight at the close of the convention with a grand political coup."[109] By preventing Republicans from passing their motions, opponents maintained the political independence of the convention, but illuminated the divisions. The delegates left Boston failing to achieve the political unity to which they had aspired at the convention's outset.

Despite divisions over the endorsement, McKinley won the presidency in 1896, and African Americans were hopeful that the Republican president would enact policies to roll back the tide of white supremacy and violence that was rising in southern states. But the tragic and widely publicized lynching of a South Carolinian postmaster and his family soon shattered any optimism. In response to this horror, African American men and women applied the energy generated in organizations such as the Colored National League, MRPA, and the Woman's Era Club to the protection of southern victims. Again, however, they faced disappointment when attempts by supposed white allies to take control of causes they had worked so hard to advance failed to bring about meaningful change. So they increasingly turned inward and looked for strategies beyond partisan electoral politics. As black Bostonians entered the final years of the nineteenth century, it became clearer that progress would continue to be elusive, and that their faith in electoral politics as a solution may have been misplaced.

## CHAPTER EIGHT

# Where There Is No Will There Is No Way

## *The Tragedy of Partisan Politics and the Hope of Solidarity*

On October 3, 1899, Boston attorney and former *Hub* editor Archibald H. Grimké, who had recently returned from his position as U.S. consul in Santo Domingo, addressed the Colored National League. Grimké read aloud a letter to the president of the United States William McKinley, written at the insistence of the executive committee of the league. "We address ourselves to you, sir," Grimké wrote, "not as suppliants, but as of right, as American citizens, whose servant you are, and to whom you are bound to listen . . . and upon occasion to act."[1] This "Open Letter to President McKinley by the Colored People of Massachusetts" expressed outrage at the lynching of African Americans in southern states and even more indignation at the perceived inaction on the part of the federal government and the McKinley administration. "We have suffered, sir,—God knows how much we have suffered!—since your accession to office," the league announced. "You have seen our sufferings, witnessed from your high place our awful wrongs and miseries, and yet you have at no time and on no occasion opened your lips on our behalf. . . . Is there no help in the federal arm for us?"[2]

The letter explained how southern violence had stifled southern black resistance and how Massachusetts residents felt especially well positioned to address the president. "The silence of death reigns over our people and their leaders at the South," the letter explained. "We of Massachusetts are free, and must and shall raise our voice to you and through you to the country, in solemn protest and warning against the fearful sin and peril of such social conditions." The letter continued, to address the contradictions in McKinley's endorsement of U.S. intervention in Cuba and his refusal to use federal troops to protect black rights in southern states. As Grimké concluded, following an ovation from the audience, the letter was signed by prominent members of the league and adopted by the meeting with "significant unanimity."[3] This letter marks a turning point in black politics and provides a point of departure to a more radical political action. With this document, activists confirmed the sentiment that no matter the administration, the rights of African Americans were not going to be protected by the federal government. In their address to McKinley, the league members affirmed their commitment to race and not party as their public political identity.

By the time the Colored National League sent its formal letter denouncing President McKinley's inaction in the face of southern atrocities, it had been embroiled in protests against lynching for nearly a decade. These sentiments intensified toward the end of the 1890s. This was partly due to the marked increase in incidents and the focused attention by local organizations such as the Colored National League and the Massachusetts Racial Protective Association.

In 1898, following the brutal attack in South Carolina on a black postmaster, the Colored National League mobilized to address the violence and to care for the victims. In their meetings, debates occurred again over what continued southern violence meant for black political afflation and the place of electoral politics in fighting lynching. League members also openly argued over the place of white leaders in the movement, with some arguing that it should be exclusively a black-led effort.

The lynching of the postmaster and the lack of federal response to this and many other occasions of racial violence led black independents to the conclusion that their faith in political parties had been misplaced. Rather than being a choice between Republican or Democrat, it had become clear that both parties rejected black interests. Pauline Hopkins captured this sentiment in her novel *Contending Forces*, and through her fiction shared it with a nationwide audience. For decades, black activists sought to bend the major political parties to their will, but the parties remained rigidly opposed to making black rights and lives a priority.

By the end of his life, Edwin Walker joined others in distrust of both Republican and Democratic candidates. They had hoped that leveraging black votes would motivate government officials to act. Disappointingly, by the end of the century, African Americans were unable to turn the tide of white supremacy, violence, and Jim Crow. The failure of black Bostonians to muster the sufficient influence to change the national agenda increased the feeling of political isolation. Condemning the lack of will on the part of political parties and abandoned by supposed allies, and coinciding with the death of Walker, the Boston activists required a shift in strategy. They concluded that neither the major political parties nor the U.S. government were serving African Americans, and that the only solution was through organization and political power grounded in race-based unity.

## The Baker Lynching and the Jewett Controversy

On February 22, 1898, following months of intense white opposition to his appointment as postmaster of Lake City, South Carolina, black postmaster Frazier Baker and his family were attacked. Armed vandals set their home ablaze and fired upon the family as they attempted to flee. Bullets flew through the burning structure as Baker and his wife, Lavinia, attempted to gather their four children. As Baker opened the front door he was immediately shot through the body and head. Lavinia, shielding her youngest child Julia in her arms, was shot through the left arm. As the bullet injured Mrs. Baker, it mortally wounded the infant, whose lifeless body fell into the flames from her mother's arms. Lavinia Baker and the rest of her children, all with gunshot wounds, fled to the home of a neighbor, leaving the bodies of Frazier Baker and his baby daughter to smolder in the burning ruins.[4]

As the sun rose the next morning, her husband and youngest daughter were dead, and she and three of her remaining children were wounded. According to a journalist for the *Charleston Weekly News and Courier* who interviewed Mrs. Baker following the attack, "There is no clue whatever to the parties that did the shooting and the consensus of opinion seems to be that no one in the immediate community is in any way connected or responsible for it."[5] In response to the lynching, the federal government immediately suspended mail service to Lake City and commenced an investigation, and after a failed local inquest, a federal grand jury issued indictments and arrested several alleged perpetrators. Ultimately, as it was in many such cases, the courts failed to convict anyone for the atrocity.[6]

News of the Baker lynching came to Boston quickly, and the response from the Colored National League was almost immediate. On March 1, 1898, the league organized a meeting at the Charles Street AME Church to denounce Baker's murder and the maiming of his family. Speakers condemned the "Baker butchery" and passed resolutions demanding that President McKinley appoint another black man to replace Baker as postmaster and insisting that the U.S. government call out the military to protect African American appointees in the South.[7] They also made an appeal for funds to send a delegation to Washington, D.C., to carry the protest of black Bostonians to the president. Among those chosen were active community leaders and antilynching spokespeople Rev. Dolphin Roberts, Edwin Walker, and William H. Lewis. Following this initial mobilization, the league met again a month later to call attention to "the apparent lukewarm efforts of the government to apprehend perpetrators of the Baker murder."[8]

Baker lynching and aftermath, *Boston Post*, August 10, 1899. (Serial and Government Publications Division, Library of Congress.)

The Baker lynching continued to occupy the agenda of the Colored National League over the following year as members watched the federal government bring charges against the alleged perpetrators, only to have the jury fail to render a guilty verdict. In addition to observing the trial, black Bostonians became increasingly concerned with the condition of Mrs. Baker and her children. The Colored National League hosted Rev. Dr. John L. Dart, one of the major conduits for aid to the Bakers and the president of the Normal and Industrial Institute in Charleston, South Carolina, during his trips to Boston where he appealed for support of the Baker family.

Dart's politics clashed with those of some black Bostonians, but the Colored National League nonetheless became an important ally in raising money to care for the Bakers. One point that conflicted with Bostonian calls for immediate action was Dart's plea for black men in the South to refrain from taking government positions. "I do not think it wise for colored men who remain in the south to jeopardize their lives by taking government positions in small localities," he told a league meeting in July 1899. Echoing the senti-ment of southern spokespeople such as Booker T. Washington, Dart advo-cated, "Instead of seeking these petty places [African Americans should] build themselves up in business, get money, get property, gain a foothold in their community . . . show the white people that they can meet them upon the nondebateable grounds of mutual local interest . . . and establish good citi-zenship among ourselves."[9]

As the league debated how best to aid the Baker family, white female activ-ist Lillian Jewett mobilized a movement to relocate the Baker family to Bos-ton. Jewett was relatively unknown by most Bostonians at the time, and the lack of knowledge of her background helped agitate the opposition to her lead-ership. In much of the discussion surrounding Jewett, speakers drew compari-sons with the antislavery movement. Rev. Benjamin W. Farris, the minister of Boston's St. Paul's Baptist Church, who had arranged for her to speak, com-pared Jewett to Harriet Beecher Stowe, declaring that "God has frequently touched the heart of a woman when he wanted a great work performed. . . . He put the pen in the hand of Harriet Beecher Stowe. Now he is once more touch-ing the heart of a woman."[10]

Jewett heartily embraced the comparison to Stowe and declared that her mission was to bring the Baker family north, not only for their own well-being, but to draw publicity for the antilynching cause. Before emancipation, abolitionists often had presented formerly enslaved black men and women to crowds, and Jewett hoped to use a similar strategy to raise sympathy and funds against lynching. "Something must be done to bring to our people a true picture of the conditions south," Jewett told the crowd. "Bring the Baker family here to Boston. Let them see the helpless children, the maimed and destitute mother, whose husband and little one were killed."[11] Jewett hoped to reignite Boston's antislavery sentiment by exhibiting the living victims of lynching. As Stowe had done with slavery, Jewett hoped to show the damage lynching had done to Baker's family and mobilize white sympathy in the North and South.

Despite Jewett's apparently altruistic motives, members of the Colored National League, already deeply disillusioned with inaction on the part of sup-posed white allies in political parties, were immediately skeptical of a relatively unknown white woman marshaling support for a cause they had advocated for years. For the members of the Colored National League, who were in a ten-uous political position in Boston already, to cede control over one of their main causes to an unknown white women would be a severe blow to their organ-ization and racial pride. As an article in the *Boston Daily Globe* explained, "It is not that the colored people of Boston as a whole are adverse to having her go south . . . but [they oppose] the alleged attempt, as some members of the Colored National League declare, to snatch from them credit which belongs to them on account of this Baker murder agitation."[12] At a league meeting to address the recent controversy, speakers revealed correspondence between the league and Mrs. Baker. The league had actively communicated with Mrs. Baker for over a year and had sent her thirty-five dollars. This was proof, the league argued, that they should have priority in deciding the best strategy.

Josephine St. Pierre Ruffin publicly declared her apprehension over the attention given to Jewett. Ruffin, the leader of Boston's Woman's Era Club, was a principal spokeswoman for the interests of African American women in Boston and the nation. Ruffin had shared the stage with Jewett at the prior meeting and was deeply concerned by her recent rise to prominence. She argued that black Boston had the strength in both resources and fortitude to bring the Baker family north if that was decided to be the best solution. "I have strong pride in New England colored people," Ruffin declared. "The Colored National League . . . should take charge of this business of bringing Mrs. Baker and her family north to Boston. . . . There are loyal, self sacrificing colored women who can go south and bring that family up north."[13]

Ruffin recognized the tenuous political position of African Americans and cautioned her fellow black Bostonians to be skeptical of any sudden emergence of white support. "We must not be governed by sentiment," she cautioned. "We must be careful how we move, for the position of the race today is a critical one, and we should carefully analyze the efforts of those who are so anxious about our people. We should not fly up when some chit of a white girl rises and declares she will go south to bring up that family." Ruffin also challenged the comparisons between Jewett and Harriet Beecher Stowe. "I am not carried away by some person who springs up like a mushroom and is heralded all over the country as the new Harriet Beecher Stowe," she announced. Stowe and other white women allies, she explained, "did not spring forth in one night." Ruffin and the other opponents of Jewett were hesitant to throw their support behind anyone before the person's true motives were understood and were not about to have their authority usurped. "Is this not a humiliation to this League," she asked, "to have this thing happen, after it had devoted so much of its time in keeping up this agitation concerning the Baker family? . . . To the league alone belongs the credit for all that has been done for that family since the unfortunate happening in Lake City."[14]

Ruffin's comments caused an uproar among some of Jewett's supporters. Rev. Ferris took exception to Ruffin's referring to Jewett as a "chit of a white girl" and thought that she had misrepresented the white activist. Ferris declared that Jewett was wealthy and was willing to fund the relocation of the Bakers. Ruffin immediately countered that she knew nothing of Jewett's being wealthy or having money to put toward the cause.[15] Other Jewett supporters rose to dispute Ruffin's allegations. Isaac Allen, a black elected official and proud supporter of the Republican Party, accused the league of accomplishing nothing and declared that the real political power of black Boston was among "those who go to colored churches and support them."[16]

Other members of the league were hesitant to pick a side in the argument. J. S. Gaines argued against the league getting dragged into a fight. Mark R. de Demortie, Boston boot maker and son-in-law to George T. Downing, declared that he just wanted the Baker family to come to Boston.[17] "I don't care who brings her, so she is brought here," Demortie told an inflamed audience. "We need not wrangle here over our shortcomings or those of others. We want to show Boston people how a Negro family suffers."[18] At the conclusion of the meeting, Ruffin's motion and the protests of others were referred to the executive committee and the meeting was adjourned. Despite the tension, Jewett made good on her promise to bring the Baker family to Boston in August 1899.[19]

The controversy over the Baker lynching placed Ruffin and the Colored National League at the center of the debates over the place of African Americans in Boston within the national antilynching movement. As a *Boston Globe* reporter observed, "The expressions of individual opinion . . . seemed to indicate that a big gulf has been made among the colored population of [Boston] by the untactful manner in which this matter of the Baker case has been handled."[20] While some might have been willing to cede power to white spokespeople, the league saw itself and the Boston community as leaders in a larger movement, and as such was highly critical of attempts by others to usurp the authority of black leadership. Through public action and the press, Ruffin and the league sought to provide an example to black women and men throughout the nation of the primacy of African Americans in their own uplift. Black men and women could not depend on the support of white leaders or the government, they felt, but must mobilize themselves behind racial and political unity.

The tragedy of the Baker family, the weak federal response, and the Jewett controversy all contributed to the rising disillusionment among black independents. For those already alienated and let down by white party leadership, ceding power to Jewett seemed to be setting up another occasion of betrayal. Just months after the controversy, the Colored National League mounted a public campaign denouncing the inaction of the Republican McKinley administration and advocating further separation of black voters from the party, and perhaps separation from party politics entirely.

## "Never Will We Efface Ourselves Politically or Otherwise"

By 1899, reluctance by the McKinley administration to prevent or punish lynching caused the Colored National League to make their most outspoken attack against the president and the federal government. Led at this time by Archibald Grimké the Colored National League held meetings advocating dividing the African American vote, and in a widely circulated pamphlet, condemned President McKinley and the hypocrisy of U.S. imperial claims in the face of southern atrocities against African Americans.

Grimké was born enslaved in Colleton County, South Carolina, in 1849. The son of Henry Grimké, a member of a prominent white Carolinian family, he was a nephew of white abolitionist sisters Sarah and Angelina Grimké. Following Henry's death in the 1850s, Grimké moved with his mother to Charleston, where he attended a school for black children. During the Civil War, he escaped slavery and eventually enrolled at Lincoln University in Pennsylvania. In 1874, he graduated from Harvard University Law School, which he attended with help from his aunt Angelina. In the 1880s Grimké edited the *Hub*, an African American newspaper known for its criticism of black political independence. Although originally a staunch Republican supporter, by the 1890s he had begun to take a more independent stance politically. By the turn of the twentieth century, he publicly denounced African American allegiance to the Republicans, eventually joining William M. Trotter and W. E. B. Du Bois in the Niagara Movement and the NAACP.[21]

During a meeting of the Colored National League in September 1899, Grimké called upon African Americans to look to themselves for support rather than to political parties. "Perhaps some put their whole trust in party action and look to the national government for aid, and mean to appeal to the American people to redress our wrongs. Well, I answer, don't. We have tried them all and in every hour of our direst need we have found them broken crutches for our arms, and extinguished lanterns for our feet."[22] Grimké rejected the "voluntary effacement" of some black leaders in the South. "Crush us with brute force, slaughter us, exterminate us, but never will we efface ourselves politically or otherwise for the sake of appeasing your hated race prejudice."[23] For Grimké and other members of the Colored National League, the federal government and the major political parties had failed to protect

African Americans and provide assistance in uplift. Racial progress, the league argued, could only come by the race's turning inward and uplifting itself. "Let our race get this saving strength," Grimké urged, "unless it is to be doomed."[24]

Only several months after the turmoil surrounding the Bakers, the Colored National League met to endorse and send the "Open Letter" to President McKinley. The league formally presented the letter on October 4, 1899. In it, they explicitly condemned the federal government for the inaction on lynching. The league argued that African Americans were entitled, as citizens, to all the rights and protections guaranteed them by the Constitution. "We ask," the letter read, "for the free and full exercise of all the rights of American freemen, guaranteed to us by the Constitution and the Union . . . for what belongs to us by the high sanction of Constitution and law, and the Democratic genius of our institutions and civilization."[25] These rights, the author argued, were infringed upon in every southern state "by mobs, by lawless legislatures, and nullifying conventions, combinations, and conspiracies."[26]

What made these violations particularly egregious, and what drew the league's ire particularly toward the Republican McKinley, was the perceived neglect of his administration in the face of such degradations. "Rights are everywhere throughout the South denied to us . . . openly, defiantly, under your eyes, in your constructive and actual presence . . . under a government, which we are bound to defend in war, and which is equally bound to furnish us in peace protection, at home and abroad."[27] The federal government, the members of the league argued, had a constitutional obligation to protect African Americans from violence and the infringement of their rights. The refusal to do so amounted to the McKinley administration's tacit consent to the atrocities.

The league was particularly outraged at the McKinley administration's defense that due to a Supreme Court decision, the president and the federal government had no authority to intervene in southern states.[28] The league argued that the rulings on constitutionality were not fixed and permanent, and that the president had the obligation to challenge unjust rulings. Writing about government inaction following the race riot in Wilmington, North Carolina, the league argued that it was a failure of political will, not unconstitutionality, that prevented the government from acting. "We well understood at the time, sir," the league explained, "notwithstanding your plea of constitutional inability to cope with the rebellion in Wilmington, that where there is a will with constitutional lawyers and rulers there is always a way, and where there is no will there is no way. We well knew that you lacked the will, and, therefore, the way to meet that emergency."[29]

The league found declarations of the constitutional limits on federal authority to stop racial violence hypocritical in the face of McKinley's involvement in the Spanish-American War and the eventual U.S. occupation of Cuba. The league argued that if the federal government had constitutional authority to intervene against the Spanish in Cuba, then it could intervene on behalf of African Americans in southern states. "[You], in your judgment, gave to the Cuban question a federal aspect, which provoked at last the armed interposition of our government in the affairs of that island, and this was 'the chronic condition of disturbance in Cuba so injurious and menacing to our interests and tranquility, as well as shocking to our sentiments of humanity.' "[30] The league asked, "Are crying national transgressions and injustices more 'injurious and menacing' to the Republic, as well as 'shocking to the sentiments of humanity,' when committed by a foreign state, in a foreign territory, against a foreign people, than when they are committed by a portion of our own people against a portion of our own people at home?"[31]

The letter concluded that the president avoided confronting racial oppression and lynching so as not to lose support for his foreign policy. "We felt," the league wrote, "that the President of the United States, in order to win the support of the South to his policy of 'criminal aggression' in the far East, was ready and willing to shut his eyes, ears and lips to the 'criminal aggression' of that section of the Constitution and the laws of the land."[32] They argued that if the president and his cabinet could make the case for the federal intervention into foreign nations, then surely, if he desired, the president could use federal authority to suppress southern violence against African Americans. The league concluded their letter, "If you have the disposition, as we know that you have the power, we are confident that you will be able to find a constitutional way to reach us in our extremity, and our enemies also, who are likewise enemies to great public interests and national tranquility."[33]

The open letter circulated widely, and Grimké received immediate responses from throughout the country and abroad. Booker T. Washington wrote to Grimké thanking him for sending the letter, which he regarded as "straight forward and manly. . . . I trust the President will be touched by the directness and of the appeal made."[34] George Downing celebrated the letter and criticized the rarity of vocal African American activism. "Would that we made such expressions and acted them out more frequently," he wrote.[35] Another letter, from St. Mary's Church in Philadelphia, declared the Colored National League's appeal "a terrible arraignment of the National Administration's neglect of duty to the Negro." This letter argued that McKinley was willing to sacrifice the welfare of African Americans for the sake of political gain and reelection. Speaking of the league's allegations of hypocrisy in McKinley's foreign policy, the author of the letter declared, "I am constrained to regard this Government as the Pharisee among the nations, condemning others whilst neglecting itself, and President McKinley is the modern Pontius Pilate. He seems to make all things subservient to the selfish expediency that will secure a second term."[36]

Katie V. Smith, from Cambridge, Massachusetts, also lauded the letter and urged Grimké and the Colored National League to continue their antilynching agitation. "I know not," Smith praised, "who else could use the English language so magnificently or so irresistibly in the cause."[37] She called for the reemergence of a protest movement in the spirit of the antislavery movement. "Then must be repeated," she announced, "the thirty years' agitation and the terrible retribution which preceded emancipation."[38]

Smith encouraged Grimké to look beyond critiques of the president and shift his attacks to Congress in the hopes of gaining legislative remedies for lynching. She urged investigating the possible solutions for ending racial violence and spreading these lessons throughout the country. "I beg, dear friend, that you who have started this fire of indignant rebuke, do not stop here. Educate the nation . . . that when the crisis comes, as it may soon, there will be knowledge how to act. . . . There is a way. Show it to the blind, ask it of the wise. Let us state it so clearly that it must be taken."[39]

Perhaps inspired by letters such as Smith's, Grimké did more than just rhetorically propose solutions to the constitutional dilemma; he sought advice and investigated judicial precedent that would make way for challenges to lynching. For example, on January 20, 1900, he received correspondence from U.S. congressmen regarding "a possible measure for the prevention and punishment of lynching."[40] "A bill for the purpose might well provide for the use of the military power to preserve the peace of the United States in neighborhoods where lynchings have actually occurred . . . and must, of course, contain a most critical provision for the selection of the jury in proceedings in the Federal courts to punish lynching."[41]

The justification for federal intervention, black congressman George White argued in a letter to fellow Republican representative James Moody forwarded to Grimké, was based on a recent Supreme Court decision, *In re Neagle*. In their opinion, the Court decided that the attorney general of the United States had the authority to appoint a U.S. marshal to protect federal judges, and thus the use of force by that marshal in his duty was protected. "We hold it to be an incontrovertible principle," the Court opined, "that the government of the United States may, by means of physical force, exercised through its official agents, execute on every foot of American soil the powers and functions that belong to it. This necessarily involves the power to command obedience to its laws, and hence the power to keep the peace to that extent."[42]

Congressman White argued that this decision gave the federal government power to protect African Americans from violence. "I see no constitutional reason against applying the same power of protection to a citizen, as to an officer, of the United States."[43] And if the United States had the power to protect the lives and property of citizens outside of the country, then "why has it not," White asked, "the same power within the states?" While White affirmed that the general power of domestic regulation fell to the states, he did not believe that this prevented the federal government from acting within the states.

White concluded his argument by asserting that the federal government had the authority to prevent lynching based on the Fourteenth Amendment. "It is not a great stretch to hold that when a state suffers lynching, by not interfering or preventing it, it deprives the victim the equal protection of the laws. . . . It also suffers him to be deprived of life without due process of law, in violation of the due process clause."[44] White argued that while the Fourteenth Amendment prohibited states from making certain types of laws, it did not exclude the United States from exercising power within that state.

The impact of the league's letter to McKinley reached beyond the borders of the United States. Through his contacts as American consul in the Dominican Republic, Grimké took messages of outrage fomented in Bostonian meetings to an international audience. James L. Drew, the interpreter for the mayor of Adjuntas, Puerto Rico, responded to Grimké, praising the letter. "I must compliment you and other leaders of our oppressed race in those United States for the manly and fearless stand which you have made on the Negro Question of the South. . . . The pen is mightier than the sword, and men like you who know how to wield it ought so to do with the energy of your manhood in defense of an oppressed and long suffering people."[45] In addition to black men such as Grimké wielding the pen in messages to the president, black women, too, turned to literature to reach a broader audience and comment on the current state of black politics.

## Contending Forces and the Politics of Literature

In her 1900 novel *Contending Forces: A Romance Illustrative of Negro Life North and South*, Pauline Hopkins outlined her vision of the political dilemma facing

Shall The Race Have a Fair Chance?

# Contending Forces.

## A Romance of Negro Life

NORTH AND SOUTH

BY

### PAULINE E. HOPKINS,
The Popular Colored Writer.

*Author of "Talma Gordon," "General Washington," etc.*

With original illustrations and cover design by R. Emmett Owen.

Over 400 pages, 8vo.  Price, $1.50.

" *The civility of no race can be perfect whilst another race is degraded.*" — EMERSON.

A most fascinating story that is pre-eminently a race-work, dedicated to the best interest of the Negro everywhere. It holds you as by a spell, from start to finish.

A book that will arouse intense interest whenever shown, as it is the most powerful narrative yet published, of the wrongs and injustice perpetrated on the race. Startling in the array of facts shown and logical in the arguments it presents.

The incidents portrayed HAVE ACTUALLY OCCURRED, ample proof of which may be found in the archives of the Court House at Newbern, N. C., and at the seat of government at Washington, D. C.

The author tells an impartial story, leaving it to the reader to draw conclusions. She has presented both sides of the dark picture — lynching and concubinage — truthfully and without vituperation, introducing enough of the exquisitely droll humor peculiar to the Negro to give a bright touch to an otherwise gruesome subject.

It is a book that will not only appeal strongly to the race everywhere, but will have a large sale among the whites. The book mailed postpaid to any address on receipt of $1.50.

AGENTS WANTED EVERYWHERE.  LIBERAL COMMISSION.

Many of our Agents are making from $15.00 to $25.00 a week. You can do the same. Address at once for full particulars and special territory,

### The Colored Co-operative Publishing Company,
5 Park Square, BOSTON, MASS.

Advertisement for *Contending Forces, Colored American Magazine,* February 1901. (Yale Collection of American Literature, Beinecke Rare Book and Manuscript Library, Yale University.)

African Americans at the turn of the twentieth century. Hopkins wrote: "Conservatism, lack of brotherly affiliation, lack of energy for the right, and the power of the almighty dollar . . . are the forces which are ruining the Negro in this country. . . . These are the Contending Forces that are dooming this race to despair." Hopkins pointedly critiqued black political leaders who placed personal success and advancement over unified racial uplift. In her analysis, personal ambition and loyalty to the political parties contended with calls for sacrifice for the greater good of racial uplift and civil rights.

In September 1900, the Bostonian publisher of the new *Colored American Magazine,* the Colored Cooperative Company, printed a "Prospectus . . . of the New Romance of Colored Life, 'Contending Forces.' "[46] Describing Hopkins as "a woman of great versatility, deep thought, and wide scope of observation," the publisher advertised the book as a "race-work dedicated to the best interest of the Negro everywhere."[47] "The book," the publisher announced, "will certainly create a sensation among a certain class of 'whites' at the South, as well as awaken a general interest among our race, not only of this country, but throughout the world."[48] Hopkins read selections from the work before an audience at Josephine Ruffin's Woman's Era Club with "instant success," and the publisher encouraged readers to invite her to give readings in woman's clubs across the country. The publisher recruited clubwomen nationally as sales agents, assuring a wide distribution and prompt delivery. Their goal, the magazine announced, was "to place a copy of this work in every household in the United States."[49]

Through her novel and the *Colored American Magazine*, Hopkins sought to use literature to reach a wide audience. As one of the editors of the *Colored American* explained, "her ambition is to become a writer of fiction . . . in this way reaching those who never read history or biography."[50] She argued for the power of fiction as an instrument to shape public opinion and unite supporters of African American rights throughout the nation and the globe. "It is the simple, homely tale, unassumingly told, which cements the bond of brotherhood among all classes and all complexions. Fiction is of great value . . . as a preserver of manners and customs—religious, political, and social."[51] Her goals transcended mere romantic literary entertainment and personal recognition. "I am not actuated," she proclaimed, "by a desire for notoriety or for profit, but to do all that I can in [a] humble way to raise the stigma of degradation from my race."[52] Through the form and wide circulation of her novel, Hopkins pressed for an end to racial violence and advocated a policy of political independence in favor of racial unity and autonomy.

Hopkins, a Maine native who had spent several decades traveling the nation as a playwright and actress, arrived in Boston in the 1890s and became an active participant in political discussions. She joined the Colored National League and participated in debates in the Massachusetts Woman Suffrage Association. Spurred on by the reports of the horrors of southern lynching and the resistance to further black political gains in their home city, Hopkins turned to the written word to collect and disseminate a call for political action. Prior to beginning her life as a full-time writer, Hopkins secured a civil service position as a stenographer in the Massachusetts government, eventually passing the civil service examination and gaining a job as a stenographer in the census division of the Massachusetts Bureau of Statistics of Labor, the first of its kind in the nation. "Hopkins's work for white Republicans," Hopkins's biographer recognizes, "not only provided her with the opportunities to see firsthand the workings of state government, but it also gave her political credibility within the city's vibrant black political milieu."[53] Hopkins built upon her new political credentials as she continued to be highly active in African American political circles, even as she worked full time in her civil service capacity.[54]

Hopkins used her experience as source material for her novel, and captures the tumultuous politics of black Boston at the turn of the century. Although publishers marketed the manuscript as a romantic novel of black urban life, it contains significant critiques of the black politics that had played out in previous decades. In particular, she deftly portrays the conflicts between loyal black partisans and more radical leaders who refused to compromise on issues of civil rights. These debates were more than fiction; as a member of the Colored National League and the Woman's Era Club, Hopkins would have seen these debates firsthand, and likely contributed herself.

*Contending Forces* focuses on southern migrant Sappho Clark and her encounters with various members of Boston's black community. Through Sappho's contact with these men and women, Hopkins draws us into the homes, churches, and organizations of black Boston. While Hopkins takes her reader into places such as Sappho's boarding house, a woman's club meeting, and a benefit fair, she also spends several chapters focusing on John Langley, a black politician and lawyer, and the activities of the fictional American Colored League. Hopkins takes the time to lay out the conflicts and competing political strategies of Boston's activists. John Langley, "the colored politician," initially stands in fervent opposition to lynching and condemns Republican inaction. However, Langley moderates his position when offered a city office by a white politician, Herbert Clapp.[55] This moderate position is countered by Will Smith, the novel's hero, who takes a more radical stance against lynching and against black Republican loyalty. By the end of the novel, John Langley dies alone and disgraced, while Will Smith marries Sappho Clark and the novel concludes with the newly married couple and their family happily sailing to Europe. By contrasting the triumph of Smith with the utter failure of Langley, Hopkins powerfully endorses Smith's political position and condemns moderate and loyalist partisan politics.

In her account of Langley's confrontation with Herbert Clapp, Hopkins criticizes black partisanship and argues for black political independence and solidarity. Hopkins, through Langley, makes a pointed critique of the Republican government's inaction in preventing lynching. "Isn't it most time for the

Administration to take it up?" Langley asks Clapp.[56] The white politician responds that the government does not have the authority to stop lynching, and that doing so would trample on the rights of southern governments. Hopkins, however, refutes calls for moderation and calls on black voters to assert their power. Through her novel, Hopkins calls for African American voters to hold the political parties accountable and in the face of inaction, unify in opposition.

Again through Langley, Hopkins advocates breaking from the two parties and starting a new organization if necessary. "There are thirty-five thousand of us in this state alone," Langley explains. "We can be organized if the work is done by the right ones and in the right way. We can help start a new party, if nothing more."[57] Hopkins continues her attack on the Republican Party for its inaction in preventing lynching. "We expect to fight you one of these days, and knock the party clear over the ropes," Langley declares to Clapp. "There would be some satisfaction in throwing you fellows out and putting others in, if a new party is the outcome of the issue."[58] In her decision to have Langley so clearly condemn the Republican Party and to advocate not just African American political independence but the formation of a new party, Hopkins makes claims for the strength of black political organization and the power of black voters' uniting under a banner of racial solidarity rather than that of one of the current political parties.

In addition to depicting the discussion between Langley and Clapp, Hopkins critiques black politics through her fictionalization of the Colored National League. Hopkins describes an American Colored League "made up of leading colored men from all over New England."[59] In her portrayal of an American Colored League meeting, Hopkins illustrates the multiple sides of the debate over African American politics and antilynching strategy. She endorses policies of political autonomy and forceful agitation against appeals for moderation. One of the major characters who voices this sentiment is Judge Watson, the president of the league. Likely based on Edwin Garrison Walker, the president of the real Colored National League, Judge Watson calls for immediate agitation against lynching, and in particular calls for the shaping of public opinion.

Through Watson, who recalls the success of notable abolitionists, Hopkins connects challenges to lynching to the legacies of abolition. "This new birth of the black race is a mighty agony," Watson exclaims. "Agitation and eternal vigilance in the formation of public opinion were the weapons which broke the power of the slaveholder and gave us emancipation. I recommend these methods to you today, knowing their value in the past."[60] Through

Watson's call for "vigilance in the formation of public opinion," Hopkins not only endorses strategies of mass publicity in newspapers, but also argues for the use of serialized fiction and the novel to educate people and shape public attitudes to African American rights and against lynching.

Hopkins uses the characters Luke Sawyer and Will Smith to make direct calls for racial unity and immediate agitation. Through Luke Sawyer, a delegate from western Massachusetts and originally from Louisiana, Hopkins calls for agitation. Through Sawyer, she offers a pointed critique of the contemporary black political dilemma created by the conflict between racial unity, partisanship, and individual ambition. She makes a direct criticism of black male political leaders who placed personal success and advancement over unified racial uplift. Hopkins also uses Sawyer to press for agitation, even if that means resorting to physical resistance. She rebukes calls for moderation and passivity, making clear her advocacy of justice at any cost. "Gentlemen call for peace, and I reply," Sawyer proclaims, "'Peace if possible, justice at any rate.' . . . Contentment, amity . . . is impossible; justice alone remains to us."[61]

Through Will Smith, Hopkins continued her calls for direct action. Smith is likely based on W. E. B. Du Bois, who, like the character Smith, worked as a bellman in a Boston hotel and was educated in Germany.[62] Through Smith, Hopkins endorses universal agitation to change American public opinion. In Smith, she draws on the collective memory of antislavery activism, arguing, "As the anti-slavery apostles went everywhere, preaching the word fifty years before emancipation, *so must we do today*."[63] Echoing Hopkins in her justification for writing the novel, Smith concludes, "It is going to take time to straighten out this problem; it will only be done by the formation of public opinion. Brute force will not accomplish anything. We must *agitate*. . . . Appeal for the justice of our cause to every civilized nation under the heavens . . . until 'Ethiopia shall indeed stretch forth her hand, and princes come out of Egypt.'"[64] By connecting an abolitionist past with calls for mass agitation, Hopkins calls on African Americans to put aside their individual ambitions and partisanship to press, united, toward the shared goal of protected African American citizenship.

Although it is difficult to gauge the breadth of *Contending Forces*'s circulation, the Colored American Cooperative attempted to make it accessible to a wide audience. The announcement in the *Colored American Magazine* noted that advance sales "have been enormous, considering this to be her first work published in book form."[65] The cooperative sold copies for $1.50 and encouraged potential sales agents to purchase a fifty-cent "Agent's Outfit" that included a copy of the novel.[66] A letter from Alberta Moore Smith, president of the Colored Women's Business Club in Chicago, Illinois, to the *Colored American Magazine* praised the novel. "It is undoubtedly the book of the century," Smith wrote. "Ethiopia is stretching forth her arm in all branches of learning. . . . This book should be classed as one of the standard works of the day."[67] According to the *Colored American Magazine*, Hopkins's novel was a success, and she continued to use literature to advocate racial pride and black political mobilization. Hopkins pushed black women to speak out against lynching and racial oppression and publicly engage in the political sphere. She directly questioned political leadership and rejected working through existing party structures and instead advocated separate, black-led organizations to achieve goals of racial uplift.

## "The Graveyard of Our Hopes and Aspirations"

Despite the best efforts of the Colored National League, the federal government did not reform federal policy on lynching. The continued inaction on the part of the government and the major political parties led Edwin Garrison Walker to accept the nomination from the National Negro Party in time for the 1900 presidential election. Former Louisiana lieutenant governor P. B. S. Pinchback joined Walker at the top of the ticket as his running mate.

The platform for this short-lived new party focused on the preservation of the rights of all U.S. citizens without regard to race, color, or condition; opposition to monopolies; and federal government control of all public conveyances and telegraph and telephone operations. When Walker received news of his potential nomination, he reiterated the independent ideology of the National Negro Party. "I believe one of the principles of the party was for colored men either to refrain from voting or to vote for this new party," Walker explained. "There is a pretty general feeling among the colored people against the Republican Party."[68]

Although the party was not successful in its campaign, the creation of the National Negro Party represented a rejection of the major political parties and a faith in the organization of African Americans based on racial unity. In 1900, at one of his final public appearances, Walker again condemned federal inaction against southern violence and charged a younger generation of African Americans with asserting themselves against injustice. "It is a terrible thing," Walker declared, "to contemplate the condition of the Negro race today, outraged and murdered by the people of the South, but the South is not alone to blame. Ninety percent of these murders could have been averted had the United States Government acted. . . . You are citizens of the United States . . .

assert your manhood, that is the remedy."[69] Walker recognized the consequence of political independence, but remained unwavering in his commitment to put race first. "Faithfulness to the race will prove to most of us the
graveyard of our hopes and aspirations," Walker warned, "for the white man
will not forgive the Negro who paints his people as they are, and works devot-
edly for their elevation."[70] Walker steadfastly continued, "With this knowledge I accept the alternative gladly. I will never cease fighting our false friends
until death seals my lips eternally."[71] Walker made good on his promise.

Edwin Garrison Walker died of pneumonia on January 13, 1901. At his funeral, friends and fellow activists remembered his tireless efforts on behalf of
black people and his personal sacrifice for political independence. Hundreds
of mourners were turned away as a multiracial crowd of more than 1,500 men
and women packed to capacity the Charles Street AME Church to commemorate his life. Walker's body was carried to the church by members of the
Robert Gould Shaw Veterans Association, which Walker, a Civil War recruiter,
helped to found. Among the honorary pallbearers were members of Boston's
black political community with whom Walker had worked during his career.
They included the now elderly George T. Downing, the Colored National
League president I. D. Barnett, former state representative John J. Smith, and
founding member of the Niagara Movement and the NAACP Clement G.
Morgan. Irish lawyer Thomas Riley also joined the black mourners.[72]

Downing, in his eulogy, remembered Walker's sacrifice to maintain an independent political position and called upon the next generation to dedicate
themselves to the uplift of the race. Walker's independent stance, according
to Downing, "cost [him] more to stand up for his race than it did any other
colored man in this country. What did he care for political parties when the
rights of his race were at stake? He made the sacrifice of money and honor for
our people." "Young people," Downing continued, "only a few remain among
us who fearlessly fight our battles. Look out for your rights, for at this moment there are those who are planning to take away from our race those rights
which have been so nobly gained and given to us to keep."[73] Downing called
upon the audience to continue working for racial justice and not be over-
taken by selfish interest, even if that meant severe personal sacrifice.

At a special memorial meeting of the Colored National League, Archibald
Grimké lamented the loss of Walker and cast his eyes toward future generations to continue his fight. Walker sought the elevation of race over party, and
only then should African Americans "ever come by what appertains to us as
American citizens." Throughout his activism, Grimké told the crowd, Walker
called for "union among ourselves, and division of our votes between the two

great political parties." Grimké called on future generations to remember Walker and embrace the power of political independence as a tool for racial justice. "Walker is dead," he passionately reminded the audience, "but his manly and uncompromising devotion to his race lives after him. May we imitate him in the single-heartedness of his service and sympathy, and fall like him, when the time comes, sword in hand and with determined faces to the foe."[74] Calls for action upon Walker's death would not go unheeded. Though abandoned by false allies in party politics, black activists of the next century renewed calls for organization to represent and fight for the future of racial justice and equality. Unable to become full political citizens in an interracial party structure, they looked to the future as a new black nation.

# Conclusion

## *The Exploits and Sacrifices for the Education and Advancement of Ages Yet Unborn*

In 1901, Boston's *Colored American Magazine* published an article by Pauline Hopkins about the life of Edwin Garrison Walker. As part of her Famous Men of the Negro Race series, Hopkins acknowledged Walker as among the most influential forces in African American history and politics. "The exploits, the sacrifices of these men," Hopkins wrote, "were performed for the education and advancement of ages yet unborn, as well as for the present generation."[1] In particular, she celebrated Walker's refusal to give his loyalty to either of the major political parties, though it cost him personally. "Lawyer Walker could not brook the crack of the party whip when it commanded him to do violence to his own best promptings in the interest of his race. . . . Such things operated against his worldly advancement."[2] She declared that Walker had embodied an ideology that placed racial uplift over personal ambition and partisan loyalty. In her memorial to Walker, Hopkins celebrated his legacy of independent politics and sought to inspire further generations to follow his model.

The life and career of Walker frames the history of black independent politics from the end of the Civil War through the turn of the twentieth century. From the denunciation of the Fourteenth Amendment, through the black support he led for Benjamin Butler, Hugh O'Brien, and Grover Cleveland, African Americans attempted to hold the political parties accountable for their positions on civil rights and to forge new alliances. In the 1890s, as racial violence and disenfranchisement increased across the South, African Americans in Boston solidified their independent position, eventually rejecting the framework of partisan politics and facing the new century with new organizations and strategies that did not depend on official government structures.

In her memorial, Hopkins recounted Walker's life and his perpetual commitment to racial justice and independence. She celebrated his service in the state legislature and his opposition to the Fourteenth Amendment. Through their outspoken critique of early Reconstruction policies, Walker joined other black Bostonians in affirming their support for black voting rights nationally. Black Bostonians could vote relatively freely under Massachusetts law, but they saw their rights as bound up with those of black men and women in southern states. Indeed, in their debates over support for Grant or Greeley in 1872, African Americans always had one eye on the southern condition, even as they looked to local events. Further, in these early challenges, activists such as Walker gained clear insight into the ease with which political parties could compromise black rights for political expediency—a harbinger of the bleak future to come.

During the 1880s, independent politics seemed to gain traction as a strategy and as a national movement. Activists celebrated the elections of Benjamin Butler and Grover Cleveland. The successes of Butler and Cleveland, they hoped, would send a message to national party leadership that Republicans could not take black votes for granted. Further, they hoped it would show Democrats the advantage of courting black voters with moderate racial policies. African Americans sought further rewards for independent politics in their pursuit of patronage. While initially optimistic, independent supporters soon discovered the limits of their support. Some, including James Trotter, received political appointments, but most, including Walker, found their commitment to independence unrewarded, at great personal and professional cost.

In her praise for Walker, Hopkins also celebrated his cooperation with Boston's Irish community. Walker and black independents hoped to secure the support of Irish Americans through their own backing of the causes of Irish Home Rule and independence. Support for Irish nationalism combined with ideologies of independent politics in the successful election of Democrat Hugh O'Brien as Boston's first Irish-born mayor and the construction of the Crispus Attucks monument. The black and Irish alliance was an example of the successes that could be achieved by political independence, but, like their relationships with the national Democrats, its failure to turn into substantive change for black Bostonians reminded activists of the tenuousness of such relationships and the shallow commitment of white partners.

By the end of the 1880s, the optimism of the beginning of the decade appeared to have been misplaced. As violence against African Americans increased and the federal government failed to pass meaningful legislation preventing it and other attacks on black freedom, independents increasingly came to understand that their future depended on activism outside the strictures of party politics. In the formations of the Colored National League, the Massachusetts Racial Protective Association, and the Woman's Era Club, black Bostonians affirmed calls for racial solidarity. As organizations looked at the inaction of the federal government in the South, they grew increasingly disillusioned with both parties and instead advocated wholesale racial solidarity and political autonomy. Locally, the city redistricting in 1895 diluted black voting strength, decreasing black representation in the legislature and city council.[3] Although during the 1890s, black independents had continued to campaign for Democratic candidates and advocate electoral action, they increasingly positioned themselves beyond party politics. Race, not party, they argued, should be the only unifying political factor.

Ultimately, Boston's independent activists were unable to achieve their goal of making the Republican Party into a long-lasting advocate of black interests, or else turning the Democratic Party into a viable electoral alternative. Several reasons account for their defeat. First, the independent political movement was never able to garner the widespread support at either the local or national level that was necessary to be truly transformative. Despite their best efforts to organize a broad movement and connections among activists across the country, they were unable to unify a significant portion of the black electorate to leave their habitual home as Republican voters. Over the decades, they attempted to expand the independent base through enticement of patronage, alliance and sympathy with nationalist movements such as Ireland's, and collective outrage over lynching. Yet, they were unable to overcome the fear of abandoning the Republican ship. As it became clear by the end of the century, however, it was unlikely that leaving the Republican Party would have made a difference.

Independent politics ultimately failed because it placed too much faith in white-dominated political structures that were fundamentally uninterested in advancing the cause of African Americans. The power of white supremacy and interests other than African American rights gave black voters little sway, even if organized collectively. The lesson of independent politics was that the government and political parties were false friends that could not be depended on for further progress. It would take a mass movement working both inside and outside of the political system to pull all levers of power, electoral and judicial, and mobilize to effect meaningful change in the government and nation. The limited tools and tactics provided by partisan politics were not enough to counteract the multifront attacks from the armies of white supremacy.

Although independent politics itself was unsuccessful in bringing transformative change to the lives of black men and women, the spirit of autonomy and willingness to publicly reject the status quo and hold powerful supposed allies accountable laid valuable groundwork for the black freedom movement in the next century. A new generation of activists such as William Monroe Trotter, whose father James was a powerful black independent, would carry the mantle of uncompromising racial solidarity.[4] Trotter's and others' continued outspoken activism would inspire powerful leaders such as W. E. B. Du Bois, Trotter's classmate at Harvard, to take up more radical politics and ultimately forge new organizations including the Niagara Movement and the NAACP.[5] Without the burden of convincing white-dominated political parties to bend to their interests, black activists could better focus on issues of racial justice and advancing the cause of black freedom and equality. By the turn of the twentieth century, black Bostonians rejected Frederick Douglass's warning that all outside the Republican Party "was the sea."[6] Increasing numbers had left the Republican hull and were now traveling on crafts of their own making. No longer castaways, they were captains. As they traveled the turbulent waters of racial violence and Jim Crow, uncharted territory lay ahead, but they took solace in piloting their own ship and charting their own course. The light of freedom remained shining just over the horizon.

# Epilogue
## *The Boston Riot and the Legacy of Independent Politics*

In 1902, William Monroe Trotter, the son of influential Boston independent James Trotter, writing in the pages of his newspaper the *Guardian*, celebrated the final placement of a new headstone for Edwin Walker. A newly christened organization, the Edwin G. Walker Tabernacle of the Brothers and Sisters of Love and Charity, donated the new three-foot-tall monument of granite and Italian marble to mark his grave site in Cambridge's famous Woodlawn Cemetery.[1] Trotter himself honored his father's and Walker's lives and legacy by taking up the cause of black freedom and becoming one of its most outspoken leaders in the early twentieth century. In his activism he represented the departure from strict party politics as a vehicle for racial justice, and continued traditions of race-first organizing fomenting in Boston since the end of the Civil War.

One would be hard-pressed to find a more likely heir to the leadership of Boston's black independents than William Monroe Trotter. Born in 1872, William lived nearly all of his early life in Boston's South End; he remained in Boston even when his father took over as recorder of deeds in Washington, D.C. He grew up in and around Boston's leading politically active families. He was especially close to the family of Archibald Grimké, who by the late 1890s was an outspoken advocate of political independence. The elder Trotter demanded high educational performance from his children and enforced a radical political orthodoxy, going so far as to prohibit visits to the family home from opponents of political independence.[2]

Graduating as president of his high school senior class, William entered Harvard in 1891, the same year as his father's death from tuberculosis. Trotter excelled at Harvard and was elected to Phi Beta Kappa, a first for an African American, and graduated magna cum laude in 1895. After prospering, like his father, in real estate for several years, Trotter accelerated his racial activism at the turn of the century. Explaining his activism later in life, Trotter recalled, "The conviction grew upon me that pursuit of business, money, civic, or literary position was like building a house upon the sands, if race prejudice and persecution and public discrimination for mere color was to spread up from the South and result in a fixed caste of color."[3] Like his father, Trotter understood his personal success was undermined by continued racism in Boston and in the South especially.

In focusing on the plight of the South, Trotter came into immediate conflict with Booker T. Washington. He eschewed Washington's more conservative politics and condemned his public calls for African Americans to downplay political activism in favor of economic uplift. Trotter joined the Massachusetts Racial Protective Association and used his position as head of the committee on business and finance to denounce Washington.[4] As an outgrowth of this association, Trotter and like-minded colleagues founded the *Guardian* newspaper in November 1901, vowing "to protest forever against being proscribed or shut off in any caste from equal rights with other citizens."[5] Trotter used the pages of the *Guardian* to spread his race-first politics to a national audience and to denounce any attempt to compromise black rights. Like his father and the previous generation of black independents, Trotter believed that victory meant wholesale freedom and equality; there could be no half measures. Echoing the legacy of black independence, he declared, "The policy of compromise has failed . . . the policy of resistance and aggression deserves a trial."[6]

Trotter channeled this sentiment into a public confrontation with Washington during a 1903 meeting of the Boston branch of the National Negro Business League that would elevate Trotter and the legacy of black independence to the national stage, influencing the trajectory and shape of the twentieth-century black freedom struggle. During what became known as the Boston Riot, the actions of Trotter and other activists garnered national attention and bolstered their reputation as radical opponents of Washington-style conservatism. This marked a transition from the party-based independent politics of the nineteenth century to the more confrontational direct action of the twentieth.

Trotter and his so-called Boston Gang were prepared to confront Washington and denounce what they viewed as his collusion with white supremacist forces. The Boston meeting followed a contentious meeting of the Afro-American Council in Louisville, Kentucky, where the Bostonians earned a reputation for militancy and confrontation with pro-Washington forces.[7] Already high tensions overflowed into violence when Washington visited Boston in July 1903. In addition to Washington, Trotter and his allies also confronted former staunch political independent turned Washington supporter T. Thomas Fortune, District Attorney William H. Lewis, and lawyer Edward Everett Brown in what the press described as a "riotous scene."[8]

In front of a crowd of nearly 2000, anti-Washington voices challenged the speakers. Adding to the already tense environment, opponents tossed hot pepper onto the stage, reducing speakers and audience members to wheezing and coughing. As Washington took the stage, the meeting immediately devolved into a confusion of scuffles and fistfights.[9]

During the confrontation with Washington, Trotter attempted to read a series of questions he had prepared for the occasion. Trotter questioned Washington's advocacy of moderation and patience and challenged Washington's calls for black southerners to place civil and political rights secondary to economic or educational uplift. For Trotter, raised by a staunch independent and taught the value of the ballot from a young age, such advice was heresy. "Do you not know," Trotter asked Washington, "that the ballot is the only self-protection for any class of people in this country? . . . Are the rope and the torch all that the race is to get under your leadership?"[10]

Before Washington could respond, the evening broke down into chaos. "Surrounded by a struggling mass of angry people of his own race, in the confusion of fainting women and fighting men," the *Boston Daily Globe* reported, "Booker T. Washington met his first really hostile demonstration in Boston."[11] By the end of the night, at least one man had been stabbed, and Trotter's sister was alleged to have attacked a police officer with a hatpin.[12] Police stormed the venue to disperse the commotion, arresting Trotter and fellow activist Granville Martin. As the room cleared and the dust settled, Trotter and Martin were in jail facing charges of disturbing a public meeting; they would each receive a thirty-day sentence.[13] Washington, shaken but not deterred, finished his speech as planned.[14] Though ultimately unsuccessful at stopping Washington, Trotter and others had made an impact and showed the nation that they represented a black politics committed above all else to full, uncompromising equality. As the *Milwaukee Sentinel* reported, "[Washington] will hereafter believe that, however tractable and receptive the average negro may be, the Boston negro is not to be fooled with."[15]

Boston's black activists were outraged at the arrests and continued to denounce Washington and any political compromise. Acting outside of official party structures, activists remained committed to the use of the ballot as a weapon. Within a week of the riot, Archibald Grimké and others met at the imprisoned Trotter's home in Dorchester to form a Massachusetts branch of the Negro Suffrage League. "The start of the league," organizers declared, "is to consolidate the colored vote into an independent mass, to segregate the negro politically."[16] In the aftermath of the Boston Riot, the league declared its opposition to Washington. "Booker Washington," the organizers argued, "while pretending to be friend of the negro, has really traded with his power. He has declared for the disenfranchisement of negroes so that southerners might be pleased."[17] The league chose Trotter to be secretary and elected Grimké as president of the Boston branch. "We mean to throw the negro vote," Grimké declared, "to the side which will give us the most of it."[18]

The league celebrated Trotter's and Martin's release from jail in November 1903 and used the event to continue its condemnation of Washington and its advocacy of racial solidarity and independent action. Grimké declared, "If we voters in the North would protect the rights of the voters in the South we have got to be an independent party.... Our position must be like the Irish party in the English parliament.... Let us get rid of the everlasting talk of gratitude to any party."[19] Looking beyond false friends in white-dominated political parties, Grimké, Trotter, and others advocated race-based political organizing to attack the white supremacist political order of American government.

While Grimké and the Negro Suffrage League attempted to galvanize activists locally, the riotous scene at the Negro Business League meeting and the subsequent incarcerations had had a national impact and were significant in pushing W. E. B. Du Bois toward a more radical position. Du Bois was born in Great Barrington, Massachusetts, and was a classmate of Trotter's at Harvard University. Unlike his outspoken classmate, Du Bois was initially moderate in his criticisms of Washington and worked closely with him while at Atlanta University and Tuskegee. In 1903 Du Bois became more critical of Washington. First, with his publication of *The Souls of Black Folk*, which included the essay "Of Booker T. Washington and Others," Du Bois attacked Washington's endorsement of industrial education over agitation for voting and civil rights. And second, following the Boston Riot, Du Bois became a more outspoken opponent of Washington. Together, Du Bois's book and Trotter's riot are a pivotal juncture in black politics and the black freedom struggle in the new century. As historian and Du Bois biographer David Levering Lewis argues, "If the impact of *The Souls of Black Folk* on civil rights was like that of *Uncle Tom's Cabin* on slavery, then Trotter's Boston 'Riot' had its civil rights analogue in John Brown's raid on Harper's Ferry."[20] Both events struck a blow against moderation and compromise and sent the message that if African Americans were to succeed in their war against white supremacy, it was going to be with black leaders firmly in command. Trotter's actions and the aftermath pushed Du Bois toward the militancy that would define the rest of his long life and career.

The opposition of Trotter and others to Washington, coupled with Trotter's incarceration, had a profound effect on Du Bois. In a letter to Tuskegee trustee George Peabody, Du Bois expressed his measured support for Trotter. "While I did then and do now condemn the disturbance, I nevertheless admire

Mr. Trotter as a man and agree with him in his main contentions. . . . As between him and Mr. Washington I unhesitantly believe Mr. Trotter to be far nearer to the right."[21] For Du Bois, Trotter's incarceration was particularly egregious and proved the extent of Washington's power, and of what was at stake for those who dared to question or oppose him. "When Trotter went to Jail," Du Bois recalled in his 1940 autobiography, "my indignation overflowed."[22] Du Bois grew even more outspoken on the impact of the Boston Riot in his later recollections. In particular, in his posthumously published autobiography, he points again to the incarceration of Trotter, by "Washington's friends," as a major catalyst. "I was not privy to this occurrence," Du Bois recalled, "but the unfairness of the jail sentence helped lead me eventually to form the Niagara Movement, which later became the founding part of the NAACP."[23]

Trotter, Du Bois, and others opposed all calls for moderation and compromise, and in doing so, channeled the disappointment of black political independents into renewed collective action. While both Trotter and Du Bois would from time to time campaign for candidates, and continued to hold the right to vote sacrosanct, they refused to measure success in terms of electoral wins or losses, political appointments, or changes to partisan platforms. They mobilized beyond the confines of the formal electoral arena and placed allegiance to race, and a resolute commitment to full equality in all areas of civil, political, and social life, first and foremost. "We will not be satisfied to take one jot or title less than our full manhood rights," the founders of the Niagara Movement declared. "We claim for ourselves every single right that belongs to a freeborn American, political, civil, and social; and until we get these rights we will never cease to protest and assail the ears of America."[24]

The founders of the Niagara Movement, and later, the NAACP, continued to demand that African Americans guard the interests of the race over all other considerations. While the tactics and strategies shifted away from the more electorally focused commitment of earlier black independents, their unwavering commitment to organize autonomous challenges to the white supremacist status quo and defeat even supposed allies continued the traditions fostered by the lives and works of independent activists such as Edwin Garrison Walker, George Downing, and James Trotter. No longer the "graveyard of our hopes and aspirations," faithfulness to race first would prove to be the seedbed of black progress and a powerful weapon in the ongoing black freedom struggle.

# Acknowledgments

Writing this book has been a long journey, and its pages have been a constant companion during my travels across land and sea. From Boston, Massachusetts, to Ann Arbor, Michigan, to Washington, D.C., to Pittsburgh, Pennsylvania, to Lilongwe, Malawi, this book reflects and embodies stories not only of the past, which is its focus, but also of the places and people around whom it was written. The completion of this project would not have been possible if it were not for the inspiration, encouragement, and support of so many friends, family, and colleagues.

My knowledge of the past and of the African American freedom struggle was shaped deeply by my opportunities to learn from and work alongside some brilliant scholars and mentors, each of whom remains a powerful influence on my thinking. Davarian Baldwin guided this project in its infancy and not only helped me unlock the treasure trove of stories to tell about black Boston but also showed me the power and nuance of African American history and politics. This project would never have happened without the careful guidance and mentorship of Martha Jones. Her constant push to make the case for the relevance of this story and to seek new and uncommon archives shapes this book on every page. Her lessons on race and the law forced me to dive ever deeper to uncover stories not obvious on the surface. Finally, Joe Trotter gave me the confidence as a young scholar to believe that I had an important story to tell. His unwavering support, along with that of the Center for Africanamerican Urban Studies and the Economy at Carnegie Mellon University, helped shape the book manuscript from a patchwork of stories into a cohesive narrative. Joe showed me that history must be something that is not just for academics behind university walls, that it can have a powerful impact on the public. Additionally, David Quigley, Lynn Lyerly, Matthew Lassiter, Matthew Countryman, J. Mills Thornton, Kevin Gaines, William Novak, Rebecca Scott, and many others taught me how to study and interpret the lives and deeds of people in the past and tell their stories in a compelling way.

This book would be nothing but empty words were it not for the difficult work of maintaining and providing access to some outstanding archives. Special thanks to the staff at the Boston Athenaeum, the Burns Library at Boston College, the newspaper archives and manuscript collections at the Boston Public Library, Harvard University's Houghton Library, the Massachusetts State Library, and the National Archives in Washington, D.C. These archivists and librarians helped me navigate complex and often confusing record sets, and their assistance was immeasurable. John Hannigan and others at the Massachusetts Archives helped me unearth the words and works of the state's black legislators. The archivists and librarians at the Moorland-Spingarn Research Center at Howard University helped with unique manuscript collections and located rare copies of the *Hub* newspaper, originally thought lost. Kristen Swett and Marta Crilly were brilliant guides of the immense collections at the Boston City Archives and helped track down last-minute requests. Thanks also to the staff of the Library of Congress, which became my office as I finished final research and writing.

This book benefited immensely from my time as a research fellow at the Massachusetts Historical Society, which allowed me to spend countless hours in one-of-a-kind manuscript collections and surrounded by excellent scholars. Thanks especially to Conrad Wright and Kate Viens for their support and excellent guidance. I could not have completed this book without the additional financial support from the University of Michigan and Carnegie Mellon University.

Time spent in research and writing was punctuated by the opportunity to teach fantastic students and work alongside colleagues at some incredible institutions. Special thanks to my students and fellow faculty at the University of Michigan, George Mason University, and the University of Maryland.

Over the years, I have had the pleasure of building an intellectual community during conference panels, workshops, roundtables, and guest lectures related to this project. Especially important were the challenging and thought-provoking reflections from audience members and other panelists. In addition to many others, special thanks go to Kate Masur, Laura Edwards, Stephen Berry, Lisa Materson, Adam Rothman, Chandra Manning, Minkah Makalani, and Clarence Lang for their important feedback and encouragement of this project.

I was lucky over the course of this project to develop a strong community of scholars dedicated to the study of African American life and politics in the nineteenth century. We became kindred spirits, sharing insights and archival discoveries. Julie Davidow, Andrew Diemer, and Mary-Elizabeth Murphy, especially, form an important cohort of excellent scholars and friends. Thanks also to Aaron Cavin, Andrew Ross, Clay Howard, Ronit Stahl, Austin McCoy, Katie Rosenblatt, Aston Gonzalez, and many others who provided intellectual and social stimulation and support. Tim Corsi and Janelle Nanos deserve my eternal gratitude for opening their home to me on numerous, and often lengthy, research trips to Boston.

In the early stages of this manuscript both Stephen Kantrowitz and Shawn Alexander served as major guides of the historical and archival landscape. Both of their path-breaking studies laid the groundwork for this book, and they both provided immeasurable encouragement and endorsement for this project. Kantrowitz especially took time to read the manuscript several times over, and his comments and critiques helped shape the final version in both form and argument.

Working with the University of North Carolina Press has been an exciting and wonderful experience. Brandon Proia shepherded this project from the beginning, and his unwavering confidence in this story and my ability to tell it kept me writing, even though thousands of miles and many time zones separated us. Brandon is not just an outstanding editor, but is also a great friend. Annette Calzone and her hardworking team at Westchester Publishing Services provided meticulous copyedits and exhibited great patience with last-minute revisions.

No thank you is enough for Jen, who has lived with this project nearly as long as I have. Her support, sacrifice, and faith in me were tireless, even when it seemed at times like the work was never going to be done, and the payoffs were few and far between. Thank you also to Zora, who was not alive when this project began, but who provided much-needed distraction and comic relief during its conclusion. Millington Samuel joined our family just as this book was going to press and the publication of this story marks the beginning of his. Special thanks also go to Susan, my mother, for her continued love and pride in my work, and to Lisa, my sister, who lives the struggle for freedom and justice daily. Finally, this book is dedicated to my father, Millington, whose love of history and personal, quiet dedication to justice and equality led me down this path a long time ago. He never got the chance to be with me on this journey, but his memory and legacy are embodied in every word.

# Notes

## Introduction

1. "Fearless Leader Sleeps," *Boston Daily Globe,* January 17, 1901.
2. "Walker's Worth," *Boston Daily Globe,* February 2, 1901; Archibald Grimké, "Edwin Garrison Walker," Grimké Papers, box 39-19, folder 358.
3. "Walker's Worth."
4. Alexander, *Army of Lions,* xiv.
5. Beatty, *Revolution Gone Backward.*
6. On postwar Boston activism and connections to abolition, see Schneider, *Boston Confronts Jim Crow;* and Kantrowitz, *More Than Freedom.*
7. Recent studies of northern black politics include Schwalm, *Emancipation's Diaspora;* Materson, *For the Freedom of Her Race;* Alexander, *Army of Lions;* Kantrowitz, *More Than Freedom;* and Garb, *Freedom's Ballot.* For histories of southern politics and independent political movements, see Hahn, *Nation under Our Feet;* and Dailey, *Before Jim Crow.* See also Ali, *In the Balance of Power.*
8. Beatty, *Revolution Gone Backward;* Mouser, *For Labor, Race, and Liberty;* Taylor, *America's First Black Socialist.*
9. See Connolly, *Triumph of Ethnic Progressivism;* Erie, *Rainbow's End;* Schneirov, *Labor and Urban Politics.* Recent exceptions are Materson, *For the Freedom of Her Race;* and Kantrowitz, *More Than Freedom.*
10. Classic studies of African American urban life paid little attention to urban electoral politics. See Katzman, *Before the Ghetto;* Kusmer, *Ghetto Takes Shape;* Osofsky, *Harlem;* Spear, *Black Chicago;* Trotter, *Black Milwaukee;* and Wright, *Life behind a Veil.*
11. Gregory P. Downs, *Declarations of Dependence: The Long Reconstruction of Popular Politics in the South, 1861–1908* (Chapel Hill: University of North Carolina Press, 2011), 1.
12. Beatty, *Revolution Gone Backward,* 49.
13. Lewis, *W. E. B. Du Bois,* 28; Taylor, *America's First Black Socialist,* 11–12; Mouser, *For Labor, Race, and Liberty,* 148.
14. "Our Colored Citizens," *Boston Daily Globe,* October 31, 1883; "Walker Not Confirmed," *New York Age,* June 16, 1888.
15. For a discussion of the importance of "symbolic representation," see Pitkin, *Concept of Representation,* 92–111.
16. Beatty, *Revolution Gone Backward,* 61–91.
17. Ibid., xi.

*Part I*

1. Quoted in "The President and Colored Citizens," *Harper's Weekly*, June 22, 1872.

2. *Life and Times of Frederick Douglass*, 508.

3. Edwin G. Walker, Charles Remond, and George L. Ruffin attended as delegates. "Convention of Colored Men," *Boston Daily Globe*, March 29, 1872.

*Chapter One*

1. "The Black North," *New York Times*, December 8, 1901.

2. Horton and Horton, *Black Bostonians*, 1–6. For further discussion of the antebellum community, see Adelaide M. Cromwell, "The Black Presence in the West End of Boston, 1800–1864: A Demographic Map," in Jacobs, *Courage and Conscience*, 155–168; Kantrowitz, *More Than Freedom*.

3. Daniels, *In Freedom's Birthplace*, 461–462.

4. Thernstrom, *Other Bostonians*, 178–179. See also Pleck, *Black Migration and Poverty*, 20; Daniels, *In Freedom's Birthplace*, 458.

5. In the late nineteenth century, only Utica, New York, and Chicago, Illinois, were as segregated as Boston. Pleck, *Black Migration and Poverty*, 32. High home prices and racial discrimination likely contributed to this residential segregation. In 1890, for example, only 6 percent of black families owned their homes. Ibid., 33.

6. Ballou, "Even in 'Freedom's Birthplace'!", 32–48. With little change to the boundaries, Ward Six became Ward Nine in 1875.

7. Daniels, *In Freedom's Birthplace*, 268–270; Cromwell, *Other Brahmins*, 49.

8. *Reports of the Proceedings of the City Council of Boston, 1896* (Boston: n.p., 1897), 583–585.

9. Pleck, *Black Migration and Poverty*, 37–38.

10. Ibid., 41.

11. Ibid., 122, 128.

12. Ibid., 125; Daniels, *In Freedom's Birthplace*, 333–334.

13. Pleck, *Black Migration and Poverty*, 34.

14. Ibid.

15. Ibid., 51–52, 140.

16. Ibid., 25.

17. Ibid., 51–52.

18. Bergeson-Lockwood, "'We Do Not Care Particularly'"; Omori, "Race-Neutral Individualism."

19. "No Colored Persons Allowed on the Surface," *Hub*, August 11, 1883, quoted in Bergeson-Lockwood, "'We Do Not Care Particularly,'" 269–270.

20. Horton and Horton, *Black Bostonians*; Horton, *Free People of Color*; Horton and Horton, *In Hope of Liberty*.

21. Horton and Horton, *Black Bostonians*, 78–81; Bergeson-Lockwood, "'We Do Not Care Particularly'"; Omori, "Race-Neutral Individualism."

22. Fox, *Guardian of Boston*, 7.

23. T. Thomas Fortune, *T. Thomas Fortune*; Thornbrough, *T. Thomas Fortune*.

24. For a larger discussion on the African American public sphere, see Elsa Barkley Brown, "Negotiating and Transforming the Public Sphere: African American Political Life in the Transition from Slavery to Freedom," in Black Public Sphere Collective, *Black Public Sphere*, 111–150.

25. Kantrowitz, " 'Intended for the Better Government of Man.' "

26. During the antebellum period African Americans faced more difficulties voting. See Litwack, *North of Slavery*, 91–92.

27. Baum, *Civil War Party System*, 10–13.

28. Ibid., 15. See also Dobson, *Politics in the Gilded Age*; McGerr, *Decline of Popular Politics*; Summers, *Rum, Romanism, and Rebellion*.

29. George L. Ruffin, "Colored Voters, Boston—1864, First List after Emancipation, New and Old Voters," Ruffin Family Papers, box 87-1, folder 34, Manuscript Division, Moorland-Spingarn Research Center, Howard University; *Boston Directory for the Year Commencing July 1, 1864* (Boston: Adams, Sampson, 1865). It is difficult to get an exact number of black voters in Boston after 1867, when, after petitions from black Bostonians, the state removed all racial designations from the tax and voting rolls.

30. Hairston and Massachusetts Black Caucus, *Blacks on Beacon Hill*.

31. Ibid., 84; State Library of Massachusetts, *Black Legislators*.

32. Handlin, *Boston's Immigrants*; O'Connor, *Boston Irish*; Ryan, *Beyond the Ballot Box*; Schneider, *Boston Confronts Jim Crow*.

33. Hopkins, "Edwin Garrison Walker"; Schneider, *Boston Confronts Jim Crow*, 167–168.

34. Shaw, "Black Club Women," 11.

35. See Kenneally, "Woman Suffrage and the Massachusetts 'Referendum.' " For more on African American woman suffrage in the nineteenth century, see Baum, "Woman Suffrage and the 'Chinese Question' "; DuBois, *Feminism and Suffrage*; DuBois, *Woman Suffrage and Women's Rights*; Gordon and Collier-Thomas, *African American Women and the Vote*; Terborg-Penn, *African American Women in the Struggle*.

## Chapter Two

1. "Convention of Colored People of New England, Boston, December 1, 1865," in Foner and Walker, *Proceedings*, 201.

2. Ibid., 204.

3. Ibid., 204–205.

4. Petition of Benjamin F. Roberts and others that the designation of "Colored" may be omitted on the City Tax Bills and Voting Lists, February 11, 1867, Board of Aldermen Docket Documents, City of Boston Archives; "Report of the Special Committee of the Common Council of Boston," February 25, 1867, *The Minutes of the Mayor and Aldermen*, City of Boston Archives.

5. Malone, *Between Freedom and Bondage*, 154; Baum, *Civil War Party System*, 10–13. The Massachusetts constitution granted African Americans the right to vote in 1780,

although the state continued to impose restrictions based on age and literacy. It also levied a poll tax.

6. Kantrowitz, *More Than Freedom*, 318.

7. Ibid.; "The Republican Meetings in This City," *Boston Evening Transcript*, November 1, 1866.

8. "Election Day and Evening in and around Boston," *Boston Daily Advertiser*, November 7, 1866; "The Colored Members," *New York Times*, January 3, 1867.

9. *Boston Daily Advertiser*, November 2, 3, 1866; "Republican Representative Caucuses," *Boston Evening Transcript*, November 1, 1866.

10. Kantrowitz, *More Than Freedom*, 318; "Ward Six," *Boston Daily Evening Transcript*, November 2, 1866; "To the Republican Voters of Ward Six," *Boston Daily Evening Transcript*, November 5, 1866.

11. *Boston Daily Advertiser*, November 3, 1866.

12. "Election Day and Evening in and around Boston."

13. Ibid.

14. Although there is some controversy in the historical record over Walker's exact birthdate, press reports identified Edwin as David's son until his death in 1901: see Contee, "Edwin Garrison Walker," 556; Hinks, *To Awaken My Afflicted Brethren*, 269–271; Hairston and Massachusetts Black Caucus, *Blacks on Beacon Hill*; Hopkins, "Edwin Garrison Walker"; "Death of the Foremost Colored Lawyer in New England," *Colored American Magazine* (February 1901): 219; "Loved His Race," *Boston Daily Globe*, January 14, 1901; "Active Life Ended," *Boston Journal*, January 15, 1901; and "A Negro Legislator," *Chicago Tribune*, November 20, 1866.

15. Contee, "Edwin Garrison Walker," 556–559; Horton and Horton, *Black Bostonians*, 61.

16. "Republican Representative Nominations," *Boston Evening Transcript*, November 1, 1866; "Republican Caucuses," *Charlestown Advertiser*, November 3, 1866.

17. "Republican Nominations," *Boston Evening Transcript*, November 5, 1866.

18. "The Republicans in Ward Three," *Charlestown Advertiser*, November 3, 1866.

19. Ibid.

20. "The Colored Members," *New York Times*, January 3, 1867; "Colored Representatives," *Right Way*, November 17, 1866.

21. "The Colored Members." The Fenians were a militant group of Irish nationalists. The event referred to here is the June 1865 invasion by the Fenians of Canada.

22. "The Colored Delegation," *Charlestown Advertiser*, November 10, 1866.

23. "The Colored Members."

24. Kantrowitz, *More Than Freedom*, 320.

25. "Election Day," *Boston Daily Advertiser*, December 11, 1866.

26. "Ward Three," *Boston Daily Advertiser*, December 12, 1866.

27. *Boston Daily Advertiser*, December 14, 1866.

28. "The Councilman Vacancy in Ward Three," *Boston Daily Advertiser*, February 2, 1867.

29. "Colored Representatives," *Right Way*, November 17, 1866.

30. "Colored Men in the Massachusetts Legislature," *Commonwealth,* quoted in *Right Way,* November 17, 1866.

31. Editorial, *Boston Daily Advertiser,* November 16, 1866.

32. "Colored Representatives."

33. Foner, *Reconstruction,* 251–261; Wang, *Trial of Democracy,* 25–28.

34. McPherson, *Struggle for Equality,* 351, 355.

35. "The Amendment to the National Constitution," *Boston Daily Advertiser,* January 25, 1867.

36. "Remonstrance of Henry T. Cheeves, George F. Hoar, Ichabod Washburn, and One Hundred Others, Citizens of Worcester, Against the Adoption of the Constitutional Amendment"; "Petition of Christopher Bryant and Fifty-five Others, Citizens of Worcester, Against the Adoption of the Constitutional Amendments"; "Petition of E. Cady Stanton, Lucy Stone, and Others, Committee Am. Equal Rights Association, Relating to the Constitutional Amendment"; "Remonstrance of Richard T. Buck and Others, Citizens of Millbury, Against the Ratification of the Constitutional Amendment"; "Remonstrance of Rev. L. A. Grimes, and Others of Boston Against the Passage of the Constitutional Amendment"; "Remonstrance of Samuel A. Collins and Forty Others of Fitchburg Against the Ratification of the Const. Amendment"; "Memorial of Richard T. Buck and Others Against the Adoption of the Proposed Amendment to the Constitution of the United States," 1867, Passed Resolves, SC1/Series 228, Massachusetts Archives; McPherson, *Struggle for Equality,* 373.

37. Horton and Horton, *Black Bostonians,* 43, 58–59, 60–61, 65–66.

38. "Remonstrance of Rev. L. A. Grimes, and Others." Another petition with the same language was submitted by Edwin Garrison Walker on behalf of Worcester residents; see "Petition of Christopher Bryant and Fifty-five Others."

39. Foner, *Reconstruction,* 469. Francis Bird was part of an influential group of Radical Republicans, known as the "Bird Club," that controlled much of Massachusetts politics in the 1860s.

40. Comm. on Federal Relations, Constitutional Amendment, H.R. Rep. No. 147, at 22 (1867); McPherson, *Struggle for Equality,* 374. At the time of the publication of the majority report from the Committee on Federal Relations on February 27, 1867, twenty former Union states had successfully ratified the amendment: Maine, New Hampshire, Vermont, Rhode Island, Connecticut, New York, New Jersey, Pennsylvania, Ohio, Michigan, Indiana, Illinois, Wisconsin, Minnesota, Missouri, Kansas, Oregon, Nevada, Tennessee, and West Virginia. Every former Confederate state (except Tennessee), Delaware, and Kentucky rejected it; and Massachusetts, Iowa, California, and Maryland had not yet made a decision.

41. H.R. Rep. No. 149, at 1 (1867).

42. Ibid., at 17 (1867). The amendment excluded "Indians and those not taxed" from the population for proportional representation.

43. U.S. Const. amend. XIV, § 2.

44. H.R. Rep. No. 149, at 9 (1867).

45. Ibid., at 18 (1867).

46. Ibid., at 6 (1867).

47. Ibid., at 8 (1867).

48. Ibid., at 17 (1867).

49. Ibid.

50. Ibid.

51. Ibid., at 23–24 (1867).

52. "Massachusetts Legislature," *Boston Daily Advertiser*, March 13, 1867.

53. Ibid.

54. Ibid.

55. Ibid.

56. *Journal of the House of Representatives of the Commonwealth of Massachusetts* [Boston: n.p., 1867], 529–530, 202). *Boston Daily Advertiser*, March 15, 1867.

57. *Boston Daily Advertiser*, October 31, 1867.

58. "Charlestown," *Boston Daily Advertiser*, November 6, 1867. Walker lost again in 1868. According to press reports, the Temperance Party voted against him. "Election Incidents," *Boston Evening Transcript*, November 4, 1868.

59. "Loved His Race," *Boston Daily Globe,* January 14, 1901; Hopkins, "Edwin Garrison Walker."

60. Hopkins, "Edwin Garrison Walker," 363.

61. U.S. Const. amend. XVI, § 1.

62. Foner, *Reconstruction*, 447.

63. *Journal of the House of Representatives of the Commonwealth of Massachusetts* (Boston: n.p., 1869), 224–227; S. Doc. No. 98 (1869); Comm. on Federal Relations, S. Doc. No. 105 (1869).

64. "The Fifteenth Amendment," *Boston Daily Advertiser*, April 15, 1870.

65. Ibid.

66. Simmons, *Men of Mark*, 740–743; Cromwell, *The Other Brahmins*, 54.

67. "The Fifteenth Amendment."

68. Ibid. This article misidentifies Walker as "David Walker, from Charlestown."

69. Ibid.

70. Ibid.

71. These statements from Walker are interesting, especially as he had been elected to office only three years earlier. Perhaps the controversy over his election and his opposition to the Fourteenth Amendment influenced his sentiments.

72. "The Fifteenth Amendment."

73. Ibid.

74. Ibid.

75. Ibid.

76. Ibid.

77. Ibid.

78. Ibid.

## Chapter Three

1. "The Colored Convention," *Boston Daily Globe*, September 6, 1872.

2. Kantrowitz, *More Than Freedom*, 367–372.

3. Foner, *Reconstruction*, 500; Baum, *Civil War Party System*, 170.

4. Ibid., 498; Richardson, *Death of Reconstruction*, xii–xv.

5. Foner, *Reconstruction*, 506.

6. Ibid., 447. This was partly due to northern interests protecting local restrictions on voting. For example, Massachusetts limited voting based on literacy.

7. Baum, *Civil War Party System*, 168–170.

8. Grossman, *Democratic Party and the Negro*, 36–37, 40–41.

9. Foner, *Reconstruction*, 506–509. For more on Sumner's support of Greeley, see James McPherson, "Grant or Greeley?"; and David Quigley, "Charles Sumner and the Political Cultures of Reconstruction in New England," in O'Toole and Quigley, *Boston's Histories*, 113–123.

10. Grossman, *Democratic Party and the Negro*, 39.

11. An Act to Enforce the Provisions of the Fourteenth Amendment to the Constitution of the United States, and for Other Purposes, ch. 22, 17 Stat. 13; Foner, *Reconstruction*, 454–455.

12. Lewis Hayden to Benjamin Butler, April 21, 1871, Benjamin Butler Papers, Library of Congress (hereafter cited as Butler Papers).

13. Ibid. See also Cong. Globe, 41st Cong., 1st Sess. 651.

14. *The Negro in Politics: Review of Recent Legislation for His Protection—Defense of the Colored Man against All Accusers* (Lowell, MA: Marden and Rowell, 1871), 8, Butler Papers.

15. Ibid., 9.

16. Ibid., 10.

17. Ibid., 13–14.

18. Ibid., 18.

19. Ibid., 19.

20. Nell also mentions that Butler assisted him with information for his book, *Colored American Patriots of the Revolution and the Rebellion*. William C. Nell to Butler, May 8, 1871, Butler Papers.

21. G. M. Brown to Butler, September 15, 1871, Butler Papers.

22. "The Disgraceful Scene . . . ," *Boston Daily Advertiser*, September 21, 1871.

23. "The Sixth Ward," *Boston Daily Advertiser*, September 22, 1871.

24. "Republican Caucuses in Boston," *Boston Daily Advertiser*, September 21, 1871.

25. Kantrowitz, *More Than Freedom*, 370.

26. "Republican Caucuses in Boston."

27. "Republican Ward Meetings," *Boston Post*, September 21, 1871.

28. "Republican Caucuses in Boston."

29. Ibid.

30. "Our Colored Citizens," *Boston Post*, September 23, 1871.

31. Kantrowitz, *More Than Freedom*, 371.

32. Ibid., 372.

33. Foner, *Reconstruction*, 506–507.

34. "Convention of Colored Men," *Boston Daily Globe*, March 29, 1872.

35. Ibid.

36. Ibid.

37. Ibid.

38. Ibid.

39. Ibid.

40. Ibid.

41. Ibid.

42. Ibid. Central State Committee: Robert Morris, George L. Ruffin, A. R. Lewis, Lewis Hayden, and J. M. Mulligan, Boston; Milton Clark and R. J. Fatall, Cambridgeport; Edwin G. Walker, Charlestown; William Brown, Worcester; W. R. Montague, Springfield; John Freedom and Andrew Bush, New Bedford; Samuel Bowman, Taunton; Joel W. Lewis, Chelsea; George W. Queen, Springfield; Ottway West, Lynn; and Horace B. Proctor, Lowell.

43. "Republican Rally," *Boston Daily Globe,* July 24, 1872.

44. Ibid.

45. Ibid.

46. Ibid. "Bring forth fruit meet for repentance" is a reference to the biblical passage, "Bring forth therefore fruits meet for repentance" (Matt. 3:8, King James Version).

47. Ibid.

48. Ibid.

49. Ibid.

50. "Politics in Ward VI," *Boston Daily Globe*, August 29, 1872.

51. Ibid.

52. "The Greeley Club in Ward XI," *Boston Daily Globe*, September 4, 1872.

53. This is similar to Sumner's complaints about Grant; see Foner, *Reconstruction*, 506–507.

54. "The Greeley Club in Ward XI."

55. Ibid.

56. "Meeting of the Colored Republicans of Ward VI," *Boston Daily Globe*, August, 15, 1872; "Address to the Colored Citizens," *Boston Daily Globe*, August 17, 1872.

57. "Address to the Colored Citizens."

58. Ibid.

59. "The Colored Convention."

60. Ibid.

61. Ibid. For more on John Langston, see Cheek and Cheek, *John Mercer Langston*.

62. Grossman, *Democratic Party and the Negro*, 39.

63. Simmons, *Men of Mark*, 1003–1006; Grossman, "George T. Downing and Desegregation."

64. "George T. Downing Declares for Grant and Wilson," *New York Times*, August 18, 1872; Grossman, *Democratic Party and the Negro*, 38–39.

65. Grossman, *Democratic Party and the Negro*, 42–43.

66. "The Voting Today," *Boston Daily Globe*, November 5, 1872; "Ward Six," *Boston Daily Globe*, November 6, 1872; "The Election," *Boston Daily Globe*, November 6, 1872; *Guide to U.S. Elections*, 1:686.

67. "Vote of Boston," *Boston Daily Globe*, November 6, 1872.

68. "Ward Six."

69. Foner, *Reconstruction*, 509; Baum, *Civil War Party System*, 172–173.

70. Richard Abbot, "Massachusetts: Maintaining Hegemony," in Mohr, *Radical Republicans in the North*, 22.


Part II

1. Editorial, *Boston Daily Globe*, August 18, 1882.

2. "The Negro and the Republican Party," *Boston Daily Globe*, August 20, 1882.

3. Ibid.


Chapter Four

1. "The State Campaign: Interview with a Prominent Colored Man," *Boston Daily Globe*, September 23, 1879.

2. Ibid.

3. "Dissatisfied Colored Men," *Boston Daily Globe*, October 5, 1877.

4. Foner, *Reconstruction*, 469–499.

5. Omori, "Race-Neutral Individualism"; Kantrowitz, *More Than Freedom*.

6. "General Butler and the Colored People," *Boston Daily Globe*, March 18, 1875.

7. Richard Harmond, "The 'Beast' in Boston: Benjamin F. Butler as Governor of Massachusetts," *Journal of American History* 55, no. 2 (September 1968): 266.

8. "Butler and the Colored Men," *Boston Daily Globe*, September 2, 1878.

9. Ibid.

10. *Record of Votes by Precinct*, 1878 and 1879, City of Boston Archives.

11. For example, in the 1880 and 1881 elections Democratic candidate Charles P. Thompson earned only 26 percent and 16 percent of the vote in Precinct Three, respectively. *Record of Votes by Precinct*, 1880 and 1881, City of Boston Archives.

12. "Bulldozing at Home," *Boston Daily Globe*, January 6, 1879.

13. Ibid.

14. Ibid.

15. Ibid.

16. Ibid.

17. "The Colored Republicans," *Boston Daily Advertiser*, October 1, 1879.

18. "In the Ninth Ward," *Boston Daily Globe*, October 1, 1879.

19. Ibid.

20. "The Colored Republicans."

21. "In the Ninth Ward."

22. *Record of Votes by Precinct*, 1882, City of Boston Archives.

23. "Independent Colored Voters," *Boston Daily Globe*, October 27, 1882.

24. Ibid. See also Grossman, *Democratic Party and the Negro*, 77–79.

25. "Butler and the Colored People," *Boston Daily Advertiser*, November 7, 1882.

26. Ibid.

27. Harmond, "The 'Beast' in Boston." See also Benjamin Butler, *Autobiography and Personal Reminiscences of Major-General Benjamin Butler–Butler's Book: A Review of His Legal, Political, and Military Career* (Boston: A. M. Thayer, 1892), 968–981; Trefousse, *Ben Butler*, 244–250; Holzman, *Stormy Ben Butler*, 217–223.

28. "Black Republicans," *Boston Daily Globe*, September 18, 1883.

29. See Summers, *Press Gang*; McGerr, *Decline of Popular Politics*, 14–22.

30. "Our Purpose and Position," *Hub*, August 25, 1883.

31. "Editor of the *Hub*," *Hub*, August 4, 1883.

32. E. D. Sanborn to John F. Andrew, November 30, 1883, John F. Andrew Papers, Massachusetts Historical Society.

33. "Prospectus," *Hub*, July 14, 1883.

34. "Our Purpose and Position."

35. "Nuts to Crack," *Hub*, August 18, 1883.

36. "Notice, Colored Voters!," *Hub*, August 4, 1883.

37. "Don't Those Colored Independents . . . ," *Hub*, November 24, 1883. See also "Wise and Otherwise," *Hub*, September 29, 1883.

38. "Vox Populi," *Hub*, September 1, 1883.

39. "Notice, Colored Voters!"

40. Ibid.

41. Ibid.

42. "The Colored Vote," *Boston Herald*, quoted in *Hub*, August 4, 1883.

43. "Mr. Editor," *Hub*, August 18, 1883. Hayden may have been influential in organizing the *Hub*. In June 1883, he proposed purchasing the anti-Republican *Boston Leader*, with Butler Wilson as the new editor, for use as an anti-Butler publication. It is unknown if this paper became the *Hub*. Lewis Hayden to John D. Long, June 17, 1883, John D. Long Papers, Massachusetts Historical Society.

44. "The Democracy," *Hub*, September 1, 1883.

45. "Where We Stand," *Hub*, July 14, 1883.

46. Harmond, "The 'Beast' in Boston," 270.

47. "The Colored Vote."

48. Ibid.

49. "Where Is the Loss?," *Hub*, August 11, 1883.

50. Ibid.

51. "Letter from Dr. Still," *Hub*, September 8, 1883.

52. Ibid.

53. Ibid.

54. "Our Hub Letter—Colored Men of Massachusetts in Council," *New York Globe*, September 22, 1883.

55. "An Important Conference," *Hub*, September 8, 1883.

56. "Our Hub Letter," September 22, 1883; "The Colored Men," *Boston Daily Advertiser*, September 18, 1883; "An Important Conference."

57. "Our Hub Letter," September 22, 1883; "The Colored Men."

58. "Colored Men in Conference," *Hub*, September 22, 1883.

59. Ibid.

60. Ibid.

61. "Our Hub Letter," September 22, 1883. This sentiment was echoed in a letter to the *Boston Daily Advertiser*; see "Butler and the Colored Men."

62. "Our Hub Letter," September 22, 1883.

63. Fox, *Guardian of Boston*, 1–13; Schneider, *Boston Confronts Jim Crow*, 109–110; Cromwell, *Other Brahmins*, 48; Daniels, *In Freedom's Birthplace*, 99.

64. "National Convention," *New York Globe*, September 29, 1883.

65. "Mr. Trotter's Statement," *New York Globe*, September 29, 1883.

66. Ibid.

67. Ibid.

68. "Colored Independents," *Boston Daily Globe*, September 27, 1883.

69. Ibid.; "Our Hub Letter," *New York Globe*, October 6, 1883.

70. *Class Memoir of George Washington Warren* (Boston: n.p., 1886).

71. Benjamin Butler, *Butler's Book*, 974.

72. George Washington Williams, "May It Please Your Honor," *New York Globe*, December 15, 1883.

73. "Our Hub Letter," *New York Globe*, August 11, 1883; "The Charlestown Judgeship," *Hub*, September 8, 1883.

74. "Our Hub Letter," August 11, 1883; "Our Hub Letter," *New York Globe*, August 25, 1883.

75. Governor's Council, Executive Records, 1879–1883, vol. 92, Massachusetts Archives (hereafter cited as Executive Records).

76. Grossman, *Democratic Party and the Negro*, 78; Charles E. Sweeny to Benjamin Butler, May 21, 1883; Joseph H. Carter to Butler, May 23, 1883; Lula Mulliken to Butler, May 22, 1883; George H. Murray to Butler, August 3, September 13, 1883; Charles E. Abbot to Butler, September 1883; Solomon Bancroft to Butler, September 3, 1883; Edward Hamilton to Butler, September 3, 1883; John W. Mahan to Butler, September 3, 1883; George W. Searle to Butler, August 30, 1883; J. Edward Bates to Butler, August 29, 1883; J. W. Converse to Butler, August 29, 1883; Edward L. Jenkins to Butler, August 22, 1883; Clarence B. Lord to Butler, August 23, 1883; N. B. Bryant to Butler, September 4, 1883; Charles E. Gibbs to Butler, September 8, 1883; John Brown to Butler, September 3, 1883. Executive Department Letters, vol. 246, District, Municipal, and Police Courts, G01/Series 567x, Massachusetts Archives (hereafter cited as Executive Department Letters).

77. "The Silver-Tongued," *Boston Daily Globe*, September 13, 1883.

78. "*The Hub* and Judge Walker," *Hub*, September 22, 1883.

79. "The Silver-Tongued."

80. West, *Lincoln's Scapegoat General*, 374; Grossman, *Democratic Party and the Negro*, 78; Holzman, *Stormy Ben Butler*, 217.

81. "Mr. Walker and the Committee," *Boston Daily Globe*, September 16, 1883.

82. Ibid.

83. "State Political Topics," *Boston Daily Globe*, September 29, 1883; "Mr. Walker's Nomination," *Boston Daily Globe*, October 1, 1883, "Mr. Walker and the Council," *Boston Daily Globe*, October 2, 1883.

84. "Is It a Conspiracy!," *Boston Daily Globe*, October 14, 1883.

85. John Brown to Benjamin Butler, September 3, 1883; Charles E. Gibbs to Butler, September 8, 1883, Executive Department Letters; "Our Hub Letter," September 22, 1883; "Simmons and Walker," *Boston Daily Globe*, October 23, 1883; George T. Downing, "A Leader in His Race," *Boston Daily Globe*, October 23, 1883.

86. "Is It a Conspiracy!"

87. "Mr. Walker Rejected," *Boston Daily Globe*, October 6, 1883.

88. "Mr. Walker Rejected."

89. Ibid.; see also "Mr. Walker's Rejection," *Boston Daily Globe*, October 6, 1883.

90. "Mr. Walker Rejected."

91. Executive Records.

92. "The Blow at the Colored Men," *Boston Daily Globe*, October 7, 1883.

93. "Indignant Colored Citizens," *Boston Daily Globe*, October 14, 1883.

94. Editorial, *New York Globe*, October 13, 1883.

95. "Mr. Walker Rejected."

96. "Mr. Walker Rejected"; "The Blow at the Colored Men."

97. "A Colored Voter Speaks," *Boston Daily Globe*, October 8, 1883.

98. "Colored Men Booming for Butler," *New York Globe*, November 3, 1883.

99. "Colored Republicans," *Boston Daily Globe*, October 30, 1883.

100. Ibid.; "Our Hub Letter," *New York Globe*, November 3, 1883.

101. "An Aroused People," *Hub*, October 20, 1883.

102. "The Issue," *Hub*, October 27, 1883.

103. Ibid.

104. "Our Colored Citizens," *Boston Daily Globe*, October 31, 1883.

105. Ibid.

106. Ibid.

107. Ibid.

108. Ibid.

109. Ibid.

110. Ibid.

111. Ibid.

112. Ibid.

113. "Ward Nine," *Hub*, October 6, October 13, October, 20, 1883.

114. "The Eve of Battle," *Hub*, November 3, 1883.

115. Ibid.

116. "Our Hub Letter," November 3, 1883.

117. *Guide to U.S. Elections*, 2:1502.

118. *Municipal Register: Containing the City Charter, the Rules and Orders of the City Council, and a List of the Officers of the City of Boston for the Year 1884* (Boston: n.p., 1884), 218; *Record of Votes by Precinct*, 1883, City of Boston Archives; "Robinson Wins!," *Boston Daily Globe*, November 7, 1883.

119. *Record of Votes by Precinct*, 1883.

120. "Victory!," *Hub*, November 10, 1883.

121. "Balance," *Hub*, November 10, 1883.

122. "Victory!"

123. "Our Hub Letter," *New York Globe*, November 17, 1883.

124. James M. Trotter, "The Latest Contest in Massachusetts," *New York Globe*, November 17, 1883.

125. Harmond, "The 'Beast' in Boston," 277.

126. "The Charlestown Judgeship," *Hub*, November 10, 1883; "Our Hub Letter," November 17, 1883; "The Executive Council," *Boston Daily Advertiser*, November 8, 1883; Executive Records.

127. "Our Hub Letter-Governor Butler's Defeat," *New York Globe*, November 10, 1883.

128. "Mr. Ruffin's Confirmation," *Boston Daily Globe*, November 20, 1883. Yet, the records of the official letters to the governor do not include any letters endorsing Ruffin, as they do for Walker, and the timing of the nomination suggests it was done quickly. If indeed Walker was rejected because of his support of a Democratic candidate, then Ruffin's Republicanism likely accounts for his being approved easily.

129. "Judge Ruffin," *Hub*, November 24, 1883.

130. "The Outlook," *Hub*, November 24, 1883.

131. "Judge Ruffin Dined," *Boston Daily Globe*, November 23, 1883; "Our Hub Letter," *New York Globe*, December 1, 1883.

132. "Our Hub Letter," *New York Globe*, December 8, 1883.

133. Editorial, *New York Globe*, February 16, 1884.

134. "Our Hub Letter," December 8, 1883; "Colored Men Organizing: The Sumner National Independents—Their Officers and Objects," *Boston Daily Globe*, November 28, 1883; "The Sumner Independents," *Boston Daily Globe*, November 28, 188; Penn, *Afro-American Press and Its Editors*, 360.

135. "Colored Men Organizing."

136. Ibid.

*Chapter Five*

1. Edwin Garrison Walker to Grover Cleveland, February 1, 1886, Grover Cleveland Papers, Library of Congress (hereafter cited as Cleveland Papers); "Street's Boston Letter," *New York Globe*, February 6, 1886.

2. Walker to Cleveland, February 1, 1886.

3. Ibid.

4. This strategy was best enunciated by George T. Downing; see "The Colored Man's Hour," *New York Globe*, February 9, 1884.

5. "Colored Men Organizing: The Sumner National Independents—Their Officers and Objects," *Boston Daily Globe*, November 28, 1883.

6. "What's in a Name!," *Hub*, December 8, 1883.

7. "Some Plain Talk," *Hub*, January 19, 1884.

8. "What's in a Name!"

9. "Some Plain Talk"; "What's in a Name!"

10. "Colored Men Organizing."

11. Ibid.

12. Ibid.

13. Ibid.

14. Ibid.

15. Ibid.

16. Ibid.

17. "Democratic Platform," in *Political Reformation of 1884*, 5; Grossman, *Democratic Party and the Negro*, 108. See also Summers, *Rum, Romanism, and Rebellion*.

18. "Democratic Platform." The platform also pointed out the overturning of Republican legislation, "to fix the status of colored citizens," by a Republican Supreme Court (ibid., 4).

19. Grossman, *Democratic Party and the Negro*, 113.

20. "An Act in Relation to Public Education in the City of New York," 1884, N.Y. Laws ch. 248.

21. Grossman, *Democratic Party and the Negro*, 127.

22. "The Address," *Hub*, September 6, 1884.

23. "An Address; Of the Wendell Phillips Club," *Hub*, September 6, 1884.

24. Ibid. The address was signed by Archibald Grimké, Lewis Hayden, John C. Chappelle, J. H. Wolff, and John J. Smith.

25. Ibid.

26. *Guide to U.S. Elections*, 1:689.

27. Commonwealth of Massachusetts, *A Manual for the Use of the General Court, 1885* (Boston: Author, 1885), 275.

28. "Vote of the State by Districts," *Boston Daily Globe*, November 5, 1884.

29. Beatty, *Revolution Gone Backward*, 72–73.

30. "Cautious Democrat" to Cleveland, November 17, 1884, Cleveland Papers. For other mentions of black anxiety, see, in Cleveland Papers: F. J. Porter to D. S. Lamont, November 17, 1884; John Snead to Lamont, November 17, 1884; A. S. H. to Cleveland, November 19, 1884; Arthur Hood to Cleveland, November 19, 1884; Merritt E. Sawyer to Cleveland, November 19, 1884. See also Grossman, *Democratic Party and the Negro*, 109.

31. Grossman, *Democratic Party and the Negro*, 109–110.

32. "The Outlook," *Hub*, November 22, 1884.

33. "Valedictory," *Hub*, January 17, 1885.

34. Ibid.

35. "Think for Themselves," *Boston Daily Globe*, October 27, 1885.

36. Ibid.

37. "A New Freedom—Colored Men Shaking Off Party Shackles," *Boston Daily Globe*, October 26, 1885.

38. Ibid.

39. Ibid.

40. Ibid.

41. Ibid.

42. "A New Freedom."

43. "Brains but No Heart," *Boston Daily Globe*, October 28, 1885.

44. J. H. Wolff to John D. Long, March 19, 1884, John D. Long Papers, Massachusetts Historical Society. See also Wolff to Long, March 22, 1884, Long Papers.

45. "Brains but No Heart."

46. "A New Freedom."

47. Ibid.

48. "The Colored Men for Prince," *Boston Daily Globe*, October 27, 1885.

49. "Think for Themselves."

50. Ibid.

51. Beatty, *Revolution Gone Backward*, 82.

52. "Think for Themselves."

53. "Independent Colored Voters," *Boston Daily Globe*, November 25, 1885; "Colored Men for O'Brien," *Boston Daily Globe*, November 27, 1885; "The Duties of Colored Citizens," *Boston Daily Globe*, December 5, 1885; "In Faneuil Hall for Colored Men," *Boston Daily Globe*, December 7, 1885; Men of Pluck," *Boston Daily Globe*, December 8, 1885; "The Massachusetts Colored League," *New York Freeman*, December 12, 1885.

54. "Men of Pluck."

55. John L. Ruffin to John F. Andrew, December 1, 1885, John F. Andrew Papers, Massachusetts Historical Society.

56. Ibid.

57. "Rally of Colored Voters at Faneuil Hall," *Boston Daily Globe*, December 8, 1885.

58. Ibid.

59. C. L. Smith to John H. Oberly, March 24, 1885, Cleveland Papers; Grossman, *Democratic Party and the Negro*, 121.

60. Smith to Oberly, March 24, 1885.

61. Ibid.

62. Walker to Cleveland, February 1, 1886.

63. Although other African Americans petitioned Cleveland, Downing's correspondence is particularly rich. For example, New York newspaper editor T. Thomas Fortune wrote letters to Cleveland seeking appointment for himself and other black independents; see T. Thomas Fortune to Patrick A. Collins, March 3, 1886, Cleveland Papers.

64. "Freedman's Village Abolished," *Washington Post*, December 6, 1887; "Freedman's Village Evictions," *Washington Post*, December 13, 1887.

65. George T. Downing to Lamont, December 10, 1887, Cleveland Papers.

66. "Freedman's Village Evictions."

67. Downing to Cleveland, April 30, 1888, Cleveland Papers.

68. Downing to Lamont, May 14, 1888, Cleveland Papers.

69. Ibid.

70. Downing to Cleveland, February 24, 1887, Cleveland Papers.

71. Downing to William C. Whitney, May 6, 1887, Cleveland Papers.

72. Ibid.

73. Ibid.

74. Downing to Cleveland, January 18, 1886, Cleveland Papers.

75. J. D. Powell to Cleveland, January 18, 1886, Cleveland Papers.

76. Ibid.

77. Ibid.

78. Downing to Patrick A. Collins, January 23, 1886, Cleveland Papers.

79. Ibid.

80. Although Downing supported Cleveland and sought recognition, he cast his ballot for Benjamin Butler as a candidate of the Greenback Party. Downing asserted that although he could support Cleveland, he could not support Hendricks as his vice president. Downing to Cleveland, September 20, 1886, Cleveland Papers.

81. Downing to Cleveland, February 23, 1886, Cleveland Papers.

82. Ibid.

83. Downing to Lamont, March 24, 1887, Cleveland Papers.

84. Ibid.

85. Ibid.

86. Ibid.

87. Ibid.

88. Ibid.

89. Downing to Lamont, April 11, 1887, Cleveland Papers.

90. Ibid.

91. Ibid.

92. Downing to Cleveland, April 8, 1886, Cleveland Papers. Although nominated, Downing lost the election, as did the whole Democratic ticket.

93. Thomas G. Williams to Cleveland, June 1887, Cleveland Papers.

94. Ibid. Downing is also recommended as a candidate for office by Ohio governor George Hoadly. See Hoadly to Lamont, March 28, 1885, Cleveland Papers.

95. Downing to Cleveland, April 8, 1886.

96. Ibid.

97. Downing to Lamont, November 2, 1886, Cleveland Papers.

98. Walker to Cleveland, February 1, 1886.

99. Downing to Lamont, June 13, 1887, Cleveland Papers.

100. Downing to Cleveland, November 21, 1888, Cleveland Papers.

101. Downing continued to support Cleveland and campaigned for his reelection, continued to request presidential appointments, and urged him to intervene in southern

states on behalf of African Americans. See Downing to Cleveland, November 4, 1891; Downing to Cleveland, July 12, 1892; Downing to W. C. Whitney, July 15, 1992; Downing et al. to Cleveland, November 16, 1893; Downing to Henry T. Thurber, September 7, 1894, Cleveland Papers.

102. Grossman, *Democratic Party and the Negro*, 128.

103. Ibid., 121.

104. Ibid., 125–128.

105. Downing applied for the position in March 1885; see Lamont to Downing, March 14, 1885, Cleveland Papers.

106. Grossman, *Democratic Party and the Negro*, 128.

107. William H. Bonaparte to William M. Evarts, February 8, 1887, William Evarts Papers, Library of Congress.

108. Grossman, *Democratic Party and the Negro*, 129–130.

109. Cleveland to Frederick Douglass, January 4, 1886, Douglass to Cleveland, January 5, 1886, Frederick Douglass Papers, Library of Congress; Douglass to George F. Hoar, March 12, 1886, George F. Hoar Papers, Massachusetts Historical Society (hereafter cited as Hoar Papers).

110. Grossman, *Democratic Party and the Negro*, 129. Matthews was responsible for writing the New York legislation preserving black schools, and thus black teachers' jobs, in New York City as ward schools within the integrated school system. See Grossman, *Democratic Party and the Negro*, 66–67, 129; Beatty, *Revolution Gone Backward*, 77–78.

111. Grossman, *Democratic Party and the Negro*, 129.

112. "Outspoken Boston Views," *New York Freeman*, February 12, 1887; Grossman, *Democratic Party and the Negro*, 133–134; Beatty, *Revolution Gone Backward*, 78–79.

113. Quoted in "Negroes No Longer Republicans," *Boston Daily Globe*, February 21, 1887.

114. Grossman, *Democratic Party and the Negro*, 136; Beatty, *Revolution Gone Backward*, 79.

115. "Try Trotter," *Boston Daily Globe*, March 2, 1887; Grossman, *Democratic Party and the Negro*, 137; Beatty, *Revolution Gone Backward*, 81.

116. Grossman, *Democratic Party and the Negro*, 139.

117. Charles C. Soule to Hoar, March 1, 1887; A. W. Beard to Hoar, March 1, 1887; Samuel Moseley to Hoar, March 1, 1887; Alfred Hartwell to Hoar, March 2, 1887, Hoar Papers.

118. Lewis Hayden to Hoar, February 29, 1887; John Warren to Senator Dawes, March 2, 1887, Hoar Papers.

119. John Warren to Senator Dawes, March 2, 1887, Hoar Papers.

120. Grossman, *Democratic Party and the Negro*, 139.

121. Bonaparte to Cleveland, March 2, 1887, Cleveland Papers.

122. "Trotter and Cleveland," *Boston Daily Globe*, March 5, 1887.

123. "Thinks It a Good Idea," *Boston Daily Globe*, March 6, 1887.

124. "Trotter and Cleveland."

125. "James Munroe Trotter," *Boston Daily Globe*, August 18, 1887.

126. Ibid.

127. "Mr. Trotter," *Boston Daily Globe*, November 6, 1887.

128. Grossman, *Democratic Party and the Negro*, 141.


*Chapter Six*

1. "First Martyrs," *Boston Daily Globe*, November 15, 1888; "It is Expected That the Crispus Attucks Monument . . . ," *Boston Pilot*, September 22, 1888; "Crispus Attucks," *Boston Pilot*, November 10, 1887; "Boston Honors the Negro Patriot," *Boston Pilot*, November 24, 1888; "Attucks and His Comrades," *New York Age*, November 17, 1888.

2. "Honoring Crispus Attucks," *Boston Daily Globe*, November 13, 1888.

3. "First Martyrs."

4. Ibid.

5. For more on the Home Rule movement, see Jackson, *Home Rule*.

6. Brown, *Irish-American Nationalism*, 102. For more on the land leagues in America, see Eric Foner, "Class, Ethnicity, and Radicalism in the Gilded Age: The Land League and Irish America," in *Politics and Ideology*, 150–200.

7. Brown, *Irish-American Nationalism*, 101–102.

8. Jackson, *Home Rule*, 57–59; Brown, *Irish-American Nationalism*, 159.

9. Brown, *Irish-American Nationalism*, 103.

10. "The Land League," *Boston Daily Globe*, March 4, 1881.

11. Ibid.

12. "National Convention," *New York Globe*, September 29, 1883.

13. "The Colored Convention and the Irish," *New York Globe*, October 20, 1883.

14. Ibid.

15. "Men of Pluck," *Boston Daily Globe*, December 8, 1885. For additional discussion of the Massachusetts Colored League, see chapter 5.

16. "Men of Pluck"; "The Massachusetts Colored League," *New York Freeman*, December 12, 1885; Shankman, "Black on Green," 291.

17. "Men of Pluck."

18. John Boyle O'Reilly to George T. Downing, December 15, 1885, DeGrasse-Howard Papers, Massachusetts Historical Society.

19. "Shall We Help Ireland," *New York Freeman*, January 2, 1886. For more on Fortune's support of Irish independence, see Alvarez, "Place Between"; Alexander, "We Know Our Rights"; Thornbrough, *T. Thomas Fortune*, 106–107.

20. "Shall We Help Ireland."

21. "Mr. Downing on Ireland," *New York Freeman*, January 9, 1886; "The Colored Man on Ireland," *Boston Pilot*, January 23, 1886.

22. "Mr. Downing on Ireland."

23. Ibid.

24. "Home Rule," *Boston Advocate*, August 14, 1886.

25. Ibid.

26. Ibid.

27. "The 108th Anniversary of the Death of Robert Emmet," *Boston Advocate*, March 13, 1886.

28. Ibid.

29. Ibid.

30. "Colored Men for Ireland," *Boston Daily Globe*, March 10, 1886. Edwin Garrison Walker and other black supporters of Benjamin Butler formed the Sumner National Independent League in the aftermath of Butler's gubernatorial loss in 1883; its members advocated political independence and separation from the Republican Party.

31. "Invitation Accepted," *Boston Advocate*, February 13, 1886.

32. "The Five Dollar Subscription," *Boston Pilot*, February 27, 1886; "Five Dollar Irish Parliamentary Fund," March 1886, John F. Andrew Papers, Massachusetts Historical Society.

33. "Invitation Accepted."

34. "For Ireland's Cause," *Boston Advocate*, February 27, 1886.

35. "Invitation Accepted."

36. "For Ireland's Cause."

37. "The Parliamentary Fund," "The Young Colored Men of Boston . . . ," *Boston Pilot*, March 13, 1886; "Concert in Aid of Parliamentary Fund," *Boston Pilot*, March 27, 1886.

38. "Streets Boston Letter," *New York Freeman*, April 4, 1886

39. "Concert in Aid of Parliamentary Fund."

40. "Colored Men for Ireland," *Boston Daily Globe*, March 31, 1886.

41. "The Young Colored Men of Boston . . . ," *Boston Pilot*, April 24, 1886.

42. "Colored Friends of the Movement," *Boston Pilot*, April 24, 1886.

43. "Colored Men Give $125 for Parnell," *Boston Daily Globe*, April 16, 1886; "Colored Friends of the Movement."

44. "The Parliamentary Fund."

45. Ibid.

46. "Home Rule."

47. "A Colored Men's Rally," *Boston Daily Globe*, November 3, 1883. For more on Maguire's career, see Galvin, "Patrick J. Maguire"; Connolly, *Triumph of Ethnic Progressivism*, 1–38; Blodgett, "Yankee Leadership in a Divided City," 371–396; Blodgett, *Gentle Reformers*.

48. O'Connor, *Boston Irish*, 118; State Street Trust, "Hugh O'Brien," in *Mayors of Boston*, 38–39.

49. "For Mayor and License," *Boston Daily Globe*, December 10, 1884; *Record of Votes by Precinct*, 1884, City of Boston Archives.

50. "Five Dollar Irish Parliamentary Fund."

51. "Thankful Colored People," *Boston Daily Globe*, July 22, 1885; "Men of Pluck." O'Brien also demonstrated his interest in African American affairs when he was the only white city official to attend a banquet in honor of Frederick Douglass held by the Wendell Phillips Club.

52. "The Colored Vote," *Boston Daily Globe*, December 10, 1886.

53. Ibid.; "Last Week There Died . . . ," *Boston Pilot*, November 27, 1886.

54. "The Colored Vote."

55. John Boyle O'Reilly to Josephine St. Pierre Ruffin, November 23, 1886, Ruffin Family Papers, box 87-2, folder 75, Manuscript Division, Moorland-Spingarn Research Center, Howard University.

56. "Colored Voters Want Recognition," *Boston Daily Globe*, November 27, 1887; "Claims of Colored Voters," *New York Age*, December 3, 1887.

57. "Claims of Colored Voters."

58. "Colored Citizens on Alert," *Boston Daily Globe*, November 28, 1887; "The Colored Voters," *Boston Daily Globe*, December 1, 1887.

59. "Discouraged," *Boston Daily Globe*, December 11, 1887.

60. "Politics Galore," *Boston Daily Globe*, December 5, 1887.

61. Ibid.

62. "Ward Eight's Colored Men," *Boston Daily Globe*, December 8, 1887.

63. Ibid.

64. "Colored Citizens Aroused," *Boston Daily Globe*, December 13, 1887.

65. Ibid.

66. Ibid.

67. "O'Brien," *Boston Daily Globe*, December 14, 1887; Record of Votes by Precinct, 1887, City of Boston Archives.

68. "O'Brien's Colored Friends," *Boston Daily Globe*, December 18, 1887.

69. Ibid.

70. Ibid.

71. Ibid.

72. Ibid.

73. Valelly, *The Two Reconstructions*, 6.

74. "First Martyrs."

75. Horton and Horton, *Black Bostonians*, 128. For more on the meanings and issues surrounding the construction of the Crispus Attucks Monument, see Kantrowitz, "A Place for 'Colored Patriots'"; Kachun, "From Forgotten Founder to Indispensable Icon"; Fitz, "Commemorating Crispus Attucks"; Nyong'o, "'The Black First'"; Browne, "Remembering Crispus Attucks"; Freeman, "The Crispus Attucks Monument Dedication"; Ryan, "The Crispus Attucks Monument Controversy"; Quarles, "Crispus Attucks."

76. "Petition of Lewis Hayden and Others for the Erection of a Suitable Monument to the Memory of Crispus Attucks and Other Early Patriots of the Revolution, January 21, 1887," 53, 1887, Passed Resolves, SC1/Series 228, Massachusetts Archives.

77. *Reports of Proceedings of the City Council of Boston* (Boston: n.p., 1886), 395–396.

78. *Reports of Proceedings of the City Council of Boston* (Boston: n.p., 1888), 800–802.

79. Ibid.

80. Ibid, 801. The "persecution" Keenan refers to is likely the general court's attempts to control city services. For example, in 1884, following O'Brien's first election, the

general court transferred control of Boston's police department from the city to an executive-appointed commission. See Blodgett, "Yankee Leadership in a Divided City," 375.

81. *Reports of Proceedings of the City Council of Boston* (Boston: n.p., 1888), 800–802.

82. "A Monument to Crispus Attucks and the Colored Race," *Boston Advocate,* January 15, 1887; Ryan, "Crispus Attucks Monument Controversy," 657.

83. Massachusetts Historical Society, *Proceedings of the Massachusetts Historical,* Series 2, Vol. 3, *1886–1887* (Boston: Author, 1888), 318.

84. "Call a Meeting at Faneuil Hall," *Boston Pilot,* May 21, 1887.

85. "Crispus Attucks," *Boston Pilot,* May 28, 1887.

86. "The Attucks Apotheosis," *Congregationalist,* May 19, 1887.

87. Ibid.

88. "Crispus Attucks."

89. Ibid.

90. Ibid.; "It Is Given Out That the Monument . . . ," *Boston Pilot,* September 17, 1887.

91. "The Crispus Attucks Monument," *Boston Pilot,* November 26, 1887. For more on the design of the memorial, see "Unveiling of the Crispus Attucks Monument," *Boston Daily Globe,* November 4, 1888.

92. "It Is Expected That the Crispus Attucks Monument. . . ." The subcommittee included E. M. Chamberlin, William O. Armstrong, Dominic Toy, Archibald Grimké, and Julius C. Chappelle.

93. "Honoring Crispus Attucks."

94. "First Martyrs."

95. "Boston Honors the Negro Patriot."

96. John Boyle O'Reilly, "Crispus Attucks," in Roche and O'Reilly, *Life of John Boyle O'Reilly,* 414; "First Martyrs;" Boston City Council, *A Memorial of Crispus Attucks.* O'Reilly also presented this poem at the AME Church on Charles Street on December 18 before a crowd of African American men and women. "O'Reilly's Crispus Attucks," *Boston Daily Globe,* December 19, 1888.

97. "First Martyrs."

98. Ibid.

99. Ibid. Lodges listed: U.S. Grant, No. 1, Worcester; Crispus Attucks, No. 2, William C. Nell, No. 3, Puritan, No. 4, George L. Ruffin, No. 5, and David Walker, No. 6, all of Boston. Among those seated on the platform were James Wolff, Edward E. Brown, Mark De Martie, John D. Powell, Rev. Peter Smith, Rev. Jesse Harrell, Rev. B. F. Combush, and H. H. Gilbert, founder of the colored Knights of Pythias in the Northern States.

100. Ibid.

101. Ibid.

102. "Walker Not Confirmed," *New York Age,* June 16, 1888.

103. Ibid.

104. Blodgett, "Yankee Leadership in a Divided City," 376.

105. "Hart Elected," *Boston Daily Globe,* December 12, 1888. In Ward Nine O'Brien received 521 of 1,687 votes. *Record of Votes by Precinct,* 1888, City of Boston Archives.

106. *A Memorial of John Boyle O'Reilly from the City of Boston.*

107. *A Memorial of John Boyle O'Reilly,* 50–54; Evans, *A Fanatic Heart,* 251–255.

108. Brown, *Irish-American Nationalism,* 178–182.

109. Schneider, *Boston Confronts Jim Crow,* 169–184.

110. "New England Politics," *New York Globe,* August 23, 1884.


Part III

1. Hopkins, *Contending Forces,* 265.


Chapter Seven

1. Beatty, *Revolution Gone Backward,* 121.

2. Alexander, *Army of Lions.*

3. Ibid., 23, 310; "Colored Men in Session," *Boston Daily Globe,* January 1, 1890.

4. "The League Convention," *New York Age,* January 25, 1890; Alexander, *Army of Lions,* 14. League organizers changed this policy in 1891 (Alexander, *Army of Lions,* 46).

5. "Boston's National League," *New York Age,* November 5, 1887.

6. *New York Age,* January 5, 1889, May 25, 1889.

7. "Claims of Colored Voters," *New York Age,* December 3, 1887.

8. Ibid.

9. "National League Meeting," *Boston Daily Globe,* November 30, 1887.

10. "Boston's National League."

11. "Claims of Colored Voters."

12. "Boston's National League."

13. "United for Protection," *New York Age,* October 15, 1887.

14. "Boston's National League."

15. "United for Protection"; "Boston's National League."

16. "Seeking Union in Boston," *New York Age,* January 7, 1888.

17. "Letters to the League," *New York Age,* February 18, 1888.

18. For more on Teamoh, see Penn, *Afro-American Press and Its Editors,* 360–364.

19. "Mr. Douglass' Advice," *New York Age,* March 3, 1888.

20. Ibid.

21. Ibid.

22. "At the Cradle of Liberty," *New York Age,* August 9, 1890; "Boston's National League," *New York Age,* August 16, 1890.

23. Grossman, *Democratic Party and the Negro,* 149–150.

24. Ibid., 151–153.

25. Ibid., 153; Richardson, *Death of Reconstruction,* 208.

26. Grossman, *Democratic Party and the Negro,* 153–154.

27. Schechter, *Ida B. Wells-Barnett,* 106–110.

28. "Miss Wells Indorsed," *Boston Daily Globe,* July 18, 1894; "Colored National League," *Boston Daily Globe,* August 8, 1894; "Protest against Lynching," *Boston Daily Globe,* August 29, 1894.

29. "They Protest in Mass Meeting," *Boston Daily Globe,* August 30, 1894.

30. Ibid.

31. Ibid.

32. Ibid.

33. "Colored National League," *Boston Daily Globe,* September 5, 1894.

34. Fox, *Guardian of Boston,* 28–29.

35. "Anti-Lynching," *Boston Daily Advertiser,* November 13, 1895.

36. It is likely that the account is referring to the notorious lynching of Henry Smith in 1893 in Paris, Texas. This lynching was publicized by Ida B. Wells in 1895. See Wells-Barnett, *Red Record,* 91–98.

37. "Anti-Lynching."

38. Ibid.

39. Ibid.

40. Ibid.

41. Ibid.

42. Ibid.

43. Ibid.

44. "Protest from Massachusetts," *Dallas Morning News,* November 13, 1885.

45. Ibid.

46. "Lynching and Burning," *Commercial Appeal,* November 13, 1895; "Boston People Are Holding Mass Meetings . . . ," *Commercial Advertiser,* November 14, 1885; "Protest against Lynching," *North American,* November 13, 1895; "Protest from Massachusetts"; "Lynching for Rape," *Daily Picayune,* November 14, 1895.

47. Editorial, *Dallas Morning News,* quoted in "Negro Lynching," *Boston Daily Advertiser,* November 20, 1895.

48. Ibid.

49. Anonymous to Edwin U. Curtis, November 16, 1895, quoted in "Incendiary Letters," *Boston Daily Advertiser,* November 20, 1895.

50. Ibid.

51. W. C. Crawford to Edwin U. Curtis, November 15, 1895, quoted in "Incendiary Letters."

52. "Lynching for Rape."

53. Ibid.

54. Ibid.

55. Ibid.

56. Anonymous to Curtis.

57. "Apply Torch," *Boston Daily Globe,* November 20, 1895.

58. Waters and New England Historic Genealogical Society, *New England Historical and Genealogical Register,* lvi–lvii; "Apply Torch."

59. "Apply Torch."

60. Ibid.

61. Ibid.

62. "Negro Lynching."

63. Ibid.

64. "Apply Torch."

65. "Negro Lynching."

66. "Apply Torch."

67. "The Federal Elections Bill," *Boston Daily Advertiser*, December 4, 1890. Cooperation with Boston's white women leaders also had beneficial financial outcomes. For
example, Ruffin sought financial assistance from Edna Cheney to support the first convention of African American women in 1896. See Josephine St. Pierre Ruffin to Edna
Cheney, May 19, 1896, Ms.A.10.1 No. 68; Ruffin to Cheney, March 24, 1896, Ms.A.10.1
no. 87; Ruffin to Cheney, May 22, 1896, Ms.A.10.1 no. 69, American Anti-Slavery Collection, Boston Public Library.

68. Kenneally, "Catholicism and Woman Suffrage."

69. Materson, "For the Freedom of Her Race," 11.

70. "Silver Ticket," *Boston Daily Globe*, November 25, 1896; "They Are Indignant,"
*Boston Daily Globe*, December 2, 1896.

71. "Boston City Election," *New York Age*, December 15, 1888.

72. For further discussion of the significance of women's involvement in elections,
see Brown, "Negotiating and Transforming the Public Sphere."

73. "Mrs. George L. Ruffin," *Boston Daily Globe*, March 4, 1894.

74. Ibid.

75. Ibid.

76. Schuppert, "Josephine St. Pierre Ruffin," in *African American Lives*, ed. Gates and
Higginbotham, 735–737; Jenkins, "She Issued the Call," 74–76; Brown, *Homespun Heroines*, 151–153. Holden, "'Earnest Women Can Do Anything.'"

77. "Greeting," *Woman's Era*, March 24, 1894.

78. "The Woman's Era Club," *Woman's Era*, March 24, 1894. Although Chant gained
the support of members of the Woman's Era Club, she was later criticized as an apolo-
gist for lynching. See "Ida B. Wells," *Woman's Era*, July 1894.

79. "The Woman's Era Club."

80. Ibid.

81. Ibid.

82. "Ida B. Wells."

83. "Woman's Place," *Woman's Era*, September 1894.

84. Ibid.

85. Ibid.

86. Editorial, *Woman's Era*, December 1894.

87. Ibid.

88. The paper also included correspondence from Elizabeth Piper Enslet on suffrage movements in Colorado. See "What Has Woman's Suffrage Done for Colorado,"
*Woman's Era*, November 1894.

89. Fannie Barrier Williams, "Woman in Politics," *Woman's Era*, November 1894.

90. Ibid.

91. "Colored Party," *Boston Daily Advertiser*, July 23, 1896.

92. Ibid.

93. Ibid.

94. Kantrowitz, *Ben Tillman and the Reconstruction of White Supremacy*.

95. "Colored Party."

96. Ibid.

97. Ibid.

98. "Negro Convention," *Boston Daily Advertiser*, August 11, 1896; "For Their Race," *Boston Daily Globe*, August 11, 1896.

99. "Negro Convention."

100. "For Their Race."

101. Ibid.

102. Ibid.

103. Ibid.

104. Ibid.

105. Ibid.

106. Ibid.

107. "In Disorder," *Boston Daily Globe*, August 13, 1896.

108. Ibid.

109. Ibid.

*Chapter Eight*

1. "Negro's Wrongs," *Boston Daily Globe*, October 4, 1899; Colored National League, "Open Letter to President McKinley," 2.

2. Ibid., 2–3.

3. "Negro's Wrongs"; "Open Letter to President McKinley," 1.

4. Waldrep, *Many Faces of Judge Lynch*, 118–119; Chestnut, "Lynching," 23; Dray, *At the Hands of Persons Unknown*, 117; "A Negro Post Master Killed," *Charleston Weekly News and Courier*, March 2, 1898.

5. "A Negro Post Master Killed."

6. Chestnut, "Lynching," 27–28.

7. "Colored People's Protest," *Boston Daily Globe*, March 2, 1898.

8. "Lively Discussion," *Boston Daily Globe*, April 13, 1898.

9. Hux, "Lillian Clayton Jewett," 14–15; "Discussed Baker Tragedy," *Boston Daily Globe*, July 12, 1899. See also Chestnut, "Lynching."

10. *Boston Herald*, July 17, 1899, quoted in Hux, "Lillian Clayton Jewett," 17.

11. *Boston Herald*, July 17, 1899.

12. "Not All Agree," *Boston Daily Globe*, July 26, 1899.

13. Ibid.

14. Ibid.

15. Ruffin's sentiment is supported by records of Jewett's filing for bankruptcy in 1898; see Hux, "Lillian Clayton Jewett," 16.

16. "Not All Agree."

17. Brown, *Pauline Elizabeth Hopkins*, 56.

18. "Not All Agree."

19. Hux, "Lillian Clayton Jewett," 21.

20. "Close to a Riot," *Boston Daily Globe*, August 2, 1899.

21. Dickson D. Bruce, "Archibald Henry Grimké," in *African American Lives*, ed. Gates and Higginbotham, 360–361; Bruce, *Archibald Grimké*.

22. "Not the Church or the State," *Boston Daily Globe*, September 20, 1899.

23. Ibid.

24. Ibid.

25. "Open Letter to President McKinley," 2.

26. Ibid.

27. Ibid.

28. See United States v. Harris, 160 U.S. 629 (1883).

29. "Open Letter to President McKinley," 5.

30. Ibid., 10. This quotation is from McKinley's Second State of the Union Address, December 5, 1898. Grimké and the members of the Colored National League criticized this speech for neglecting to address incidents of racial violence in favor of focusing on the United States' interventions in Cuba and the Philippines.

31. "Open Letter to President McKinley," 10.

32. Ibid., 7. The statement of "'criminal aggression' in the far East" is in reference to McKinley's invasion of the Philippines.

33. "Open Letter to President McKinley," 11.

34. Booker T. Washington to Grimké, November 20, 1899, Archibald Grimké Papers, box 39-6, folder 121, Manuscript Division, Moorland-Spingarn Research Center, Howard University (hereafter cited as Grimké Papers).

35. George T. Downing to Grimké, December 2, 1899, Grimké Papers, box 39-4, folder 91.

36. James McDermott to Grimké, April 12, 1900, Grimké Papers, box 39-7, folder 129.

37. Katie V. Smith to Grimké, November 23, 1899, Grimké Papers, box 39-5, folder 103.

38. Ibid.

39. Ibid.

40. Albert E. Pillsbury to Grimké, November 20, 1900, Grimké Papers, box 39-5, folder 101. Pillsbury forwarded a letter to white Republican congressman James Moody from African American congressman George H. White discussing how to pass legislation to stop lynching. White was one of the last black men to serve in the U.S. Congress until the late twentieth century, and he introduced the first federal antilynching bill to Congress.

41. Pillsbury to Grimké.

42. In re Neagle, 135 U.S. 1, 60.

43. Pillsbury to Grimké.

44. Ibid.

45. James L. Drew to Archibald Grimké, January 14, 1900, Grimké Papers, box 39-4, folder 91.

46. "Prospectus . . . ," *Colored American Magazine* (September 1900): 195.

47. "Editorial and Publisher's Announcement," *Colored American Magazine* (October 1900): 333; "Prospectus. . . ."

48. "Editorial and Publisher's Announcement," *Colored American Magazine* (September 1900): 262.

49. "Time of Publication," *Colored American Magazine* (September 1900): 196.

50. "The Story of Our Magazine," *Colored American Magazine* (May 1901): 47.

51. Hopkins, *Contending Forces*, 13.

52. Ibid.

53. Brown, *Pauline Elizabeth Hopkins*, 167.

54. Ibid., 163–164.

55. Hopkins, *Contending Forces*, 16.

56. Ibid., 229.

57. Ibid.

58. Ibid., 230.

59. Ibid., 224.

60. Ibid., 244–245.

61. Ibid., 262.

62. Richard Yarborough, introduction to Hopkins, *Contending Forces*, xxxvii.

63. Hopkins, *Contending Forces*, 272 (emphasis in original).

64. Ibid. (emphasis in original).

65. "Editorial and Publisher's Announcement," *Colored American Magazine* (October 1900): 333

66. "Editorial and Publisher's Announcement," *Colored American Magazine* (October 1901): 479.

67. Ibid.

68. "Negroes to Put Up a Ticket," *Baltimore Sun,* June 7, 1900.

69. "Negroes Attack Roosevelt," *New York Times,* August 17, 1900; "For the Negro," *Boston Daily Globe,* August 17, 1900.

70. Quoted in Hopkins, "Edwin Garrison Walker," 365.

71. Ibid.

72. "Fearless Leader Sleeps," *Boston Daily Globe,* January 17, 1901; "Loved His Race," *Boston Daily Globe,* January 14, 1901; "Funeral Will Be Imposing," *Boston Daily Globe,* January 15, 1901; "Active Life Ended," *Boston Journal,* January 15, 1901; "Death of the Foremost Lawyer in New England," *Colored American Magazine* (February 1901): 291. A later memorial was also held by the Colored National League, on February 12, 1901; see "Walker's Worth," *Boston Daily Globe,* February 13, 1901.

73. "Fearless Leader Sleeps."

74. "Walker's Worth," Archibald Grimké, "Edwin Garrison Walker," Grimké Papers, box 39-19, folder 358.

## Conclusion

1. Hopkins, "Edwin Garrison Walker," 358.

2. Ibid.

3. Daniels, *In Freedom's Birthplace*, 268–270; Cromwell, *Other Brahmins*, 49; *Reports of the Proceedings of the City Council of Boston, 1896* (Boston: n.p., 1897), 583–585.

4. Beatty, *Revolution Gone Backward*, 178.

5. W. E. B. Du Bois to George Foster Peabody, December 28, 1903, in Aptheker, *Correspondence of W. E. B. Du Bois*, 66–69; Lewis, *W. E. B. Du Bois*, 300–304; Du Bois, *Autobiography of W. E. B. Du Bois*, 87; Du Bois, *Dusk of Dawn*, 44.

6. "The President and Colored Citizens," *Harper's Weekly*, June 22, 1872.

## Epilogue

1. "In Honor of Edwin G. Walker," *Guardian*, October 25, 1902.

2. Fox, *Guardian of Boston*, 15.

3. *Harvard College Class of 1895: Thirtieth Anniversary Report* (Cambridge, MA: Harvard University Press, 1925), 303, quoted in Fox, *Guardian of Boston*, 27.

4. Fox, *Guardian of Boston*, 29.

5. *Guardian*, November 9, 1901, quoted in Fox, *Guardian of Boston*, 30.

6. *Guardian*, October 22, 1904, quoted in Fox, *Guardian of Boston*, 33.

7. Fox, *Guardian of Boston*, 47–49; Lewis, *W. E. B. Du Bois*, 299; Alexander, *Army of Lions*, 206–212.

8. "Negroes Make a Riotous Scene," *Boston Daily Globe*, July 31, 1903.

9. Fox, *Guardian of Boston*, 51–52.

10. "Negroes Make a Riotous Scene"; Fox, *Guardian of Boston*, 50.

11. "Negroes Make a Riotous Scene."

12. Ibid.; Fox, *Guardian of Boston*, 49–58; Lewis, *W. E. B. Du Bois*, 300–301.

13. "Got Thirty Days Each," *Boston Daily Globe*, August 8, 1903.

14. Fox, *Guardian of Boston*, 52.

15. *Milwaukee Sentinel*, August 2, 1903, quoted in Fox, *Guardian of Boston*, 53.

16. "Anti-Washington," *Boston Daily Globe*, August 18, 1903; Alexander, *Army of Lions*, 214.

17. "Anti-Washington."

18. Ibid.

19. "For His Rights," *Boston Daily Globe*, November 8, 1903; see also "For a Black Man's Party," *New York Times*, November 8, 1903.

20. Lewis, *W. E. B. Du Bois*, 301.

21. W. E. B. Du Bois to George Foster Peabody.

22. Du Bois, *Dusk of Dawn*, 44.

23. Du Bois, *Autobiography of W. E. B. Du Bois*, 87. See also Lewis, *W. E. B. Du Bois*, 300–304.

24. Niagara Movement, "The Niagara Movement: Address to the Country," in Aptheker, *Pamphlets and Leaflets by W. E. B. Du Bois*, 64.

# Bibliography

*Manuscript Collections*

Boston City Archives, Boston, MA
    Boston City Council Minutes
    Boston City Documents, 1784–1970
    Boston Municipal Registers 1834–1991
    City Council Committee Records, 1822–1909
    City Council Meeting and Hearing Transcripts, 1886–2009
    City Council Proceedings, 1822–2002
    Docket Documents for the Common Council and the Board of Aldermen
    Election Scrapbooks, 1867–1901
    List of Qualified Male Voters, 1889
    List of Women Returned by the Assessors Circa 1880–1890
    The Minutes of the Mayor and Aldermen
    Miscellaneous Committee Records
    Office of the City Clerk Records, 1829–1984
    Organization of the City Government of Boston, 1880–2002
    Personal Records of Members of the City Council, 1861–1890
    Real Estate, Personal, Estate, and Poll Tax Records, 1822–1985
    Record of Returns of Votes from the Several Wards in the City of Boston,
        1822–1853, 1862–1894
    Record of Votes by Precinct, 1878–1894
    Registers of Native Voters
    Registers of Naturalized Voters
    Voter Registrations, 1857–1940
    Ward and Precinct Maps, 1878–1925
    Women Voter Registrations, 1884–1920
Boston Public Library, Boston, MA
    Anti-Slavery Collection
    George W. Forbes Papers
Houghton Library, Harvard University, Cambridge, MA
    Wendell Phillips Papers
    Charles Sumner Papers
Library of Congress, Washington, DC
    Benjamin F. Butler Papers
    Grover Cleveland Papers
    Frederick Douglass Papers

William Evarts Papers
Mary Church Terrell Papers
Booker T. Washington Papers
Records of the National Association of Colored Women's Clubs, 1895–1992
Massachusetts Archives, Boston, MA
Executive Department Letters
Governor's Council Executive Records
Judicial Archives
Passed Acts and Resolves
Unpassed Acts and Resolves
Massachusetts Historical Society, Boston, MA
John F. Andrew Papers
Association of Officers of the 55th Massachusetts Volunteer Infantry Records
Boston Central Labor Union (Mass.) Records
DeGrasse–Howard Papers
George F. Hoar Papers
John D. Long Papers
Massachusetts Reform Club Records
New England Freedmen's Aid Society Papers
Young Men's Republican and Independent Club Records
Young Men's Republican Committee Records
Moorland-Spingarn Research Center, Howard University, Washington, DC
George T. Downing Papers
Archibald Grimké Papers
Ruffin Family Papers
National Archives and Records Administration, Washington, DC
Civil War Pension Records
Freedmen's Bureau Records
United States Census
Special Collections, State Library of Massachusetts, Boston, MA
Burrill File
Legislative Documents

*Newspapers and Periodicals*

BALTIMORE, MD

*Baltimore Sun*

BOSTON, MA

*Boston Advocate*  
*Boston Courant*  
*Boston Daily Advertiser*  
*Boston Daily Globe*

*Boston Evening Transcript*  
*Boston Guardian*  
*Boston Herald*  
*Boston Investigator*

*Colored American Magazine*
*Commonwealth*
*Congregationalist and Boston Recorder*
*Emancipator & Republican*

*Hub*
*Liberator*
*Right Way*
*Woman's Era*

CHARLESTOWN, MA
*Charlestown Advertiser*

CHARLESTON, SC
*Charleston Weekly News and Courier*

DALLAS, TX
*Dallas Morning News*

MEMPHIS, TN
*Commercial Advertiser*
*Commercial Appeal*

NEW ORLEANS, LA
*Daily Picayune*

NEW YORK, NY
*New York Age*
*New York Freeman*
*New York Globe*
*New York Times*

PHILADELPHIA, PA
*North American*

WASHINGTON, DC
*Washington Bee*
*Washington Post*

*Published Primary Sources*

Boston Board of Alderman. *A Memorial of John Boyle O'Reilly from the City of Boston.* Boston: Rockwell and Churchill, 1891.
Boston City Council. *A Memorial of Crispus Attucks, Samuel Maverick, James Caldwell, Samuel Gray, and Patrick Carr.* Boston: Boston City Council, 1889.
Butler, Benjamin F. *Autobiography and Personal Reminiscences of Major-General Benjamin Butler-Butler's Book: A Review of His Legal, Political, and Military Career.* Boston: A. M. Thayer, 1892.

Colored National League, "Open Letter to President McKinley by Colored People of Massachusetts." Boston: Colored National League, 1899.

Cooper Nell, William. *William Cooper Nell: Nineteenth-Century African American Abolitionist, Historian, Integrationist: Selected Writings from 1832–1874.* Edited by Dorothy Porter Wesley and Constance Porter Uzelac. Baltimore: Black Classic Press, 2002.

Douglass, Frederick. *Life and Times of Frederick Douglass, Written By Himself.* Boston: De Wolfe & Fiske Co., 1892.

Du Bois, W. E. B. *The Autobiography of W. E. B. Du Bois: A Soliloquy on Viewing My Life from the Last Decade in Its First Century.* 1968. Reprint, New York: Oxford University Press, 2007.

———. *The Correspondence of W. E. B. Du Bois.* Vol. 1, *Selections, 1877–1934.* Edited by Herbert Aptheker. Amherst: University of Massachusetts Press, 1973.

———. *Dusk of Dawn: An Essay Toward an Autobiography of a Race Concept.* 1940. Reprint, New York: Oxford University Press, 2007.

———. *Pamphlets and Leaflets by W. E. B. Du Bois.* Edited by Herbert Aptheker. White Plains, NY: Kraus-Thomson, 1986.

Foner, Philip S., and George E. Walker, eds. *Proceedings of the Black National and State Conventions, 1865–1900.* Vol. 1. Philadelphia: Temple University Press, 1986.

Fortune, T. Thomas. *T. Thomas Fortune, the Afro-American Agitator: A Collection of Writings, 1880–1928.* Edited by Shawn Leigh Alexander. Gainesville: University Press of Florida, 2008.

Hayden, Lewis. *Caste among Masons: Address before Prince Hall Grand Lodge of Free and Accepted Masons of the State of Massachusetts, at the Festival of St. John the Evangelist, December 27, 1865 / By Lewis Hayden.* Boston: Edward S. Coombs, 1866.

———. *Grand Lodge Jurisdictional Claims, or, War of the Races: An Address before Prince Hall Grand Lodge of Free and Accepted Masons for the State of Massachusetts, at the Festival of Saint John the Baptist, June 24, 1868 / By Lewis Hayden, Grand Master.* Boston: Edward S. Coombs, 1868.

———. *A Letter from Lewis Hayden, of Boston, Massachusetts, to Hon. Judge Simms, of Savannah, Georgia.* Boston: Committee on Masonic Jurisprudence, Prince Hall Grand Lodge, 1874.

———. *Masonry among Colored Men in Massachusetts: To the Right Worshipful J. G. Findel, Honorary Grand Master of the Prince Hall Grand Lodge, and General Representative Thereof to the Lodges upon the Continent of Europe.* Boston: Author, 1871.

Harvard College. *Harvard College Class of 1895: Thirtieth Anniversary Report.* Cambridge, MA: Harvard University Press, 1925.

Hopkins, Pauline E. *Contending Forces: A Romance Illustrative of Negro Life North and South.* 1901. Reprint, New York: Oxford University Press, 1988.

———. *Daughter of the Revolution: The Major Nonfiction Works of Pauline E. Hopkins.* Edited by Ira Dworkin. New Brunswick, NJ: Rutgers University Press, 2007.

———. "Famous Men of the Negro Race: Edwin Garrison Walker." *Colored American Magazine* (March 1901): 358–366.

Massachusetts Historical Society. *Proceedings of the Massachusetts Historical.* Series 2, Vol. 3, *1886–1887.* Boston: Massachusetts Historical Society, 1888.

*The Political Reformation of 1884: A Democratic Campaign Book.* New York: National Democratic Committee, 1884.

*The Record of Benjamin F. Butler Compiled from the Original Sources.* Boston, 1883.

*The Record of Benjamin F. Butler since His Election as Governor of Massachusetts.* Boston, 1883.

Roche, James Jeffrey, and John Boyle O'Reilly. *Life of John Boyle O'Reilly . . . Together with His Complete Poems and Speeches.* New York: Cassell, 1891.

Savage, Edward H. *A Chronological History of the Boston Watch and Police, from 1631 to 1865; Together with the Recollections of a Boston Police Office, or, Boston by Daylight and Gaslight, from the Diary of an Officer Fifteen Years in the Service.* 2nd ed. Boston: Author, 1865.

*Sumner Memorial Meeting: Oration of Robert B. Elliott, Delivered in Faneuil Hall, April 14, 1874, under the Auspices of the Colored Citizens of Boston. With the Address of Edwin G. Walker, and a Sketch of the Proceedings.* Boston: Charles L. Mitchell, 1874.

Usher, J. M. *Boston By-ways to Hell: A Visit to the Dens of North Street.* Boston: Nation Office, 1867.

Washington, Booker T. *The Booker T. Washington Papers.* Edited by Louis Harlan. Urbana: University of Illinois Press, 1972.

Wells-Barnett, Ida B. *A Red Record: Tabulated Statistics and Alleged Causes of Lynchings in the United States, 1892–1893–1894.* In *Southern Horrors and Other Writings,* edited by Jacqueline Jones Royster, 73–157. Boston: Bedford Books, 1997.

*Published Government Documents*

*Acts and Resolves Passed by the General Court of Massachusetts.* Boston: Secretary of the Commonwealth, 1661–.

*Boston Directory for the Year Commencing July 1, 1864.* Boston: Adams, Sampson, and Co., 1865.

*A Catalogue of the City Councils of Boston (1822–1908), Roxbury (1846–1867), Charlestown (1847–1873) and of The Selectmen of Boston, 1634–1822, also of Various Other Town and Municipal Officers.* Boston: City of Boston, 1909.

*City Marshal's Annual Report on the Police Department of the City of Boston.* Boston: n.p., 1851.

*Guide to US Elections.* 5th ed. 2 vols. Washington, DC: Congressional Quarterly Press, 2005.

*Journal of the House of Representatives of the Commonwealth of Massachusetts.* Boston: n.p., 1864–1897.

*Journal of the Senate of the Commonwealth of Massachusetts.* Boston: n.p., 1868–.

*A Manual or the Use of the General Court.* Boston: n.p., 1885.

*Municipal Register: Containing the City Charter the Rules and Orders of the City Council; and a List of Officers of the City of Boston for the Year 1880. Reports of the Proceedings of the City Council of Boston.* Boston: 1876–1909.

*Special Schedule of the Eleventh Federal Census, 1890. Enumerating Union Veterans and Widows of Union Veterans of the Civil War, Suffolk County, MA.* Washington, DC: National Archives (film).


*Secondary Sources*

Alexander, Shawn Leigh. *An Army of Lions: The Civil Rights Struggle before the NAACP.* Philadelphia: University of Pennsylvania Press, 2012.

———. "Vengeance without Justice, Injustice without Retribution: The Afro-American Council's Struggle against Racial Violence." *Great Plains Quarterly* 27, no. 2 (2007): 117–133.

———. " 'We Know Our Rights and Have the Courage to Defend Them': The Spirit of Agitation in the Age of Accommodation, 1883–1909." PhD diss., University of Massachusetts, 2004.

Ali, Omar H. *In the Balance of Power: Independent Black Politics and Third-Party Movements in the United States.* Athens: Ohio University Press, 2008.

Alvarez, Thomas. "The Place Between: The New York Independent Colored Movement and the Democratic Party, 1883–1905." PhD diss., University of Michigan, 2007.

Anderson, Eric. *Race and Politics in North Carolina, 1872–1901: The Black Second.* Baton Rouge: Louisiana State University Press, 1981.

Arblaster, Anthony. *The Rise and Decline of Western Liberalism.* Oxford: Blackwell, 1984.

Arnesen, Eric. "The 1890s Crisis in Context: The Pullman Strike, Labor Politics, and the New Liberalism." *Journal of the Illinois State Historical Society* 92, no. 3 (1999): 299–305.

———. "Labor and Urban Politics: Class Conflict and the Origins of Modern Liberalism in Chicago, 1864–97." *Journal of the Illinois State Historical Society* 92, no. 3 (1999): 299–305.

Avins, Alfred. "The Civil Rights Act of 1875 and the Civil Rights Cases Revisited: State Action, the Fourteenth Amendment, and Housing." *UCLA Law Review* 14, no. 1 (1966): 1966–1967.

Baker, Bruce E. *This Mob Will Surely Take My Life: Lynchings in the Carolinas, 1871–1947.* London: Hambledon Continuum, 2009.

Baker, John R. "Citizen Participation and Neighborhood Organizations." *Urban Affairs Review* 30, no. 6 (July 1995): 880–887.

Ballou, Richard Alan. "Even in 'Freedom's Birthplace'!: The Development of Boston's Black Ghetto, 1900–1940." PhD diss., University of Michigan, 1984.

Baum, Dale. *The Civil War Party System: The Case of Massachusetts, 1848–1876.* Chapel Hill: University of North Carolina Press, 1984.

————. "Woman Suffrage and the 'Chinese Question': The Limits of Radical Republicanism in Massachusetts, 1865–1876." *New England Quarterly* 56, no. 1 (March 1983): 60–77.

Bay, Mia. *To Tell the Truth Freely: The Life of Ida B. Wells*. New York: Hill and Wang, 2009.

————. *The White Image in the Black Mind: African-American Ideas about White People, 1830–1925*. New York: Oxford University Press, 2000.

Beatty, Bess. *A Revolution Gone Backward: The Black Response to National Politics, 1876–1896*. Westport, CT: Greenwood Press, 1989.

Beckert, Sven. *The Monied Metropolis: New York City and the Consolidation of the American Bourgeoisie, 1850–1896*. Cambridge: Cambridge University Press, 2001.

Bensel, Richard Franklin. *The Political Economy of American Industrialization, 1877–1900*. Cambridge: Cambridge University Press, 2000.

Bergeson-Lockwood, Millington W. "'We Do Not Care Particularly about the Skating Rinks': African American Challenges to Racial Discrimination in Places of Public Amusement in Nineteenth-Century Boston, Massachusetts." *Journal of the Civil War Era* 5, no. 2 (June 2015): 254–288.

Bernard, Emily. "Pauline E. Hopkins: A Literary Biography." *New England Quarterly* 79, no. 2 (June 2006): 336–338.

Bernstein, Iver. *The New York City Draft Riots: Their Significance for American Society and Politics in the Age of the Civil War*. New York: Oxford University Press, 1990.

Betts, John R. "The Negro and the New England Conscience in the Days of John Boyle O'Reilly." *Journal of Negro History* 51, no. 4 (1966): 246–261.

Black Public Sphere Collective. *The Black Public Sphere*. Chicago: University of Chicago Press, 1995.

Bland, T. A. *Life of Benjamin F. Butler*. Boston: Lee and Shepard, 1879.

Blodgett, Geoffrey. "Ethno-Cultural Realities in Presidential Patronage: Grover Cleveland's Choices." *New York History* 81, no. 2 (April 2000): 189–210.

————. *The Gentle Reformers: Massachusetts Democrats in the Cleveland Era*. Cambridge, MA: Harvard University Press, 1966.

————. "Yankee Leadership in a Divided City: Boston, 1860–1910." *Journal of Urban History* 8, no. 4 (August 1982): 371–396

Borchert, James. *Alley Life in Washington: Family, Community, Religion, and Folklife in the City, 1850–1970*. Urbana: University of Illinois Press, 1980.

Boydston, Jeanne. "Gender as a Question of Historical Analysis." *Gender and History* 20, no. 3 (November 2008): 558–583.

Brown, Elsa Barkley. "Negotiating and Transforming the Public Sphere: African American Political Life in the Transition from Slavery to Freedom." *Public Culture* 7, no. 1 (Fall 1994): 107–146.

————. "Womanist Consciousness: Maggie Lena Walker and the Independent Order of Saint Luke." *Signs* 14, no. 3 (Spring 1989): 610–633.

Brown, Elsa Barkley, and Gregg D. Kimball. "Mapping the Terrain of Black Richmond." *Journal of Urban History* 21, no. 3 (March 1995): 296–346.

Brown, Hallie Q. *Homespun Heroines and Other Women of Distinction*. Xenia: Aldine Press, 1926; New York: Oxford University Press, 1988.

Brown, Lois. *Pauline Elizabeth Hopkins: Black Daughter of the Revolution*. Chapel Hill: University of North Carolina Press, 2008.

Brown, Thomas J., ed. *Reconstructions: New Perspectives on the Postbellum United States*. New York: Oxford University Press, 2006.

Brown, Thomas N. *Irish-American Nationalism, 1870–1890*. Westport, CT: Greenwood Press, 1980. First published in 1966 by Lippincott.

Browne, Stephen H. "Remembering Crispus Attucks: Race, Rhetoric, and the Politics of Commemoration." *Quarterly Journal of Speech* 85, no. 2 (1999): 169–187.

Bruce, Dickson D. *Archibald Grimké: Portrait of a Black Independent*. Baton Rouge: Louisiana State University Press, 1993.

Carby, Hazel V. *Reconstructing Womanhood: The Emergence of the Afro-American Woman Novelist*. New York: Oxford University Press, 1987.

Cathcart, Dolita Dannêt. "White Gloves, Black Rebels: The Decline of Elite Black National Political Leadership in Boston, 1870–1929." PhD diss., Boston College, 2004.

Chandler, Alfred D. *The Visible Hand: The Managerial Revolution in American Business*. Cambridge, MA: Belknap Press, 1977.

Cheek, William, and Aimee Lee Cheek. *John Mercer Langston and the Fight for Black Freedom, 1829–65*. Urbana: University of Illinois Press, 1989.

Chestnut, Trichita M. "Lynching: Ida B. Wells Barnett and the Outrage over the Frazier Baker Murder." *Prologue* 40, no. 3 (Fall 2008): 20–29.

Chittenden, Elizabeth F. "As We Climb: Mary Church Terrell." *Negro History Bulletin* 38, no. 2 (March 1975): 351–354.

Christopher, Maurine. *America's Black Congressmen*. New York: Crowell, 1971.

Coben, Stanley. "Northeastern Business and Radical Reconstruction: A Re-examination." *Mississippi Valley Historical Review* 46, no. 1 (January 1959): 67–90.

Cohen, Nancy. *The Reconstruction of American Liberalism, 1865–1914*. Chapel Hill: University of North Carolina Press, 2002.

Connolly, James J. *The Triumph of Ethnic Progressivism: Urban Political Culture in Boston, 1900–1925*. Cambridge, MA: Harvard University Press, 1998.

Contee, Clarence G. "Edwin Garrison Walker: Son of David Walker of Boston." *Negro History Bulletin* 39 no. 3 (March 1976): 556–559.

Countryman, Matthew. *Up South: Civil Rights and Black Power in Philadelphia*. Philadelphia: University of Pennsylvania Press, 2006.

Cromwell, Adelaide M. *The Other Brahmins: Boston's Black Upper Class, 1750–1950*. Fayetteville: University of Arkansas Press, 1994.

Dailey, Jane Elizabeth. *Before Jim Crow: The Politics of Race in Post-Emancipation Virginia*. Chapel Hill: University of North Carolina Press, 2000.

Dale, Elizabeth. "'Social Equality Does Not Exist among Themselves, Nor among Us': Baylies vs. Curry and Civil Rights in Chicago, 1888." *The American Historical Review* 102, no. 2 (April 1997): 311–339.

Daniels, John. *In Freedom's Birthplace: A Study of the Boston Negroes.* Boston: Houghton Mifflin, 1914.

Davis, Abraham L., and Barbara Luck Graham. *The Supreme Court, Race, and Civil Rights.* Teller Oaks, CA: Sage Publications, 1995.

Deutsch, Sarah. "Learning to Talk More Like a Man: Boston Women's Class-Bridging Organizations, 1870–1940." *American Historical Review* 97, no. 2 (April 1992): 379–404.

Diemer, Andrew. "Reconstructing Philadelphia: African Americans and Politics in the Post–Civil War North." *Pennsylvania Magazine of History and Biography* 133, no. 1 (January 2009): 29–58.

Dobson, John M. *Politics in the Gilded Age: A New Perspective on Reform.* New York: Praeger Publishers, 1972.

Doenecke, Justus D. "Grover Cleveland and the Enforcement of the Civil Service Act." *Hayes Historical Journal* 4, no. 3 (January 1984): 44–58.

Dormon, James H. "Ethnic Stereotyping in American Popular Culture: The Depiction of American Ethnics in the Cartoon Periodicals of the Gilded Age." *Amerikastudien* 30, no. 4 (December 1985): 489–507.

Douglas, Davison M. *Jim Crow Moves North: The Battle over Northern School Segregation, 1865–1954.* Cambridge: Cambridge University Press, 2005.

Dray, Philip. *At the Hands of Persons Unknown: The Lynching of Black America.* New York: Random House, 2003.

DuBois, Ellen Carol. *Feminism and Suffrage: The Emergence of an Independent Women's Movement in America, 1848–1869.* Ithaca, NY: Cornell University Press, 1978.

———. *Woman Suffrage and Women's Rights.* New York: New York University Press, 1998.

Edwards, Rebecca. *Angels in the Machinery: Gender in American Party Politics from the Civil War to the Progressive Era.* New York: Oxford University Press, 1997.

Edwards, Rheable M., and Laura B. Morris. *The Negro in Boston.* Boston: Action for Boston Community Development, 1961.

Einhorn, Robin L. *Property Rules: Political Economy in Chicago, 1833–1872.* Chicago: University of Chicago Press, 1991.

Erby, Kelly. "Worthy of Respect: Black Waiters in Boston before the Civil War." *Food & History* 5, no. 2 (2007): 205–217.

Erie, Steven P., *Rainbow's End: Irish Americans and the Dilemmas of Urban Machine Politics, 1840–1985.* Berkeley: University of California Press, 1988.

Ershkowitz, Miriam, and Joseph Zikmund, eds. *Black Politics in Philadelphia.* New York: Basic Books, 1973.

Ethington, Philip J. "Recasting Urban Political History: Gender, the Public, the Household, and Political Participation in Boston and San Francisco during the Progressive Era." *Social Science History* 16, no. 2 (Summer 1992): 301–333.

Evans, A. G. *Fanatic Heart: A Life of John Boyle O'Reilly, 1844–1890.* Nedlands, Australia: University of Western Australia Press, 1997.

Feimster, Crystal Nicole. *Southern Horrors: Women and the Politics of Rape and Lynching.* Cambridge, MA: Harvard University Press, 2009.

Fields, Barbara J. "Slavery, Race and Ideology in the United States of America." *New Left Review* 181 (May–June 1989): 95–118

Fishel, Leslie H. "The Negro in Northern Politics, 1870–1900." *Mississippi Valley Historical Review* 42, no. 3 (December 1955): 466–489.

———. "The North and the Negro, 1865–1900: A Study in Race Discrimination." PhD diss., Harvard University, 1954.

———. "Northern Prejudice and Negro Suffrage, 1865–1870." *Journal of Negro History* 39, no. 1 (January 1954): 8–26.

Fitz, Karsten. "Commemorating Crispus Attucks: Visual Memory and the Representations of the Boston Massacre, 1770–1857." *Amerikastudien* 50, no. 3 (2005): 463–484.

Fitzgerald, Michael W. *Splendid Failure: Postwar Reconstruction in the American South.* Chicago: Ivan R. Dee, 2007.

Flewellen, Kathryn. "The National Black Independent Political Party: Will History Repeat?" *Freedomways* 21, no. 2 (March 1981): 93–105.

Foner, Eric. *Freedom's Lawmakers: A Directory of Black Officeholders during Reconstruction.* Rev. ed. Baton Rouge: Louisiana State University Press, 1996.

———. *Politics and Ideology in the Age of the Civil War.* New York: Oxford University Press, 1980.

———. *Reconstruction: America's Unfinished Revolution, 1863–1877.* New York: Harper Perennial Modern Classics, 2002.

Foner, Philip S. "A Labor Voice for Black Equality: The *Boston Daily Evening Voice*, 1864–1867." *Science and Society* 38, no. 3 (Fall 1974): 304–325.

Foreman, P. Gabrielle. *Activist Sentiments: Reading Black Women in the Nineteenth Century.* Urbana: University of Illinois Press, 2009.

Formisano, Ronald P., and Constance K. Burns, eds. *Boston, 1700–1980: The Evolution of Urban Politics.* Westport, CT: Greenwood Press, 1984.

Fox, Stephen R. *The Guardian of Boston: William Monroe Trotter.* New York: Athenaeum, 1971.

Fraser, Nancy. "Rethinking the Public Sphere: A Contribution to the Critique of Actually Existing Democracy." In *Habermas and the Public Sphere*, edited by Craig Calhoun, 109–142. Cambridge, MA: MIT Press, 1992.

Fredrickson, George M. *The Black Image in the White Mind: The Debate on Afro-American Character and Destiny, 1817–1914.* New York: Harper and Row, 1972.

Freeman, Dale H. "The Crispus Attucks Monument Dedication." *Historical Journal of Massachusetts* 26, no. 2 (1997): 125–138.

Frisch, Michael. "Better City Government: Innovation in American Urban Politics, 1850–1937." *Journal of Urban History* 7, no. 2 (February 1981): 205–218.

Gaines, Kevin. "Rethinking Race and Class in African-American Struggles for Equality, 1885–1941." *The American Historical Review* 102, no. 2 (April 1997): 378–387.

Gaines, Kevin Kelly. *Uplifting the Race: Black Leadership, Politics, and Culture in the Twentieth Century.* Chapel Hill: University of North Carolina Press, 1996.

Galvin, John T. "Patrick J. Maguire: Boston's Last Democratic Boss." *New England Quarterly* 55, no. 3 (September 1982): 392–415.

Garb, Margaret. *Freedom's Ballot: African American Political Struggles in Chicago from Abolition to the Great Migration.* Chicago: University of Chicago Press, 2014.

Gates, Henry Louis, and Evelyn Brooks Higginbotham, eds. *African American Lives.* New York: Oxford University Press, 2004.

Gatewood, Willard B., Jr. *Black Americans and the White Man's Burden, 1898–1903.* Urbana: University of Illinois Press, 1975.

———. *"Smoked Yankees" and the Struggle for Empire: Letters from Negro Soldiers, 1898–1902.* Urbana: University of Illinois Press, 1971.

Gavins, Raymond. "Literature on Jim Crow." *Organization of American Historians Magazine of History* (January 2004): 13–16.

Gems, Gerald, et al. *Sports in American History: From Colonization to Globalization.* Champaign, IL: Human Kinetics, 2008.

Giddings, Paula. *Ida: A Sword among Lions: Ida B. Wells and the Campaign against Lynching.* New York: Amistad, 2008.

Gilmore, Glenda Elizabeth. *Gender and Jim Crow: Women and the Politics of White Supremacy in North Carolina, 1896–1920.* Chapel Hill: University of North Carolina Press, 1996.

Glickman, Lawrence B. *A Living Wage: American Workers and the Making of Consumer Society.* Ithaca, NY: Cornell University Press, 1997.

Goldstein, Michael L. "Preface to the Rise of Booker T. Washington: A View from New York City of the Demise of Independent Black Politics, 1889–1902." *Journal of Negro History* 62, no. 1 (January 1977): 81–99.

Gonzales-Day, Ken. *Lynching in the West: 1850–1935.* Durham, NC: Duke University Press, 2006.

Gordon, Ann D., and Bettye Collier-Thomas. *African American Women and the Vote, 1837–1965.* Amherst: University of Massachusetts Press, 1997.

Grant, Donald Lee. *The Anti-Lynching Movement, 1883–1932.* San Francisco: R and E Research Associates, 1975.

Greenwood, Janette Thomas. *First Fruits of Freedom: The Migration of Former Slaves and Their Search for Equality in Worcester, Massachusetts, 1862–1900.* Chapel Hill: University of North Carolina Press, 2009.

Grossman, Lawrence. *The Democratic Party and the Negro: Northern and National Politics, 1868–92.* Urbana: University of Illinois Press, 1976.

———. "George T. Downing and Desegregation of Rhode Island Public Schools, 1855–1866." *Rhode Island History* 36 no. 4 (November 1977): 99–105.

Gruesser, John Cullen, Hanna Wallinger, and Collegium for African American Research. *Loopholes and Retreats: African American Writers and the Nineteenth Century.* Münster, Germany: LIT Verlag, 2009.

Gurin, Patricia, Shirley Hatchett, and James S. Jackson. *Hope and Independence: Blacks' Response to Electoral and Party Politics.* New York: Russell Sage Foundation, 1989.

Habermas, Jürgen. *The Structural Transformation of the Public Sphere: An Inquiry into a Category of Bourgeois Society.* Cambridge, MA: MIT Press, 1989.

Habermas, Jürgen, Sara Lennox, and Frank Lennox. "The Public Sphere: An Encyclopedia Article (1964)." *New German Critique* 3 (Autumn 1974): 49–55.

Hahn, Steven. *A Nation under Our Feet: Black Political Struggles in the Rural South, from Slavery to the Great Migration.* Cambridge, MA: Belknap Press of Harvard University Press, 2003.

———. *The Roots of Southern Populism: Yeoman Farmers and the Transformation of the Georgia Upcountry, 1850–1890.* 2nd ed. New York: Oxford University Press, 2006.

Hairston, Curtis M., and Massachusetts Black Caucus. *Blacks on Beacon Hill: A History of Blacks in the Massachusetts Legislature.* Boston: Massachusetts Black Caucus, 1983.

Hale, Grace Elizabeth. *Making Whiteness: The Culture of Segregation in the South, 1890–1940.* New York: Pantheon Books, 1998.

Hall, Jacquelyn Dowd. "The Long Civil Rights Movement and the Political Uses of the Past." *Journal of American History* 91, no. 4 (2005): 1233–1263.

———. *Revolt against Chivalry: Jessie Daniel Ames and the Women's Campaign against Lynching.* New York: Columbia University Press, 1979.

Hamilton, Tullia Kay Brown. "The National Association of Colored Women, 1896–1920." *Dissertation Abstracts International* 40, no. 1 (July 1979): 405.

Handlin, Oscar. *Boston's Immigrants, 1790–1880: A Study in Acculturation.* Rev. and enl. ed. Cambridge, MA: Belknap Press, 1959.

Harlan, Louis R. *Booker T. Washington: The Making of a Black Leader, 1856–1901.* New York: Oxford University Press, 1975.

———. *Booker T. Washington: The Wizard of Tuskegee, 1901–1915.* New York: Oxford University Press, 1983.

Harrison, William. "Phylon Profile IX: William Monroe Trotter-Fighter." *Phylon (1940–1956)* 7, no. 3 (1946): 237–245.

Hellwig, David J. "Black Attitudes toward Irish Immigrants." *Mid-America* 49 (January 1977): 39–49.

Hesseltine, William B. "Economic Factors in the Abandonment of Reconstruction." *Mississippi Valley Historical Review* 22, no. 2 (1935): 191–210.

Higginbotham, Evelyn Brooks. "African-American Women's History and the Metalanguage of Race." *Signs* 17, no. 2 (1992): 251–274.

———. "Beyond the Sound of Silence, Afro-American Women in History." *Gender & History* 1, no. 1 (1989): 50–67.

———. *Righteous Discontent: The Women's Movement in the Black Baptist Church, 1880–1920.* Cambridge, MA: Harvard University Press, 1993.

Hine, Darlene Clark. *Hine Sight: Black Women and the Re-Construction of American History.* Brooklyn, NY: Carlson Publishing, 1994.

Hinks, Peter. *To Awaken My Afflicted Brethren: David Walker and the Problem of Antebellum Slave Resistance.* University Park: Pennsylvania State University Press, 1997.

Hirshson, Stanley P. *Farewell to the Bloody Shirt: Northern Republicans and the Southern Negro, 1877–1893.* Gloucester, MA: P. Smith, 1968.

Hofstadter, Richard. *The Age of Reform: From Bryan to F.D.R.* New York: Vintage Books, 1955.

Hohendahl, Peter, and Patricia Russian. "Jürgen Habermas: 'The Public Sphere' (1964)." *New German Critique* 3 (Autumn 1974): 45–48.

Holden, Teresa Blue. "'Earnest Women Can Do Anything': The Public Career of Josephine St. Pierre Ruffin, 1842–1904." PhD diss., Saint Louis University, 2005.

Holt, Thomas C. *Black over White: Negro Political Leadership in South Carolina during Reconstruction.* Urbana: University of Illinois Press, 1977.

Holzman, Robert S. *Stormy Ben Butler.* 1954. Reprint, New York: Octagon Books, 1978.

Hoogenboom, Ari A. *Outlawing the Spoils: A History of the Civil Service Reform Movement, 1865–1883.* Urbana: University of Illinois Press, 1961.

Horton, James Oliver. *Free People of Color: Inside the African American Community.* Washington, DC: Smithsonian Institution Press, 1993.

Horton, James Oliver, and Lois E. Horton. *Black Bostonians: Family Life and Community Struggle in the Antebellum North.* Rev. ed. New York: Holmes and Meier Publishers, 1999.

———. *In Hope of Liberty: Culture, Community, and Protest among Northern Free Blacks, 1700–1860.* New York: Oxford University Press, 1997.

Horton, Lois E. "From Class to Race in Early America: Northern Post-Emancipation Racial Reconstruction." *Journal of the Early Republic* 19, no. 4 (1999): 629–649.

Howard, Brett. *Boston, A Social History.* New York: Hawthorn Books, 1976.

Hunter, Tera. *To 'Joy My Freedom: Southern Black Women's Lives and Labors after the Civil War.* Cambridge, MA: Harvard University Press, 1997.

Hux, Roger K. "Lillian Clayton Jewett and the Rescue of the Baker Family, 1899–1900." *Historical Journal of Massachusetts* 19, no. 1 (April 1991): 13–23.

Ignatiev, Noel. *How the Irish Became White.* New York: Routledge, 2008.

Innes, C. L. "Language in Black and Irish Nationalist Literature." *Massachusetts Review* 16, no. 1 (1975): 77–91.

Jackson, Alvin. *Home Rule: An Irish History, 1800–2000.* New York: Oxford University Press, 2004.

Jacobs, Donald M., ed. *Courage and Conscience: Black and White Abolitionists in Boston.* Bloomington: Indiana University Press, 1993.

Jacobs, Meg, Julian E. Zelizer, and William J. Novak, eds. *The Democratic Experiment: New Directions in American Political History.* Princeton, NJ: Princeton University Press, 2003.

Jacobson, Matthew Frye. *Barbarian Virtues: The United States Encounters Foreign Peoples at Home and Abroad, 1876–1917.* New York: Hill and Wang, 2000.

Jelks, Randal Maurice. *African Americans in the Furniture City: The Struggle for Civil Rights in Grand Rapids.* Urbana: University of Illinois Press, 2006.

Jenkins, Lee. "'The Black O'Connell': Frederick Douglass and Ireland." *Nineteenth-Century Studies* 13 (1999): 22–46.

Jenkins, Maude T. "The History of the Black Woman's Club Movement in America." PhD diss., Columbia University Teacher's College, 1984.

————. "She Issued the Call: Josephine St. Pierre Ruffin, 1842–1924." *Sage: A Scholarly Journal on Black Women* 5, no. 2 (July 1988): 74–76.

Johnson, Violet Showers. *The Other Black Bostonians: West Indians in Boston, 1900–1950.* Bloomington: Indiana University Press, 2006.

Jones, Beverly W. "Mary Church Terrell and the National Association of Colored Women, 1896 to 1901." *Journal of Negro History* 67, no. 1 (January 1982): 20–33.

Jones, Jacqueline. *Labor of Love, Labor of Sorrow: Black Women, Work, and the Family from Slavery to the Present.* New York: Basic Books, 1985.

Jones, Martha S. *"All Bound Up Together": The "Woman Question" in African-American Public Culture, 1830–1900.* Chapel Hill: University of North Carolina Press, 2007.

Kachun, Mitch. "From Forgotten Founder to Indispensable Icon: Crispus Attucks, Black Citizenship, and Collective Memory, 1770–1865." *Journal of the Early Republic* 29, no. 2 (Summer 2009): 249–286.

Kantrowitz, Steven. *Ben Tillman and the Reconstruction of White Supremacy.* Chapel Hill: University of North Carolina Press, 2000.

————. " 'Intended for the Better Government of Man': The Political History of African American Freemasonry in the Era of Emancipation." *Journal of American History* 96, no. 4 (March 2010): 1001–1026.

————. *More Than Freedom: Fighting for Black Citizenship in a White Republic, 1829–1889.* New York: Penguin, 2012.

————. "A Place for 'Colored Patriots.' " *Massachusetts Historical Review* 11 (January 2009): 96–117.

Katzman, David M. *Before the Ghetto: Black Detroit in the Nineteenth Century.* Urbana: University of Illinois Press, 1973.

Kelley, Blair Murphy. *Right to Ride: Streetcar Boycotts and African American Citizenship in the Era of Plessy v. Ferguson.* Chapel Hill: University of North Carolina Press, 2010.

Kelley, Robin D. G. *Race Rebels: Culture, Politics, and the Black Working Class.* New York: Free Press, 1994.

————. " 'We Are Not What We Seem': Rethinking Black Working-Class Opposition in the Jim Crow South." *Journal of American History* 80, no. 1 (June 1993): 75–112.

Kelly, Brian. "Ambiguous Loyalties: The Boston Irish, Slavery, and the Civil War." *Historical Journal of Massachusetts* 24, no. 2 (October 1996): 165–204.

Kelly, Patrick J. *Creating a National Home: Building the Veterans' Welfare State, 1860–1900.* Cambridge, MA: Harvard University Press, 1997.

Kenneally, James J. "Catholicism and Woman Suffrage in Massachusetts." *Catholic Historical Review* 53, no. 1 (April 1967): 43–57.

————. "Woman Suffrage and the Massachusetts 'Referendum' of 1895." *Historian* 30, no. 4 (Fall 1968): 617–633.

Kennedy, Lawrence W. "Young Patrick A. Collins and Boston Politics after the Civil War." *Historical Journal of Massachusetts* 38, no. 1 (Spring 2010): 38–59.

King, Desmond S., and Stephen G. N. Tuck. "De-centering the South: America's Nationwide White Supremacist Order after Reconstruction." *Past & Present* 194 (2007): 213–254.

Kleppner, Paul. *The Third Electoral System, 1853–1892: Parties, Voters, and Political Cultures.* Chapel Hill: University of North Carolina Press, 1979.

Koren, John. *Boston, 1822 to 1922: The Story of Its Government and Principal Activities during One Hundred Years.* Boston: City of Boston, 1923.

Kousser, J. Morgan. "'The Onward March of Right Principles': State Legislative Actions on Racial Discrimination in Schools in Nineteenth-Century America." *Historical Methods* 35, no. 4 (2002): 177–204.

———. "'The Supremacy of Equal Rights': The Struggle against Racial Discrimination in Antebellum Massachusetts and the Foundations of the Fourteenth Amendment." *Northwestern University Law Review* 82, no. 4 (1988): 941–1010.

Kousser, J. Morgan, and James M. McPherson, eds. *Region, Race, and Reconstruction: Essays in Honor of C. Vann Woodward.* New York: Oxford University Press, 1982.

Kusmer, Kenneth L. *A Ghetto Takes Shape: Black Cleveland, 1870–1930.* Urbana: University of Illinois Press, 1976.

Lassiter, Matthew D., and Joseph Crespino, eds. *The Myth of Southern Exceptionalism.* New York: Oxford University Press, 2009.

Leonard, William. "Black and Irish Relations in Nineteenth-Century Boston: The Interesting Case of Lawyer Robert Morris." *Historical Journal of Massachusetts* 37, no. 1 (Spring 2009): 64–85.

———. "Growing Together: Blacks and the Catholic Church in Boston." *Historian* 66, no. 2 (Summer 2004): 254–277.

Levesque, George A. "Before Integration: The Forgotten Years of Jim Crow Education in Boston." *The Journal of Negro Education* 48, no. 2 (Spring 1979): 113–125.

———. *Black Boston: African American Life and Culture in Urban America, 1750–1860.* New York: Garland Publishing, 1994.

———. "Inherent Reformers–Inherited Orthodoxy: Black Baptists in Boston, 1800–1873." *Journal of Negro History* 60, no. 4 (October 1975): 491–525.

Lewis, David L. *W. E. B. Du Bois: Biography of a Race, 1868–1919.* New York: Henry Holt, 1994.

Litwack, Leon F. *Been in the Storm So Long: The Aftermath of Slavery.* New York: Knopf, 1981.

———. *North of Slavery: The Negro in the Free States, 1790–1860.* Chicago: University of Chicago Press, 1961.

———. *Trouble in Mind: Black Southerners in the Age of Jim Crow.* New York: Knopf, 1998.

Logan, Rayford W. *The Negro in American Life and Thought: The Nadir, 1877–1901.* 1954. Reprint, New York: Collier Books, 1965.

Logan, Shirley Wilson. *We Are Coming: The Persuasive Discourse of Nineteenth-Century Black Women.* Carbondale: Southern Illinois University Press, 1999.

Love, Eric Tyrone Lowery. *Race over Empire: Racism and U.S. Imperialism, 1865–1900.* Chapel Hill: University of North Carolina Press, 2004.

Madison, James H. *A Lynching in the Heartland: Race and Memory in America.* New York: Palgrave Macmillan, 2003.

Magnum, Charles Staples. *The Legal Status of the Negro*. New York: D. Appleton-
Century Company, 1939.

Malone, Christopher. *Between Freedom and Bondage: Race, Party, and Voting Rights in
the Antebellum North*. New York: Routledge, 2008.

Marks, George P., III, ed. *The Black Press Views American Imperialism, 1898–1900*.
New York: Arno Press, 1971.

Masur, Kate. *An Example for All the Land: Emancipation and the Struggle over Equality
in Washington, D.C.* Chapel Hill: University of North Carolina Press, 2010.

Materson, Lisa G. *For the Freedom of Her Race: Black Women and Electoral Politics in
Illinois, 1877–1932*. Chapel Hill: University of North Carolina Press, 2009.

McCann, Sean. "'Bonds of Brotherhood': Pauline Hopkins and the Work of
Melodrama." *ELH* 64, no. 3 (Fall 1997): 789–822.

McCormick, Richard L. "The Republican Party's Tortuous Path to 'Victorious
Defeat.'" *Reviews in American History* 16, no. 3 (September 1988): 396–402.

McDonald, Terence J. "The Politics of Urban History versus the History of Urban
Politics." *History Teacher* 21, no. 3 (May 1988): 299–305.

———. "Rediscovering the Active City." *Journal of Urban History* 16, no. 3
(May 1990): 304–311.

McGerr, Michael E. *The Decline of Popular Politics: The American North, 1865–1928*.
New York: Oxford University Press, 1986.

McKay, Robert. "Segregation and Public Recreation." *Virginia Law Review* 40, no. 6
(October 1954): 697–731.

McLemore, Leslie Burl. "Towards a Theory of Black Politics—The Black and Ethnic
Models Revisited." *Journal of Black Studies* 2, no. 3 (January 1972): 323–331.

McMath, Robert C. *American Populism: A Social History, 1877–1898*. New York: Hill
and Wang, 1993.

McPherson, James. "Grant or Greeley? The Abolitionist Dilemma in the Election of
1872." *American Historical Review* 71 (October 1865): 43–61.

———. *Struggle for Equality: Abolitionists and the Negro in the Civil War and
Reconstruction*. Princeton, NJ: Princeton University Press, 1964.

Meier, August. "Booker T. Washington and the Negro Press: With Special Reference
to the Colored American Magazine." *Journal of Negro History* 38, no. 1
(January 1953): 67–90.

———. "The Negro and the Democratic Party, 1875–1915." *Phylon* 17, no. 2 (1956):
173–191.

———. "Negro Class Structure and Ideology in the Age of Booker T. Washington."
*Phylon* 23, no. 3 (1962): 258–266.

———. "Negro Protest Movements and Organizations." *Journal of Negro Education*
32, no. 4 (Autumn 1963): 437–450.

———. *Negro Thought in America, 1880–1915: Racial Ideologies in the Age of Booker T.
Washington*. Ann Arbor: University of Michigan Press, 1963.

———. "Toward a Reinterpretation of Booker T. Washington." *Journal of Southern
History* 23, no. 2 (May 1957): 220–227.

Melish, Joanne Pope. *Disowning Slavery: Gradual Emancipation and Race in New England, 1780–1860*. Ithaca, NY: Cornell University Press, 2000.

Miller, Edward H. "They Vote Only for the Spoils: Massachusetts Reformers, Suffrage Restriction, and the 1884 Civil Service Law." *Journal of the Gilded Age & Progressive Era* 8, no. 3 (July 2009): 341–363.

Miller, M. Sammy. "Black Gentility and American Education: A Profile of Judge Robert H. Terrell in the Capital City, 1860–1900." *Negro Educational Review* 29, no. 3–4 (July–October 1978): 225–236.

Mitchell, Michele. *Righteous Propagation: African Americans and the Politics of Racial Destiny after Reconstruction*. Chapel Hill: University of North Carolina Press, 2004.

———. "Silences Broken, Silences Kept: Gender and Sexuality in African American History." *Gender and History* 11, no. 3 (November 1999): 433–444.

Mohr, James C., ed. *Radical Republicans in the North: State Politics during Reconstruction*. Baltimore: Johns Hopkins University Press, 1976.

Montgomery, David. *Beyond Equality: Labor and the Radical Republicans, 1862–1872*. New York: Knopf, 1967.

———. *Citizen Worker: The Experience of Workers in the United States with Democracy and the Free Market during the Nineteenth Century*. New York: Cambridge University Press, 1993.

———. *The Fall of the House of Labor: The Workplace, the State, and Labor Activism, 1865–1925*. New York: Cambridge University Press, 1987.

Moore, John Hammond. *Carnival of Blood: Dueling, Lynching, and Murder in South Carolina, 1880–1920*. Columbia: University of South Carolina Press, 2006.

Moses, Wilson Jeremiah. *The Golden Age of Black Nationalism, 1850–1925*. New York: Oxford University Press, 1988.

Mouser, Bruce L. *For Labor, Race, and Liberty: George Edwin Taylor, His Historic Run for the White House, and the Making of Independent Black Politics*. Madison: University of Wisconsin Press, 2011.

Mulderink, Earl Francis. "'We Want a Country': African American and Irish American Community Life in New Bedford, Massachusetts, during the Civil War Era." PhD diss., University of Wisconsin, 1995.

Murray, Frank. "The Irish and Afro-Americans in U.S. History." *Freedomways* 22, no. 1 (January 1982): 21–31.

National Association for the Advancement of Colored People. *Thirty Years of Lynching in the United States, 1889–1918*. New York: Arno Press, 1969.

Newman, Richard S. "Faith in the Ballot: Black Shadow Politics in the Antebellum North." *Common-Place: The Interactive Journal of Early American Life* 9, no. 1 (2008). http://www.common-place.org/vol-09/no-01/newman/.

Norrell, Robert J. *Up from History: The Life of Booker T. Washington*. Cambridge, MA: Belknap Press, 2009.

Novak, William J. *The People's Welfare: Law and Regulation in Nineteenth-Century America*. Chapel Hill: University of North Carolina Press, 1996.

Nyong'o, Tavia. "'The Black First': Crispus Attucks and William Cooper Nell." *Dublin Seminar for New England Folklife Annual Proceedings* 28 (2003): 141–152.

O'Brien, Colleen C. "'Blacks in All Quarters of the Globe': Anti-Imperialism, Insurgent Cosmopolitanism, and International Labor in Pauline Hopkins's Literary Journalism." *American Quarterly* 61, no. 2 (2009): 245–270.

O'Connor, Thomas H. *The Boston Irish: A Political History*. Boston: Northeastern University Press, 1995.

———. *Civil War Boston: Home Front and Battlefield*. Boston: Northeastern University Press, 1997.

Omori, Kazuteru. "Burden of Blackness: Quest for 'Equality' among Black 'Elites' in Late-Nineteenth-Century Boston." PhD diss., University of Massachusetts, 2001.

———. "Race-Neutral Individualism and Resurgence of the Color Line: Massachusetts Civil Rights Legislation, 1855–1895." *Journal of American Ethnic History* 22, no. 1 (Fall 2002): 32–58.

Osofsky, Gilbert. "Abolitionists, Irish Immigrants, and the Dilemmas of Romantic Nationalism." *American Historical Review* 80, no. 4 (1975): 889–912.

———. *Harlem: The Making of a Ghetto: Negro New York, 1890–1930*. New York: Harper and Row, 1966.

———. "Wendell Phillips and the Quest for a New American National Identity." *Canadian Review of Studies in Nationalism* 1, no. 1 (1973): 15–46.

O'Toole, James M., and David Quigley, eds. *Boston's Histories: Essays in Honor of Thomas H. O'Connor*. Boston: Northeastern University Press, 2004.

Pearson, Henry G. *The Life of John A. Andrew: The Governor of Massachusetts, 1861–1865*. Boston: Houghton, Mifflin, 1904.

Pegram, Thomas R. "Who's the Boss?: Revisiting the History of American Urban Rule." *Journal of Urban History* 28, no. 6 (September 2002): 821–835.

Penn, I. Garland. *The Afro-American Press and Its Editors*. New York: Arno Press, 1969.

Pitkin, Hanna Fenichel. *The Concept of Representation*. Berkeley: University of California Press, 1967.

Pleck, Elizabeth Hafkin. *Black Migration and Poverty: Boston, 1865–1900*. New York: Academic Press, 1979.

Polgar, Paul. "Fighting Lightning with Fire: Black Boston's Battle against *The Birth of a Nation*." *Massachusetts Historical Review* 10 (January 2008): 84–113.

Pride, Armistead Scott, and Clint C. Wilson. *A History of the Black Press*. Washington, DC: Howard University Press, 1997.

Quarles, Benjamin. "Crispus Attucks." *American History Illustrated* 5, no. 7 (1970): 38–42.

Quigley, David. "Constitutional Revision and the City: The Enforcement Acts and Urban America, 1870–1894." *Journal of Policy History* 20, no. 1 (January 2008): 64–75.

———. *Second Founding: New York City, Reconstruction and the Making of American Democracy*. New York: Hill and Wang, 2004.

Rabinowitz, Howard N. "From Exclusion to Segregation: Southern Race Relations, 1865–1890." *Journal of American History* 63 (September 1976): 325–350.

————. "More Than the Woodward Thesis: Assessing *The Strange Career of Jim Crow*." *Journal of American History* 75 (December 1988): 842–856.

————. *Race, Ethnicity, and Urbanization: Selected Essays*. Columbia: University of Missouri Press, 1994.

————. *Race Relations in the Urban South, 1865–1890*. New York: Oxford University Press, 1978.

Rael, Patrick. *Black Identity and Black Protest in the Antebellum North*. Chapel Hill: University of North Carolina Press, 2002.

Richardson, Heather Cox. *The Death of Reconstruction: Race, Labor, and Politics in the Post–Civil War North, 1865–1901*. Cambridge, MA: Harvard University Press, 2001.

————. *West from Appomattox: The Reconstruction of America after the Civil War*. New Haven, CT: Yale University Press, 2007.

Riegel, Stephen J. "The Persistent Career of Jim Crow: Lower Federal Courts and the 'Separate but Equal' Doctrine, 1865–1896." *American Journal of Legal History* 28, no. 1 (January 1984): 17–40.

Robinson, Harriet Jane Hanson. *Massachusetts in the Woman Suffrage Movement: A General, Political, Legal and Legislative History from 1774 to 1881*. Boston: Roberts Brothers, 1883.

Roediger, David R. *The Wages of Whiteness: Race and the Making of the American Working Class*. London: Verso, 2007.

Rolston, Bill. "Frederick Douglass: A Black Abolitionist in Ireland." *History Today* 53, no. 6 (2003): 45–51.

Roy, Jessie H. "Colored Judges: Judge George Lewis Ruffin." *Negro History Bulletin* 28, no. 6 (1965): 135–137.

Rudwick, Elliott M., and August Meier. "Black Man in the 'White City': Negroes and the Columbian Exposition, 1893." *Phylon* 26, no. 4 (1965): 354–361.

Ryan, Dennis P. *Beyond the Ballot Box: A Social History of the Boston Irish, 1845–1917*. Amherst: University of Massachusetts Press, 1989.

————. "The Crispus Attucks Monument Controversy of 1887." *Negro History Bulletin* 40, no. 1 (1977): 656–657.

Samito, Christian G. *Becoming American under Fire: Irish Americans, African Americans, and the Politics of Citizenship during the Civil War Era*. Ithaca, NY: Cornell University Press, 2009.

————. "Proof of Loyalty: Irish Americans, African Americans, and the Redefinition of Citizenship during the Civil War Era." PhD diss., Boston College, 1996.

Sanders, Elizabeth. *Roots of Reform: Farmers, Workers, and the American State, 1877–1917*. Chicago: University of Chicago Press, 1999.

Sandoval-Strausz, A. K. "Travelers, Strangers, and Jim Crow: Law, Public Accommodations, and Civil Rights in America." *Law and History Review* 23, no. 1 (Spring 2005): 53–94.

Sawaya, Francesca. *Modern Women, Modern Work: Domesticity, Professionalism, and American Writing, 1890–1950*. Philadelphia: University of Pennsylvania Press, 2004.

Schechter, Patricia Ann. *Ida B. Wells-Barnett and American Reform, 1880–1930.* Chapel Hill: University of North Carolina Press, 2001.

Schneider, Mark R. *Boston Confronts Jim Crow, 1890–1920.* Boston: Northeastern University Press, 1997.

———. "The Boston NAACP and the Decline of the Abolitionist Impulse." *Massachusetts Historical Review* 1 (1999): 95–113.

———. "The Colored American and Alexander's: Boston's Pro–Civil Rights Bookerites." *Journal of Negro History* 80, no. 4 (Autumn 1995): 157–169.

———. "Confronting Jim Crow: Boston's Antislavery Tradition, 1890–1920." PhD diss., Boston College, 1995.

Schneirov, Richard. *Labor and Urban Politics: Class Conflict and the Origins of Modern Liberalism in Chicago, 1864–97.* Urbana: University of Illinois Press, 1998.

Schuppert, Roger. "Archibald Grimké: Radical Writer in a Conservative Age." *American Journalism* 12, no. 1 (Winter 1995): 39–44.

Schwalm, Leslie A. *Emancipation's Diaspora: Race and Reconstruction in the Upper Midwest.* Chapel Hill: University of North Carolina Press, 2009.

Scott, James C. *Domination and the Arts of Resistance: Hidden Transcripts.* New Haven, CT: Yale University Press, 1990.

Scott, Joan W. "Gender: A Useful Category of Historical Analysis." *The American Historical Review* 91, no. 5 (December 1986): 1053–1075.

Shankman, Arnold. "Black on Green: Afro-American Editors on Irish Independence, 1840–1921." *Phylon* 41, no. 3 (1980): 284–299.

Shaw, Stephanie J. "Black Club Women and the Creation of the National Association of Colored Women." *Journal of Women's History* 3, no. 2 (Summer 1991): 10–25.

———. *What a Woman Ought to Be and to Do: Black Professional Women Workers during the Jim Crow Era.* Chicago: University of Chicago Press, 1996.

Shklar, Judith N. *American Citizenship: The Quest for Inclusion.* Cambridge, MA: Harvard University Press, 1991.

Shockley, Ann Allen. "Pauline Elizabeth Hopkins: A Biographical Excursion into Obscurity." *Phylon* 33, no. 1 (March 1972): 22–26.

Simmons, William J. *Men of Mark: Eminent, Progressive, and Rising.* Cleveland, OH: George M. Rewell, 1887.

Singer, Joseph William. "No Right to Exclude: Public Accommodations and Private Property." *Northwestern University Law Review* 90, no. 4 (1996): 1283–1497.

Sklar, Martin J. *The Corporate Reconstruction of American Capitalism, 1890–1916: The Market, the Law, and Politics.* Cambridge: Cambridge University Press, 1988.

Slap, Andrew L. *The Doom of Reconstruction: The Liberal Republicans in the Civil War Era.* New York: Fordham University Press, 2006.

Smith, John David. "Black Intellectuals as Activists in the Age of Jim Crow." *Reviews in American History* 22, no. 2 (June 1994): 328–334.

Snay, Mitchell. *Fenians, Freedmen, and Southern Whites: Race and Nationality in the Era of Reconstruction.* Baton Rouge: Louisiana State University Press, 2007.

Spear, Allan H. *Black Chicago: The Making of a Negro Ghetto, 1890–1920*. Chicago: University of Chicago Press, 1967.

Sproat, John G. *"The Best Men": Liberal Reformers in the Gilded Age*. Chicago: University of Chicago Press, 1982.

Stanley, Amy Dru. *From Bondage to Contract: Wage Labor, Marriage, and the Market in the Age of Slave Emancipation*. Cambridge: Cambridge University Press, 1998.

State Library of Massachusetts. *Black Legislators in the Massachusetts General Court: 1867–Present*. Boston: Author, 2001.

State Street Trust. *Mayors of Boston: An Illustrated Epitome of Who the Mayors Have Been and What They Have Done*. Boston: Author, 1914.

Stephenson, Gilbert Thomas. *Race Distinctions in American Law*. New York: Association Press, 1911.

Straughan, Dulcie. "'Lifting as We Climb': The Role of 'The National Association Notes' in Furthering the Issues Agenda of the National Association of Colored Women, 1897–1920." *Media History Monographs* 8, no. 2 (June 2005): 1–19.

Streitmatter, Rodger. "Economic Conditions Surrounding Nineteenth-Century African-American Women Journalists: Two Case Studies." *Journalism History* 18 (January 1992): 33–40.

———. "Maria W. Stewart: The First Female African-American Journalist." *Historical Journal of Massachusetts* 21, no. 2 (October 1993): 44–59.

———. *Raising Her Voice: African-American Women Journalists Who Changed History*. Lexington: University Press of Kentucky, 1994.

Summers, Mark Wahlgren. *Party Games: Getting, Keeping, and Using Power in Gilded Age Politics*. Chapel Hill: University of North Carolina Press, 2004.

———. *The Press Gang: Newspapers and Politics, 1865–1878*. Chapel Hill: University of North Carolina Press, 1994.

———. *Rum, Romanism, and Rebellion: The Making of a President, 1884*. Chapel Hill: University of North Carolina Press, 2000.

Sutherland, Steven. "Patron's Right of Access to Premises Generally Open to the Public." *University of Illinois Law Review* (1983): 533–552.

Taylor, Nikki M. *America's First Black Socialist: The Radical Life of Peter H. Clark*. Lexington: University of Kentucky Press, 2013.

Terborg-Penn, Rosalyn. *African American Women in the Struggle for the Vote, 1850–1920*. Bloomington: Indiana University Press, 1998.

Thelen, David P. "Urban Politics: Beyond Bosses and Reformers." *Reviews in American History* 7, no. 3 (September 1979): 406–412.

Thernstrom, Stephan. *The Other Bostonians: Progress in the American Metropolis, 1880–1970*. Cambridge, MA: Harvard University Press, 1973.

Thornbrough, Emma Lou. "The National Afro-American League, 1887–1908." *Journal of Southern History* 27, no. 4 (1961): 494–512.

———. *T. Thomas Fortune: Militant Journalist*. Chicago: University of Chicago Press, 1972.

Thornton, J. Mills. *Dividing Lines: Municipal Politics and the Struggle for Civil Rights in Montgomery, Birmingham, and Selma.* Tuscaloosa: University of Alabama Press, 2002.

Tolnay, Stewart E., and E. M. Beck. *A Festival of Violence: An Analysis of Southern Lynchings, 1882–1930.* Urbana: University of Illinois Press, 1995.

Trefousse, Hans Louis. *Ben Butler: The South Called Him Beast!* New York: Twayne Publishers, 1957.

Trotter, Joe William. *Black Milwaukee: The Making of an Industrial Proletariat, 1915–45.* Urbana: University of Illinois Press, 2007.

Trotter, Joe William, Earl Lewis, and Tera W. Hunter, eds. *African American Urban Experience: Perspectives from the Colonial Period to the Present.* New York: Palgrave Macmillan, 2004.

Turner, Max W., and Frank R. Kennedy. "Exclusion and Segregation of Theater Patrons." *Iowa Law Review* 32, no. 4 (May 1947): 625–658.

Valelly, Richard M. *The Two Reconstructions: The Struggle for Black Enfranchisement.* Chicago: University of Chicago Press, 2004.

Vandiver, Margaret. *Lethal Punishment: Lynchings and Legal Executions in the South.* New Brunswick, NJ: Rutgers University Press, 2006.

Waldrep, Christopher. *The Many Faces of Judge Lynch: Extralegal Violence and Punishment in America.* New York: Palgrave Macmillan, 2002.

Walton, Hanes. *Black Political Parties: An Historical and Political Analysis.* New York: Free Press, 1972.

———. *The Negro in Third Party Politics.* Philadelphia: Dorrance, 1969.

———. *The Study and Analysis of Black Politics: A Bibliography.* Metuchen, NJ: Scarecrow Press, 1973.

Wang, Xi. *The Trial of Democracy: Black Suffrage and Northern Republicans, 1860–1910.* Athens: University of Georgia Press, 1997.

Washburn, Patrick Scott. *The African American Newspaper: Voice of Freedom.* Evanston, IL: Northwestern University Press, 2006.

Waters, Henry Fitz-Gilbert, and New England Historic Genealogical Society. *The New England Historical and Genealogical Register.* Boston: New England Historic Genealogical Society, 1908.

Welke, Barbara Young. *Recasting American Liberty: Gender, Race, Law, and the Railroad Revolution, 1865–1920.* Cambridge: Cambridge University Press, 2001.

West, Richard Sedgewick. *Lincoln's Scapegoat General: A Life of Benjamin F. Butler, 1818–1893.* Boston: Houghton Mifflin, 1965.

White, Deborah G. *Too Heavy a Load: Black Women in Defense of Themselves, 1894–1994.* New York: W. W. Norton, 1999.

Whitehill, Walter Muir, and Lawrence W. Kennedy. *Boston: A Topographical History.* Cambridge, MA: Belknap Press of Harvard University Press, 2000.

Wiebe, Robert H. *The Search for Order, 1877–1920.* New York: Hill and Wang, 1967.

Williamson, Joel. "Wounds Not Scars: Lynching, the National Conscience, and the American Historian." *Journal of American History* 83, no. 4 (March 1997): 1221–1253.

Wilson, Dreck Spurlock. *African American Architects: A Biographical Dictionary, 1865–1945*. New York: Routledge, 2004.

Wolcott, Victoria W. *Remaking Respectability: African American Women in Interwar Detroit*. Chapel Hill: University of North Carolina Press, 2001.

Wood, Amy. "A Spectacular Secret: Lynching in American Life and Literature." *Journal of American History* 94, no. 1 (June 2007): 288–289.

Woodward, C. Vann. *The Strange Career of Jim Crow*. 3rd ed. New York: Oxford University Press, 1974.

Wright, George C. *Life Behind a Veil: Blacks in Louisville, Kentucky, 1865–1930*. Baton Rouge: Louisiana State University Press, 1985.

———. *Racial Violence in Kentucky, 1865–1940: Lynchings, Mob Rule, and "Legal Lynchings."* Baton Rouge: Louisiana State University Press, 1990.

Wynes, Charles E. "President Grover Cleveland's Black Correspondent." *Southern Studies: An Interdisciplinary Journal of the South* 26, no. 1 (January 1987): 63–69.

# Index

*Page numbers in italics refer to figures and tables.*